ALA-LC ROMANIZATION TABLES

Transliteration Schemes for Non-Roman Scripts

1997 Edition

Approved by the

LIBRARY OF CONGRESS

and the

AMERICAN LIBRARY ASSOCIATION

Tables compiled and edited by

RANDALL K. BARRY

Network Development and MARC Standards Office

Library of Congress ■ *Washington*
Cataloging Distribution Service

Library of Congress-in-Publication Data

ALA-LC romanization tables: transliteration schemes for
    non-Roman scripts/approved by the Library of Congress
    and the American Library Association; tables compiled
    and edited by Randall K. Barry. — 1997 ed.

    239 p.: ill.; 28 cm.

    Some tables originally published in: *Cataloging service bulletin.*
    Includes index.
    ISBN 0–8444–0940–5 (pbk. only)

    1. Transliteration. 2. Oriental languages—Transliteration.
3. Semitic languages—Transliteration. 4. Slavic languages—
Transliteration. 5. Cataloging of foreign language publications.
I. Barry, Randall K. (Randall Keigan), 1955— II. Library of Congress.
III. American Library Association. IV. Cataloging Service Bulletin.
P226.A4 1997
411—dc20   97–012740

For sale by the Cataloging Distribution Service,
Library of Congress, Washington, D.C. 20540–4910

This publication will be reissued from time to time as needed to incorporate revisions.

Library of Congress • CDS • 101 Independence Ave., S.E. • Washington, D.C. 20540-4910

Contents

Contents (continued)

Introduction

The 1997 edition of *ALA-LC Romanization Tables* contains 54 romanization and transliteration schemes, the majority of which have also appeared in the Library of Congress *Cataloging Service Bulletin*. These tables were developed for use when the consistent transliteration of a non-Roman (vernacular) script (e.g., Arabic script) into the Roman alphabet is needed. This publication covers more than 150 languages written in various non-Roman scripts.

Transliteration of non-Roman scripts is done by librarians, archivists, information specialists, writers, etc. when translation into English or some other Roman script language is not desirable or possible. This is often the case with proper names, titles, and terms for which no appropriate Roman script equivalent exists. For some scripts the process of romanization or transliteration involves imparting characteristics of the Roman script such as capitalization and word division. The Thai script is typical of one that has neither of these characteristics. (There are no separate upper and lower case forms for letters in the Thai script and words are not separated by spaces.) *ALA-LC Romanization Tables* provides special guidelines for capitalization and word division for certain scripts.

Development of ALA-LC Romanization Tables

Romanization schemes have been developed over the years by foreign language specialists at Library of Congress, often with the help of scholars and experts at other institutions. This work is done to support the cataloging of foreign language materials. Bibliographic information appearing in vernacular scripts is routinely romanized so that it can be incorporated into the Library's large catalog and shared with other institutions. Cataloging information in the vernacular is often included with the romanization.

As tables for new scripts are developed they are reviewed and approved by the American Library Association. This provides input from a wider group of potential users. The development of romanization schemes is an ongoing process. Periodically new romanization schemes are developed for scripts for which no scheme exists. Existing schemes are occasionally revised to reflect better understanding of a script or to provide an improved rendering of it in the Roman script.

Changes in this Edition

The tables in the 1997 edition include four new tables that cover Azerbaijani, Balinese, Javanese, Madurese, Malay, and Sundanese. As with existing tables, information has been formatted for legibility. Many of the older tables have been changed to correct typographical errors and omissions.

Special Features of the Tables

For each non-Roman script, a font was selected that presents each character (i.e., alphabetic, syllabic, ideographic, etc.) as unambiguously as possible. For some scripts certain characters are stylized. This was done to make similar characters more easily distinguished from one another.

The organization of characters belonging to each script follows the traditional arrangement of characters for the script. Often, this is not in the order of the Roman alphabet.

For scripts where certain characters and character modifiers can appear in combination with others (e.g., vowel marks written above or below other characters), an unspecified character is represented by the convention "□" (e.g., ◌́ represents the acute accent which can appear over a variety of alphabetic characters). This convention is only used for characters which are normally written in combination with other characters. These characters are referred to as *character modifiers* and are generally considered *non-spacing*.

Most scripts included special characters that are used in addition to the regular letters of an alphabet, syllabary, or system of ideographs. These special characters occupy a space by themselves (e.g., ' *apostrophe*). When presented in one of these romanization tables, they are not shown in conjunction with any □.

The romanization shown for each character often includes one or more special characters or character modifiers. Special attention should be paid to this part of each romanization scheme. For characters that might be misidentified, a special legend (e.g., *(soft sign)*) is included in parentheses following the character. When a character has no roman value this is indicated by the presence of a hyphen (-), the word "*omit*", or "*disregard*" in the romanization table.

Examples have been included of vernacular text for some scripts. These examples are intended to be descriptive of the rule or principle presented.

NOTE: In the application of the *ALA-LC Romanization Tables*, familiarity with the language involved is helpful, if not essential, for many scripts.

BLANK PAGE

Amharic

Syllables

1st Order		2nd Order		3rd Order		4th Order		5th Order		6th Order		7th Order	
ሀ	ha	ሁ	hu	ሂ	hi	ሃ	hā	ሄ	hé	ህ	he or h	ሆ	ho
ለ	la	ሉ	lu	ሊ	li	ላ	lā	ሌ	lé	ል	le or l	ሎ	lo
ሐ	ḥa	ሑ	ḥu	ሒ	ḥi	ሓ	ḥā	ሔ	ḥé	ሕ	ḥe or ḥ	ሖ	ḥo
መ	ma	ሙ	mu	ሚ	mi	ማ	mā	ሜ	mé	ም	me or m	ሞ	mo
ሠ	śa	ሡ	śu	ሢ	śi	ሣ	śā	ሤ	śé	ሥ	śe or ś	ሦ	śo
ረ	ra	ሩ	ru	ሪ	ri	ራ	rā	ሬ	ré	ር	re or r	ሮ	ro
ሰ	sa	ሱ	su	ሲ	si	ሳ	sā	ሴ	sé	ስ	se or s	ሶ	so
ሸ	ša	ሹ	šu	ሺ	ši	ሻ	šā	ሼ	šé	ሽ	še or š	ሾ	šo
ቀ	qa	ቁ	qu	ቂ	qi	ቃ	qā	ቄ	qé	ቅ	qe or q	ቆ	qo
በ	ba	ቡ	bu	ቢ	bi	ባ	bā	ቤ	bé	ብ	be or b	ቦ	bo
ተ	ta	ቱ	tu	ቲ	ti	ታ	tā	ቴ	té	ት	te or t	ቶ	to
ቸ	ča	ቹ	ču	ቺ	či	ቻ	čā	ቼ	čé	ች	če or č	ቾ	čo
ኀ	ẖa	ኁ	ẖu	ኂ	ẖi	ኃ	ẖā	ኄ	ẖé	ኅ	ẖe or ẖ	ኆ	ẖo
ነ	na	ኑ	nu	ኒ	ni	ና	nā	ኔ	né	ን	ne or n	ኖ	no
ኘ	ña	ኙ	ñu	ኚ	ñi	ኛ	ñā	ኜ	ñé	ኝ	ñe or ñ	ኞ	ño
አ	ʼa	ኡ	ʼu	ኢ	ʼi	ኣ	ʼā	ኤ	ʼé	እ	ʼe	ኦ	ʼo
ከ	ka	ኩ	ku	ኪ	ki	ካ	kā	ኬ	ké	ክ	ke or k	ኮ	ko
ኸ	xa	ኹ	xu	ኺ	xi	ኻ	xā	ኼ	xé	ኽ	xe or x	ኾ	xo
ወ	wa	ዉ	wu	ዊ	wi	ዋ	wā	ዌ	wé	ው	we or w	ዎ	wo
ዐ	ʻa	ዑ	ʻu	ዒ	ʻi	ዓ	ʻā	ዔ	ʻé	ዕ	ʻe	ዖ	ʻo
ዘ	za	ዙ	zu	ዚ	zi	ዛ	zā	ዜ	zé	ዝ	ze or z	ዞ	zo
ዠ	ža	ዡ	žu	ዢ	ži	ዣ	žā	ዤ	žé	ዥ	že or ž	ዦ	žo
ጘ	ža	ጙ	žu	ጚ	ži	ጛ	žā	ጜ	žé	ጝ	že or ž	ጞ	žo
	-		-		-		-		-	ኇ	že or ž		-
የ	ya	ዩ	yu	ዪ	yi	ያ	yā	ዬ	yé	ይ	ye or y	ዮ	yo
ደ	da	ዱ	du	ዲ	di	ዳ	dā	ዴ	dé	ድ	de or d	ዶ	do
ጀ	ǧa	ጁ	ǧu	ጂ	ǧi	ጃ	ǧā	ጄ	ǧé	ጅ	ǧe or ǧ	ጆ	ǧo
ገ	ga	ጉ	gu	ጊ	gi	ጋ	gā	ጌ	gé	ግ	ge or g	ጎ	go
ጠ	ṭa	ጡ	ṭu	ጢ	ṭi	ጣ	ṭā	ጤ	ṭé	ጥ	ṭe or ṭ	ጦ	ṭo
ጨ	čˌa	ጩ	čˌu	ጪ	čˌi	ጫ	čˌā	ጬ	čˌé	ጭ	čˌe or čˌ	ጮ	čˌo
ጰ	p̣a	ጱ	p̣u	ጲ	p̣i	ጳ	p̣ā	ጴ	p̣é	ጵ	p̣e or p̣	ጶ	p̣o
ጸ	ṣa	ጹ	ṣu	ጺ	ṣi	ጻ	ṣā	ጼ	ṣé	ጽ	ṣe or ṣ	ጾ	ṣo
ፀ	ṥa	ፁ	ṥu	ፂ	ṥi	ፃ	ṥā	ፄ	ṥé	ፅ	ṥe or ṥ	ፆ	ṥo
ፈ	fa	ፉ	fu	ፊ	fi	ፋ	fā	ፌ	fé	ፍ	fe or f	ፎ	fo
ፐ	pa	ፑ	pu	ፒ	pi	ፓ	pā	ፔ	pé	ፕ	pe or p	ፖ	po
ቨ	va	ቩ	vu	ቪ	vi	ቫ	vā	ቬ	vé	ቭ	ve or v	ቮ	vo

Combinations with *w*:

1st Order		2nd Order		3rd Order		4th Order		5th Order		6th Order		7th Order	
ቈ	qwa		-	ቊ	qwi	ቋ	qwā	ቌ	qwé	ቍ	qwe		-
ኈ	ẖwa		-	ኊ	ẖwi	ኋ	ẖwā	ኌ	ẖwé	ኍ	ẖwe		-
ኰ	kwa		-	ኲ	kwi	ኳ	kwā	ኴ	kwé	ኵ	kwe		-
ጐ	gwa		-	ጒ	gwi	ጓ	gwā	ጔ	gwé	ጕ	gwe		-

Combinations with *wa*:

ኈ	lwa	በ	bwa	ዠ	zwa	ጧ	ṭwā̄
ኈ Ꭿ Ꮉ	mwa	ቷ	twa	ዠ	žwa	ጯ	čwā̄
ፈ Ꮌ	rwa	ፗ	čwa	Ꮍ	ywa	ጿ	ṣwā̄
ሷ	swa	ኋ Ꮍ	nwa	Ꮍ	dwa	ፈ Ꮍ Ꮍ	fwā̄
ሿ	šwa	ኋ	ñwa	Ꮍ	gwa	-	

Combinations with *ya*:

Ꮎ Ꮎ	rya	Ꮎ Ꮎ	mya	Ꮎ	fya

Special Initial:

ኸ   ă̆

Numerals:

፩	1	፪	2	፫	3	፬	4	፭	5	፮	6	፯	7	፰	8	፱	9
፲	10	፳	20	፴	30	፵	40	፶	50	፷	60	፸	70	፹	80	፺	90
፻	100

Notes

1. The Ethiopic script used for Amharic is also used for other languages, including Ge'ez, Argobba, Gurage, and Tigre. Ge'ez, which is chiefly a liturgical language, uses only 26 basic letter forms from this table.

SPECIAL CHARACTERS AND CHARACTER MODIFIERS IN ROMANIZATION

Special character	*Name*	*USMARC hexadecimal code*
ʼ	alif	AE
ʻ	ayn	B0

Character modifiers	*Name*	*USMARC hexadecimal code*
́	acute	E2
̃	tilde	E4
̄	macron	E5
̆	breve	E6
̇	dot above	E7
̌	hachek	E9
̣	dot below	F2
̱	underscore	F6

Arabic

Letters of the Alphabet

Initial	Medial	Final	Alone	Romanization
ا	ا	ا	ا	omit (see Note 1)
بـ	ـبـ	ـب	ب	b
تـ	ـتـ	ـت	ت	t
ثـ	ـثـ	ـث	ث	th
جـ	ـجـ	ـج	ج	j
حـ	ـحـ	ـح	ح	ḥ
خـ	ـخـ	ـخ	خ	kh
دـ	ـدـ	ـد	د	d
ذـ	ـذـ	ـذ	ذ	dh
رـ	ـرـ	ـر	ر	r
زـ	ـزـ	ـز	ز	z
سـ	ـسـ	ـس	س	s
شـ	ـشـ	ـش	ش	sh
صـ	ـصـ	ـص	ص	ṣ
ضـ	ـضـ	ـض	ض	ḍ
طـ	ـطـ	ـط	ط	ṭ
ظـ	ـظـ	ـظ	ظ	ẓ
عـ	ـعـ	ـع	ع	' (ayn)
غـ	ـغـ	ـغ	غ	gh
فـ	ـفـ	ـف	ف	f (see Note 2)
قـ	ـقـ	ـق	ق	q (see Note 2)
كـ	ـكـ	ـك	ك	k
لـ	ـلـ	ـل	ل	l
مـ	ـمـ	ـم	م	m
نـ	ـنـ	ـن	ن	n
هـ	ـهـ	ـه ، ة	ه ، ة	h (see Note 3)
وـ	ـوـ	ـو	و	w
يـ	ـيـ	ـى	ى	y

Vowels and Diphthongs

◌َ	a	اَ	ā (see Rule 5)	◌ِىْ	ī
◌ُ	u	◌َى	á (see Rule 6(a))	◌َوْ	aw
◌ِ	i	◌ُو	ū	◌َىْ	ay

Letters Representing Non-Arabic Consonants

This list is not exhaustive. It should be noted that a lettter in this group may have more than one phonetic value, depending on the country or area where it is used, and that the romanization will vary accordingly.

گ	g	چ	ch	ڨ	v
ڭ	g	چ	zh	ۋ	v
پ	p	ژ	zh	ڤ	v

Notes

1. For the use of *alif* to support *hamzah*, see rule 2. For the romanization of *hamzah* by the consonantal sign ʼ (alif) see rule 8(a). For other orthographic uses of *alif* see rules 3-5.
2. The *Maghribī* variations ڢ and ڧ are romanized *f* and *q* respectively.
3. ة in a word in the construct state is romanized *t*. See rule 7(b).

RULES OF APPLICATION

Arabic Letters Romanized in Different Ways Depending on Their Context

1. As indicated in the table, و and ي may represent:
   (a) The consonants romanized *w* and *y*, respectively

waḍʻ	وضع
ʻiwaḍ	عوض
dalw	دلو
yad	يد
ḥiyal	حيل
ṭahy	طهي

   (b) The long vowels romanized *ū*, *ī*, and *ā* respectively

ūlá	اولى
ṣūrah	صورة
dhū	ذو
īmān	ايمان
jīl	جيل
fī	في
kitāb	كتاب
saḥāb	سحاب
jumān	جمان

   See also rules 11(a) and 11(b1-2).

(c)   The diphthongs romanized *aw* and *ay*, respectively

awj	اوج
nawm	نوم
law	لو
aysar	ايسر
shaykh	شيخ
‘aynay	عينى

See also rules 11(a)(2) and 11(b)(3).

2.   ا (*alif*), و and ى when used to support ء (*hamzah*) are not represented in romanization. See rule 8(a).

3.   ا (*alif*) when used to support ٱ (*waṣlah*) and آ (*maddah*) is not represented in romanization. See rules 9 and 10.

4.   ا (*alif*) and و when used as orthographic signs without phonetic significance are not represented in romanization.

fa‘alū	فعلوا
ulā’ika	اولائك
‘ilman wa-‘amalan	علما وعملا

See also rule 12 and examples cited in rules 23-26.

5.   ا (*alif*) is used to represent the long vowel romanized *ā*, as indicated in the table.

fā‘il	فاعل
riḍā	رضا

This ا, when medial, is sometimes omitted in Arabic; it is always indicated in romanization. See rule 19.

6.   Final ى appears in the following special cases:

(a)   As ىٰ (*alif maqṣūrah*) used in place of اٰ to represent the long vowel romanized *á*.

ḥattá	حتّىٰ
maḍá	مضىٰ
kubrá	كبرىٰ
Yaḥyá	يحيىٰ
musammá	مسمّىٰ
Muṣṭafá	مصطفىٰ

(b)   As ىّ ـ in nouns and adjectives of the form *faʻīl* which are derived from defective roots. This ending is romanized *ī*, not *īy*, without regard to the presence of ـّ (*shaddah*). See rule 11(b2).

Raḍī al-Dīn   رضىّ الدين

Compare the *faʻīl* form of the same root الرضى [with out *shaddah*] *al-Raḍī*.

(c)   As ىّ ـ in the relative adjective (*nisbah*). The ending, like (b) above, is romanized *ī*, not *īy*.

al-Miṣrī   المصرىّ

Compare المصريّة *al-Miṣrīyah* and see rule 11(b1).

7.   ة (*tāʼ marbūṭah*)

(a)   When the noun or adjective ending in ة is indefinite, or is preceded by the definite article, ة is romanized *h*. The ة in such positions is often replaced by ﻩ.

salāh   صلاة
al-Risālah al-bahīyah   الرسالة البهية
mirʻāh   مرآة
Urjūzah fī al-ṭibb   ارجوزة فى الطب

(b)   When the word ending in ة is in the construct state, ة is romanized *t*.
Wizārat al-Tarbiyah   وزارة التربية
Mirʼāt al-zamān   مرآة الزمان

(c)   When the word ending in ة is used adverbally, ة (vocalized ةً) is romanized *tan*. See rule 12(b).

Romanization of Arabic Orthographic Symbols Other than Letters and Vowel Signs

The signs listed below are frequently omitted from unvocalized Arabic writing and printing; their presence or absence must then be inferred. They are represented in romanization according to the following rules:

8.   ء (*hamzah*)

(a)   In initial position, whether at the beginning of a word, following a prefixed preposition or conjunction, or following the definite article, ء is not represented in romanization. When medial or final, ء is romanized as ʼ (alif).

asad	أسـد
uns	أنـس
idha	إذا
mas'alah	مسـألة
mu'tamar	مؤتمر
dā'im	دائم
mala'a	ملأ
khaṭi'a	خطـئ

(b) ء , when replaced by the sign ٱ *(waslah)* and then known as *hamzat al-waṣl*, it is not represented in romanization. See rule 9 below.

9. ٱ *(waslah)*, like initial ء , is not represented in romanization. See also rule 8(b) above. When the *alif* which supports *waṣlah* belongs to the article ال , the initial vowel of the article is romanized *a*. See rule 17(b). In other words, beginning with *hamzat al-waṣl*, the initial vowel is romanized *i*.

Riḥlat Ibn Jubayr	رحلة آبن جبير
al-istidrāk	الآستدراك
kutub iqtanat'hā	كتب آقتنتها
bi-ihtimām 'Abd al-Majīd	بآهتمام عبد آلمجيد

10. آ *(maddah)*

(a) Initial آ is romanized *ā*

ālah	آلة
Kullīyat al-Ādāb	كلية الآداب

(b) Medial آ, when it represents the phonetic combination '*ā*, is so romanized.

ta'ālīf	تآليف
ma'āthir	مآثر

(c) آ is otherwise not represented in romanization.

khulafā'	خلفآء

11. ّ *(shaddah* or *tashdīd)*

(a) Over و :
(1) وّ , representing the combination of long vowel plus consonant, is romanized *ūw*.

'adūw	عدُوّ
qūwah	قُوّة

See also rule 1(b).

(2) وّ◌, representing the combination of diphthong plus consonant, is romanized *aww*.

Shawwāl شَوّال

ṣawwara صَوّر

jaww جَوّ

See also rule 1(c).

(b)   Over ى :

(1)   Medial يّ◌, representing the combination of long vowel plus consonant, is romanized *īy*.

al-Miṣrīyah المصريّة

See also rule 1(b)

(2)   Final ىّ◌ is romanized *ī*.   See rules 6(b) and 6(c).

(3)   Medial and final ىّ◌, representing the combination of diphthong plus consonant, is romanized *ayy*.

ayyām أيّام

sayyid سَيّد

Quṣayy قُصَىّ

See also rule 1(c)

(c)   Over other letters, ◌ّ is represented in romanization by doubling the letter or digraph concerned.

al-Ghazzī الغزّى

al-Kashshāf الكشّاف

12.   *Tanwīn* may take the written form ◌ٌ, ◌ً (اً), or ◌ٍ, romanized *un*, *an*, and *in*, respectively. *Tanwīn* is normally disregarded in romanization, however.   It is indicated in the following cases:

(a)   When it occurs in indefinite nouns derived from defective roots.

qāḍin قاضٍ

maʻnan معنًى

(b)   When it indicates the adverbial use of a noun or adjective.

ṭabʻan طبعًا

fajʼatan فجأةً

al-Mushtarik waḍʻan wa-al-muftariq المشترك وضعاً والمفترق

ṣuqʻan صقعاً

Grammatical Structure as It Affects Romanization

13.   Final inflections of verbs are retained in romanization, except in pause.

man waliya Miṣr	من ولى مصر
maʻrifat mā yajibu la-hum	معرفة ما يجب لهم
ṣallá Allāh ʻalayhi wa-sallam	صلى الله عليه وسلم
al-Luʼluʼ al-maknūn fī ḥukm al-akhbār	اللؤلؤ المكنون فى حكم
ʻammā sayakūn	الاخبار عما سيكون

14.   Final inflections of nouns and adjectives:

(a)   Vocalic endings are not represented in romanization, except preceding pronominal suffixes, and except when the text being romanized is in verse.

Maʻhad Mawlāya al-Ḥasan	معهد مولاى الحسن
uṣūluhā al-nafsīyah wa-ṭuruq tadrīsihā	اصولها النفسية وطرق تدريسها
ilá yawminā hādhā	الى يومنا هذا

(b)   *Tanwīn* is not represented in romanization, except as specified in rule 12.

(c)   ة (*tāʼ marbūṭah*) is romanized *h* or *t* as specified in rule 7.

(d)   For the romanization of the relative adjective (*nisbah*) see rule 6(c).

15.   Pronouns, pronominal suffixes, and demonstratives:

(a)   Vocalic endings are retained in romanization.

anā wa-anta	انا وانت
hādhihi al-ḥāl	هذه الحال
muʼallafātuhu wa-shurūḥuhā	مؤلفاته وشروحها

(b)   At the close of a phrase or sentence, the ending is romanized in its pausal form.

ḥayātuhu wa-ʻaṣruh	حياته وعصره
Tawfīq al-Ḥakīm,	توفيق الحكيم ، أفكاره،
afkāruh, āthāruh	آثاره

16.   Prepositions and conjunctions:

(a)   Final vowels of separable prepositions and conjunctions are retained in romanization.

anna	ان
annahu	انه
bayna yadayhu	بين يديه

Note the special cases: مما *mimmā*, ممن *mimman*.

(b)   Inseparable prepositions, conjunctions, and other prefixes are connected with what follows by a hyphen.

bi-hi	به
wa-maʻahu	ومعه
lā-silkī	لاسلكى

17.   The definite article:

(a)   The romanized form *al* is connected with the following word by a hyphen.

al-kitāb al-thānī	الكتاب الثانى
al-ittiḥād	الاتحاد
al-aṣl	الاصل
al-āthār	الآثار

(b)   When ال is initial in the word, and when it follows an inseparable preposition or conjunction, it is always romanized *al* regardless of whether the preceding word, as romanized, ends in a vowel or a consonant.

ilá al-ān	الى الآن
Abū al-Wafāʼ	ابو الوفاء
Maktabat al-Nahḍah al-Miṣrīyah	مكتبة النهضة المصرية
bi-al-tamām wa-al-kamāl	بالتمام والكمال

Note the exceptional treatment of the preposition ل followed by the article:

lil-Shirbīnī	للشربينى

See also rule 23.

(c)   The ل of the article is always romanized *l*, whether it is followed by a "sun letter" or not, i.e., regardless of whether or not it is assimilated in pronunciation to the initial consonant of the word to which it is attached.

al-ḥurūf al-abjadīyah	الحروف الابجدية
Abū al-Layth al-Samarqandī	ابو الليث السمرقندى

Orthography of Arabic in Romanization

18.   Capitalization:

(a)   Rules for the capitalization of English are followed, except that the definite article *al* is given in lower case in all positions.

(b)   Diacritics are used with both upper and lower case letters.

al-Ījī	الايجى
al-Ālūsī	الآلوسى

19. The macron or the acute accent, as appropriate, is used to indicate all long vowels, including those which in Arabic script are written defectively. The macron or the acute accent, as the case may be, is retained over final long vowels which are shortened in pronunciation before *hamzat al-waṣl*.

Ibrāhīm	ابراهيم ، ابرهيم
Dā'ūd	داؤود ، داؤد
Abū al-Ḥasan	ابو الحسن
ru'ūs	رؤس
dhālika	ذلك
'alá al-'ayn	على العين

20.   The hyphen is used:

(a)   To connect the definite article *al* with the word to which it is attached. See rule 17(a).

(b)   Between an inseparable prefix and what follows. See rules 16(b) and 17(b) above.

(c)   Between *bin* and the following element in personal names when they are written in Arabic as a single word. See rule 25.

21.   The prime (ʹ) is used:

(a)   To separate two letters representing two distinct consonantal sounds, when the combination might otherwise be read as a digraph.

Adʹham	ادهم
akramatʹhā	اكرمتها

(b)   To mark the use of a letter in its final form when it occurs in the middle of a word.

Qalʻahʹjī	قلعةجى
Shaykhʹzādah	شيخزاده

22.   As in the case of romanization from other languages, foreign words which occur in an Arabic context and are written in Arabic letters are romanized according to the rules for romanizing Arabic.

Jārmānūs (*not* Germanos *nor* Germanus)	جارمانوس
Lūrd Ghrānfīl (*not* Lord Granville)	لورد غرانفيل
Īsāghūjī (*not* Isagoge)	ايساغوجى

For short vowels not indicated in the Arabic, the Arabic vowel nearest to the original pronunciation is supplied.

Gharsiyā Khayin (*not* García Jaén)	غرسيا خين

Examples of Irregular Arabic Orthography

23.   Note the romanization of الله, alone and in combination.

        Allāh   الله

        billāh   بالله

        lillāh   لله

        bismillāh   بسم الله

        al-Mustanṣir billāh   المستنصر بالله

24.   Note the romanization of the following personal names.

        Ṭāhā   طه

        Yāsīn   يس ، يسن

        ‘Amr   عمرو

        Bahjat   بهجت ، بهجة

25.   ابن and بن are both romanized *ibn* in all positions.

        Aḥmad ibn Muḥammad ibn Abī al-Rabīʻ   احمد بن محمد بن ابى الربيع

        Sharḥ Ibn ‘Aqīl ‘alá Alfīyat   شرح ابن عقيل على الفية

        Ibn Mālik   ابن مالك

Exception is made in the case of modern names, typically North African, in which the element بن is pronounced *bin*.

        Bin Khiddah   بن خده

        Bin-‘Abd Allāh   بنعبد الله

26.   Note the anomalous spelling مائة, romanized *mi’ah*.

SPECIAL CHARACTERS AND CHARACTER MODIFIERS IN ROMANIZATION

Special Characters	Name	USMARC hexadecimal code
′	soft sign (prime)	A7
’	alif (hamzah)	AE
‘	ayn	B0

Character Modifiers	Name	USMARC hexadecimal code
́	acute	E2
̄	macron	E5
̣	dot below	F2

Armenian

Vernacular	Romanization		Vernacular	Romanization	
Upper case letters			*Lower case letters*		
Ա	A		ա	a	
Բ	B [P]	(see Note 1)	բ	b [p]	(see Note 1)
Գ	G [K]	(see Note 1)	գ	g [k]	(see Note 1)
Դ	D [T]	(see Note 1)	դ	d [t]	(see Note 1)
Ե	{ E / Y }	(see Note 2)	ե	{ e / y }	(see Note 2)
Զ	Z		զ	z	
Է	Ē		է	ē	
Ը	Ĕ		ը	ĕ	
Թ	T'		թ	t'	
Ժ	Zh	(see Note 3)	ժ	zh	(see Note 3)
Ի	I		ի	i	
Լ	L		լ	l	
Խ	Kh	(see Note 3)	խ	kh	(see Note 3)
Ծ	Ts [Dz]	(see Notes 1, 3)	ծ	ts [dz]	(see Notes 1, 3)
Կ	K [G]	(see Note 1)	կ	k [g]	(see Note 1)
Հ	H		հ	h	
Ձ	Dz [Ts]	(see Notes 1, 3)	ձ	dz [ts]	(see Notes 1, 3)
Ղ	Gh	(see Note 3)	ղ	gh	(see Note 3)
Ճ	Ch [J]	(see Note 1)	ճ	ch [j]	(see Note 1)
Մ	M		մ	m	
Յ	{ Y / H }	(see Note 4)	յ	{ y / h }	(see Note 4)
Ն	N		ն	n	
Շ	Sh	(see Note 3)	շ	sh	(see Note 3)
Ո	O		ո	o	
Չ	Ch'		չ	ch'	
Պ	P [B]	(see Note 1)	պ	p [b]	(see Note 1)
Ջ	J [Ch]	(see Note 1)	ջ	j [ch]	(see Note 1)
Ռ	Ṙ		ռ	ṛ	
Ս	S		ս	s	
Վ	V		վ	v	
Տ	T [D]	(see Note 1)	տ	t [d]	(see Note 1)
Ր	R		ր	r	
Ց	Ts'		ց	ts'	
Ւ	W		ւ	w	
Ու	U		ու	u	
Փ	P'		փ	p'	
Ք	K'		ք	k'	
Եւ	Ew	(see Note 5)	եւ	ew	(see Note 5)
Եվ	Ev	(see Note 6)	եվ	ev	(see Note 6)
Օ	Ō		o	ō	
Ֆ	F		ֆ	f	

Notes

1. The table is based on the phonetic values of Classical and East Armenian. The variant phonetic values of West Armenian are included in brackets but are intended solely for use in preparing references from West Armenian forms of name when this may be desirable.
2. This value is used only when the letter is in initial position of a name and followed by a vowel, in Classical orthography.
3. The soft sign (prime) is placed between the two letters representing two different sounds when the combination might otherwise be read as a digraph (e.g., Դզնունի *D′znuni*)
4. This value is used only when the letter is in initial position of a word or of a stem in a compound, in Classical orthography.
5. Romanization for letters in Classical orthography, sometimes appears as Ու .
6. Romanization for letters in Reformed orthography, sometimes appears as Ու .

SPECIAL CHARACTERS AND CHARACTER MODIFIERS IN ROMANIZATION

Special character	Name	USMARC hexadecimal code
′	Soft sign (prime)	A7
‘	ayn	B0

Character modifiers	Name	USMARC hexadecimal code
ō	macron	E5
ŏ	hachek	E9
ọ	dot below	F2

Assamese

Vowels and Diphthongs (see Note 1)

অ	a		ঋ	r̥̄
আ	ā		৯	l̥
ই ঈ	i		এ	e
ঈ ঊ উ	ī		ঐ	ai
উ ঊ উ	u		ও	o
উ ঊ উ	ū		ঔ	au
ঋ	r̥			

Consonants (see Note 2)

Gutturals		**Palatals**		**Cerebrals**		**Dentals**	
ক	ka	চ	ca	ট	ṭa	ত	ta
খ	kha	ছ	cha	ঠ	ṭha	ৎ	ṯa
গ	ga	জ	ja	ড	ḍa	থ	tha
ঘ	gha	ঝ	jha	ড়	ṛa	দ	da
ঙ	ṅa	ঞ	ña	ঢ	ḍha	ধ	dha
				ঢ়	ṛha	ন	na
				ণ	ṇa		

Labials		**Semivowels**		**Sibilants**		**Aspirate**	
প	pa	য	ya	শ	śa	হ	ha
ফ	pha	য়	ẏa	ষ	sha		
ব	ba	ৰ	ra	স	sa		
ভ	bha	ল	la				
ম	ma	ৱ	wa				

Anusvāra		*Bisarga*		*Candrabindu (anunāsika)* (see Note 3)		*Abagraha* (see Note 4)	
ং	ṃ	ঃ	ḥ	ঁ	n̐, m̐	ঽ	' (apostrophe)

Notes

1. Only the vowel forms that appear at the beginning of a syllable are listed; the forms used for vowels following a consonant can be found in grammars; no distinction between the two is made in transliteration.

2. The vowel *a* is implicit after all consonants and consonant clusters and is supplied in transliteration, with the following exceptions:

    (a) when another vowel is indicated by its appropriate sign; and

    (b) when the absence of any vowel is indicated by the subscript sign (ˎ) called *hasanta* or *birāma*.

3. *Candrabindu* before gutteral, palatal, cerebral, and dental occlusives is transliterated *ṅ*. Before labials, sibilants, semivowels, the aspirate, vowels, and in final position it is transliterated *m̐*.

4. When doubled, *abagraha* is transliterated by two apostrophes (″).

SPECIAL CHARACTERS AND CHARACTER MODIFIERS IN ROMANIZATION

Special character	*Name*	*USMARC hexadecimal code*
ʼ	apostrophe	27

Character modifiers	*Name*	*USMARC hexadecimal code*
́◌	acute	E2
̃◌	tilde	E4
̄◌	macron	E5
̇◌	dot above	E7
̆◌	candrabindu	EF
◌̣	dot below	F2
◌̥	circle below	F4
◌̱	underscore	F6

Azerbaijani

Letters of the Alphabet

Initial	Medial	Final	Alone	Romanization
ا	ـا	ـا	ا	(see **Vowels and Digraphs**)
بـ	ـبـ	ـب	ب	b
پـ	ـپـ	ـپ	پ	p
تـ	ـتـ	ـت	ت	t
ثـ	ـثـ	ـث	ث	s̲
جـ	ـجـ	ـج	ج	c
چـ	ـچـ	ـچ	چ	ç
حـ	ـحـ	ـح	ح	ḥ
خـ	ـخـ	ـخ	خ	x
دـ	ـدـ	ـد	د	d
ذـ	ـذـ	ـذ	ذ	z̲
رـ	ـرـ	ـر	ر	r
زـ	ـزـ	ـز	ز	z
ژـ	ـژـ	ـژ	ژ	j
سـ	ـسـ	ـس	س	s
شـ	ـشـ	ـش	ش	ş
صـ	ـصـ	ـص	ص	ṣ
ضـ	ـضـ	ـض	ض	ẓ̤
طـ	ـطـ	ـط	ط	ṭ
ظـ	ـظـ	ـظ	ظ	ẓ
عـ	ـعـ	ـع	ع	ʻ (ayn)
غـ	ـغـ	ـغ	غ	ğ
فـ	ـفـ	ـف	ف	f
قـ	ـقـ	ـق	ق	q
كـ	ـكـ	ـك	ك	k
گـ	ـگـ	ـگ	گ	g
لـ	ـلـ	ـل	ل	l
مـ	ـمـ	ـم	م	m
نـ	ـنـ	ـن	ن	n
وـ	ـوـ	ـو	و	v
هـ	ـهـ	ـه	ه	h
یـ	ـیـ	ـی	ی	y

Vowels and Digraphs	Value	Examples	
a	◌َ	barakat	بركت
i	◌ِ	sāḥil	ساحل
ı	◌ِ	bādımcān	بادمجان
u	◌ُ	qudrat	قدرت
ū	◌ُو	būg̱ā	بوغا
ā	آ ، ا	ārām	آرام
e	ائِ	enlī	ائنلی
ī	◌ِى	dalīl	دلیل
ı	◌ِى	qārānlıq	قارانلیق
ī	◌ِاى	īş	ایش
ı	◌ِاى	ışıq	ایشیق
o	◌ُاُو	on	اُون
ū	◌ُاو	ūn	اون
ö	◌ُاؤ	ön	اؤن
ü	◌ُاُو	üzüm	أوزوم
ey	◌َىْ	eyvān	ایوان
aw	◌َو	Awḥadī	اوحدی
a	◌َا	avval	اوّل
i	◌ِا	istiqlāl	استقلال

Notes to the Tables

1. As seen in the examples above, vowel harmony, which is found in Modern Turkish, applies to Azerbaijani as well.

2. The letter ى in final position may represent the long vowel romanized *á*, in addition to the vowels romanized *ī* and *ı*. This occurs in Arabic names, such as:
   Muṣṭafá
   al-Muṯanná

3. Vowel points are used sparingly in Azerbaijani publications. For romanization, they must be supplied from a dictionary.

RULES OF APPLICATION

Letters Which May Be Romanized in Different Ways Depending on Their Context

1. ء (*hamzah*)

   (a) When initial, ء is not represented in romanization.

           üzdah   أوزده

(b) When medial or final in words of Perso-Arabic origin, ء is romanized as ' (alif), except when it accompanies the phonetic sound *e* (as in *men*), in which case it is romanized by *e*.

	mas'alah	مسئله
but	gecah	گنجه
	neçah	نئچه

2. ٓ (*maddah*)

    (a) Initial آ is romanized *ā*.

        ādām   آدام

    (b) Medial آ, when it represents the phonetic combination '*ā*, is so romanized.

        Ḥeydar'ābād   حیدرآباد

3. ّ (*shaddah* or *tashdīd*) is represented by doubling the letter or digraph concerned.

        sāqqāl   ساققال

Note the exceptional case where ّ is written over و and ى to represent the combination of long vowel plus consonants.

        madanīyat   مدنیّت

4. *Tanvīn* (written ٌ, ٍ, ً, اً), which occurs chiefly in Arabic words, is romanized *un, in, an,* and *an*, respectively.

5. The consonant letter ة at the end of Arabic words in the genetive construction (*iẓāfah*) is romanized by *t*.

        takmilat al-axbār   تكملة الاخبار

Grammatical Structure as It Affects Romanization

6. *Iẓāfah*. When two Persian words are used in an Azerbaijani context in a relationship known as *iẓāfah*, the first word (the *muẓāf*) is followed by an additional letter or syllable in romanization. This is added according to the following rules:

    (a) When the *muẓāf* bears no special mark of *iẓāfah*, it is followed by *-i*.

        Sāzmān-i tabliğāti-Islāmī   سازمان تبلیغات اسلامی

    (b) When the *muẓāf* is marked by the addition of ء, it is followed by *-'i*.

        Nābiğah-'i dahr   نابغهٔ دهر

    (c) When the *muẓāf* is marked by the addition of ى, it is followed by *-yi*.

        daryā-yi nūr   دریای نور

(d) *Iẓāfah* is represented in romanization of personal names only when implied in the Persian
script.

Mucīr-i Beylaqānī	مجیر بیلقانی
Maktabī-i Şīrāzī	مکتبی شیرازی

Affixes and Compounds

7.   Affixes.

(a) When the affix and the word with with it is connected grammatically are written separately in
Azerbaijani, the two are separated in romanization by a single prime (ʹ).

gecahʹlar	گنجه لر
ʻālimʹlar	عالم لر
Nacafʹzādah	نخف زاده
Vahābzādahʹnīn	وهابزادهنین
YāzıçıʹĪdī	یازیچی ایدی
O ādāmlārʹīdīlār	او آداملاراید یلار
ḥayaṭdahʹkī	حیطدهکی

(b) The Arabic article *al* is separated by a hyphen, in romanization, from the word to which it is
prefixed.

maqbarat al-şuʻarā	مقبرة الشعرا
ʻAbd al-Karīm	عبد الکریم

8.   Compounds. When the elements of a compound (except a compound personal name) are written
separately in Azerbaijani, they are separated in romanization by a single prime (ʹ).

	Islāmʹ şinās	اسلام شناس
but	Naqd ʻAlī	نقد علی
	ʻAvaẕ ʻAlī	عوضعلی

Orthography of Azerbaijani in Romanization

9.   Capitalization.

(a) Rules for the capitalization of English are followed, except that the Arabic article *al* is lower
cased in all positions.

(b) Diacritics are used with both upper and lower case letters in romanization.

10.   Foreign words. Foreign words in an Azerbaijani context, including Persian and Arabic words, are
romanized according to the rules for Azerbaijani. For short vowels not indicated in the script, the
Azerbaijani vowels nearest the original pronunciation of the word are supplied in romanization.

safīnat al-nacāt	سفینة النجات
Şāhanşāhī	شاهنشاهی
kāpītālāsyon	کاپیتالاسیون

SPECIAL CHARACTERS AND CHARACTER MODIFIERS IN ROMANIZATION

Special Characters	Name	USMARC hexadecimal code
′	soft sign (prime)	A7
᾿	alif	AE
ʻ	ayn	B0
ı	Turkish i (lower case)	B8

Character Modifiers	Name	USMARC hexadecimal code
́	acute	E2
̃	tilda	E4
̄	macron	E5
̆	breve	E6
̇	dot above	E7
̈	umlaut (diearesis)	E8
̧	cedilla	F0
̣	dot below	F2
̤	double dot below	F3
̲	underscore	F6

BLANK PAGE

Balinese

1. Principal consonants[1]

ᬳ	ᬳ	(h)a[2]	ᬧ	ᬧ	pa
ᬦ	ᬦ	na	ᬤ	ᬤ	ḍa
ᬘ	ᬘ	ca	ᬥ	ᬥ	dha
ᬭ	ᬭ	ra	ᬚ	ᬚ	ja
ᬓ	ᬓ	ka	ᬬ	ᬬ	ya
ᬤ	ᬤ	da	ᬜ	ᬜ	ña
ᬢ	ᬢ	ta	ᬫ	ᬫ	ma
ᬲ	ᬲ	sa	ᬕ	ᬕ	ga
ᬯ	ᬯ	wa	ᬩ	ᬩ	ba
ᬮ	ᬮ	la	ᬝ	ᬝ	ṭa
			ᬗ	ᬗ	nga

2. Other consonant forms[3]

ᬡ	ᬡ	na (ṇa)		ᬂ	'a
	ᬙ	ca (cha)		ᬳ	ha
ᬣ		ta (tha)		ᬔ	kha
ᬰ	ᬰ	sa (śa)		ᬨ	fa
ᬱ	ᬱ	sa (ṣa)		ᬚ	za
ᬨ	ᬨ	pa (pha)		ᬖ	gha
ᬖ	ᬖ	ga (gha)			
ᬪ	ᬪ	ba (bha)			

3. Vowels and other agglutinating signs[4]

	ᬅ[5]	a			ya, ia[6]
[7]	ᬆ	ā			r [8]
		e			ra
		ai			rĕ
		ĕ			
		ö			rö
		i			lĕ
		ī			lö
		o			h
		au			ng
		u [9]			ng
		ū			

4. Numerals

	1		2		3		4		5
	6		7		8		9		0

Notes

1. Each consonant has two forms, the regular and the appended, shown on the left and right respectively in the romanization table. The vowel *a* is implicit after all consonants and consonant clusters and should be supplied in transliteration, unless:
   (a) another vowel is indicated by the appropriate sign; or
   (b) the absence of any vowel is indicated by the use of an *adeg-adeg* sign (ᬳ᭄). (Also known as the *tengenen* sign; *paten* in Javanese.)

2. This character often serves as a neutral seat for a vowel, in which case the *h* is not transcribed. Generally speaking, *ha* in word-initial or vowel-medial position in a root word, is transcribed without the *h*. Root word-final *ha* followed by suffixal vowels, on the other hand, is always written with *h*. When questions arise as to whether the *h* should be represented, consult a standard dictionary of Balinese in Latin script.

3. "Other consonant forms" refers to *aksara wayah* ("on the left") and *aksara rekan* ("on the right"). The *aksara rekan*, which are most frequently encountered in texts originating from north Bali and Lombok, are used to indicate phonemes alien to Balinese, particularly words of Arabic or Dutch origin. When used in purely Balinese words, the *aksara wayah* are similar to capital letters and have an honorific effect which is not preserved in standard romanization. In words of Sanskrit origin, or in writing Sanskrit, Old Javanese, or Old Balinese text, the same characters represent aspiriated or other consonants and should be romanized with the alternative equivalents provided in parentheses.

4. Vowels are almost always indicated by one of a class of agglutinating signs (*pangangge-suara*) added above, below, before, or after the consonant or consonant cluster which they affect. Other signs are used to indicate the various forms of the semi-vowels *r*, *l*, and *y*, as well as the consonants *h* and *ng*, when they occur in certain positions within a syllable. Free standing vowels (shown to the right in romanization table) are most commonly found in initial syllables only. No difference between vowels indicated by free standing characters and those represented by agglutinating signs is preserved in romanization.

5. Sometimes this character, the *a-kara*, is used as a neutral seat that, when marked with the appropriate sign, can also be transliterated as *i*, *u*, etc. Thus ꦇ is romanized *i*, and so forth.

6. This character, the *nania*, is used in consonant clusters within words. Consonant clusters between words formed when the second word begins with *y* use the ordinary appended form of *ya*. In romanization these two forms are not distinguished. In some words (for example: *siap*), the *nania* is transcribed as *ia* instead of *ya*. Familiarity with the orthographical conventions is necessary to assure proper romanization of such words.

7. This mark, the *ledung*, forms optional ligatures with all letters except *ba*, *nga*, *ja*, and *nya*, slightly changing their morphology. For example, ꦤꦸꦌ may also be written ꦤꦸꦌ.

8. This character, the *surung-i*, takes the special form ꜀ following the *suku-i*. Thus ꦫꦶ is romanized *rhi*.

9. This character, the *suku-u*, takes the form √ with certain consonants and semi-vowels. Thus ꦲꦸ, is romanized *hru* and ꦚꦸ is romanized *nyu*.

SPECIAL CHARACTERS AND CHARACTER MODIFIERS IN ROMANIZATION

Special character	*Name*	*USMARC hexadecimal code*
ʻ	ayn	B0

Character modifiers	*Name*	*USMARC hexadecimal code*
́	acute	E2
̃	tilde	E4
̄	macron	E5
̆	breve	E6
̈	dieresis (umlaut)	E8
̣	dot below	F2

Belorussian

Vernacular	Romanization		Vernacular	Romanization
Upper case letters			*Lower case letters*	
А	A		а	a
Б	B		б	b
В	V		в	v
Г	H		г	h
Ґ	G		ґ	g
Д	D		д	d
Е	E		е	e
Ё	ĪŌ		ё	ī͡o
Ж	Z͡H		ж	z͡h
З	Z		з	z
І	I		і	i
Й	Ĭ		й	ĭ
К	K		к	k
Л	L		л	l
М	M		м	m
Н	N		н	n
О	O		о	o
П	P		п	p
Р	R		р	r
С	S		с	s
Т	T		т	t
У	U		у	u
Ў	Ŭ		ў	ŭ
Ф	F		ф	f
Х	Kh		х	kh
Ц	Ts		ц	ts
Ч	Ch		ч	ch
Ш	Sh		ш	sh
Щ	Shch		щ	shch
Ы	Y		ы	y
Ь	′ (soft sign)		ь	′ (soft sign)
Э	Ė		э	ė
Ю	Ī͡U		ю	ī͡u
Я	Ī͡A		я	ī͡a

SPECIAL CHARACTERS AND CHARACTER MODIFIERS IN ROMANIZATION

Special character	*Name*	*USMARC hexadecimal code*
ʹ	soft sign (prime)	A7

Character modifiers	*Name*	*USMARC hexadecimal code*
̆	breve	E6
̇	dot above	E7
͡	ligature, 1st half	EB
͡	ligature, 2nd half	EC

Bengali

Vowels and Diphthongs (see Note 1)

অ	a		ঋ	r̥̄
আ	ā		৯	l̥
ই ঈ	i		এ	e
উ ঊ	ī		ঐ	ai
	u		ও	o
	ū		ঔ	au
ঋ	r̥			

Consonants (see Note 2)

Gutturals		Palatals		Cerebrals		Dentals	
ক	ka	চ	ca	ট	ṭa	ত	ta
খ	kha	ছ	cha	ঠ	ṭha	ৎ	ṯa
গ	ga	জ	ja	ড	ḍa	থ	tha
ঘ	gha	ঝ	jha	ড়	ṛa	দ	da
ঙ	ṅa	ঞ	ña	ঢ	ḍha	ধ	dha
				ঢ়	ṛha	ন	na
				ণ	ṇa		

Labials		Semivowels		Sibilants		Aspirate	
প	pa	য	ya	শ	śa	হ	ha
ফ	pha	য়	ẏa	ষ	sha		
ব	ba (See Note 3)	র	ra	স	sa		
ভ	bha	ল	la				
ম	ma	ব	ba (see Note 3)				

Anusvāra		*Bisarga*		*Candrabindu* *(anunāsika)* (see Note 4)		*Abagraha* (see Note 5)	
ং	ṃ	ঃ	ḥ	ঁ	n̐, m̐	ঽ	' (apostrophe)

Notes

1. Only the vowel forms that appear at the beginning of a syllable are listed; the forms used for vowels following a consonant can be found in grammars; no distinction between the two is made in transliteration.

2. The vowel *a* is implicit after all consonants and consonant clusters and is supplied in transliteration, with the following exceptions:
    (a) when another vowel is indicated by its appropriate sign; and
    (b) when the absence of any vowel is indicated by the subscript symbol (ˏ) called *hasanta* or *birāma*.

3. ব is used both as a labial and as a semivowel. When it occurs as the second consonant of a consonant cluster, it is transliterated *va*. When ব is doubled, it is transliterated *bba*.

4. *Candrabindu* before guttural, palatal, cerebral, and dental occlusives is transliterated *n̐*. Before labials, sibilants, semivowels, the aspirate, vowels, and in final position it is transliterated *m̐*.

5. When doubled, *abagraha* is transliterated by two apostrophes (”).

SPECIAL CHARACTERS AND CHARACTER MODIFIERS IN ROMANIZATION

Special character	Name	USMARC hexadecimal code
’	apostrophe	27

Character modifiers	Name	USMARC hexadecimal code
́	acute	E2
̃	tilde	E4
̄	macron	E5
̆	breve	E6
̇	dot above	E7
̐	candrabindu	EF
̣	dot below	F2
̱	underscore	F6

Bulgarian

Vernacular	Romanization		Vernacular	Romanization	
Upper case letters			*Lower case letters*		
А	A		а	a	
Б	B		б	b	
В	V		в	v	
Г	G		г	g	
Д	D		д	d	
Е	E		е	e	
Ж	Zh		ж	zh	
З	Z		з	z	
И	I		и	i	
Й	Ĭ		й	ĭ	
К	K		к	k	
Л	L		л	l	
М	M		м	m	
Н	N		н	n	
О	O		о	o	
П	P		п	p	
Р	R		р	r	
С	S		с	s	
Т	T		т	t	
У	U		у	u	
Ф	F		ф	f	
Х	Kh		х	kh	
Ц	T͡S		ц	t͡s	
Ч	Ch		ч	ch	
Ш	Sh		ш	sh	
Щ	Sht		щ	sht	
Ъ	Ŭ	(see Note 1)	ъ	ŭ	(see Note 1)
Ь	-	[disregarded]	ь	-	[disregarded]
Ѣ	I͡E	(see Note 2)	ѣ	i͡e	(see Note 2)
Ю	I͡U		ю	i͡u	
Я	I͡A		я	i͡a	
Ѫ	Ŭ	(see Note 2)	ѫ	ŭ	(see Note 2)

Notes

1. ъ is romanized as *ŭ* when it appears in the middle of a word. It is disregarded when it appears at the end of a word.
2. Letter is found chiefly in older texts.

CHARACTER MODIFIERS IN ROMANIZATION

Character Modifiers	*Name*	*USMARC hexadecimal code*
̆	breve	E6
͡	ligature, first half	EB
͜	ligature, second half	EC
̐	candrabindu	EF

Burmese

1. Consonants

က	ka	ဋ	ṭa	ပ	pa
ခ	kha	ဌ	ṭha	ဖ	pha
ဂ	ga	ဍ	ḍa	ဗ	ba
ဃ	gha	ဎ	ḍha	ဘ	bha
င	ṅa	ဏ	ṇa	မ	ma
စ	ca	တ	ta	ယ	ya
ဆ	cha	ထ	tha	ရ	ra
ဇ	ja	ဒ	da	လ	la
ဈ	jha	ဓ	dha	ဝ	va
ဉ	ñña	န	na	သ	sa
ဉ	ña			ဟ	ha
				ဠ	ḷa
				အ	'a

2. Vowels (see Note 1)

□ာ , □ါ	□ā	ေ□	□e	အ	i
□ိ	□i	ဲ့	□ai	ဤ	ī
□ီ	□ī	ေ□ာ , ေ□ါ	□o	ဥ	u
□ု , □ု	□u	ေ□ာ် , ေ□ၟ	□o'	ဦ	ū
□ူ , □ူ	□ū	ုံ , ုံ	□ui	ဧ	e
				ဩ	o
				ဩ်	o'

3. Medials

□ျ	□y	□ြ	□r		
□ွ	□v	□ှ	□h		

Medials are written in the order: *y* or *r - v - h*; for example:

မျှ	myha	ကြွ	krva	လွှ	lvha	မြွင်း	mrvhaṅ ' //

Notes

1. Some symbols in the Burmese script are attached above, below, or beside a consonant. Where such symbols are listed in this table, the symbol "□" is used to represent the consonant.

2. Absence of a vowel symbol in the script is represented by *a* in romanization, with the following exceptions:
   (a) when a different vowel is indicated by its appropriate symbol (see 2. Vowels);
   (b) when the absence of any vowel is indicated by the symbol ◌် (see 5. Final symbols).

4. Conjunct consonants

Romanize an upper consonant before a lower one:

တက္ကသိုလ်	takkasuil‘	တိရစ္ဆာန်	tiracchān‘	ကမ္ဘာ	kambhā

Note that the following consonants have modified forms when conjunct:

င်္□	ṅ□	ဉ္ဈ	□ñjh	ဍ္ဎ	□ḍḍh
ဏ္ဍ	□ṇḍ	ဇ္ဈ	□jjh	ဋ္ဌ	□ṭṭh
ဏ္ဌ	□ṇṭh	ဿ	□ss		

5. Final Symbols

□်	□‘	□ံ	□ṃ

6. Tone Marks

□့	□′	□း	□″

Examples:	ပို့	pui′	ပိုး	pui″

7. Punctuation

၊	, (comma)	။	(period)

8. Numerals

The numerals are: ၀ (0), ၁ (1), ၂ (2), ၃ (3), ၄ (4), ၅ (5), ၆ (6), ၇ (7), ၈ (8), ၉ (9).

9. Abbreviations

၏	e*	၍	r*
၌	n*	၎	l*

10. Word Division

For Burmese words, leave a space after each syllable.

For loanwords, use the same word division as in the original language. Apply the same practice to loanwords with modified forms in Burmese.

ကော်မီတီ	ko'mītī	*(English)*
ဥပုသ်	upus'	*(modified Pali)*
ပန်းကန်	pan'"kan'	*(Mon)*
ကော်ပြန့်	ko'pran''	*(Chinese)*

11. Capitalization

Capitalize words according to the rules that apply to English.

For personal names composed of Burmese elements, or of elements treated as Burmese, capitalize the initial letter of each syllable.

မောင်မောင်စိုးတင့်	Moṅ' Moṅ' Cui" Taṅ''
စောစိုင်မောင်	Co Cuiṅ' Moṅ'
ချန်ရီစင်	Khyan' Rī Cin'

Note the following names with non-Burmese elements:

ကဲနက်ဘစိန်	Kainak' Bha Cin'
မြသီတာ	Mra Sītā
ပဒေသရာဇာ	Padesarājā

12. Examples

မဟာသမိုင်းတော်ကြီးညွှန့်ပေါင်း	Mahā samuiṅ'" to' krī" ññvan'' poṅ'"
ယောအတွင်းဝန်ဦးဖိုးလှိုင်	Yo 'A tvaṅ'" van' Ū" Phui" Lhuiṅ'
ဒုဋ္ဌဂါမဏိမင်းကြီးဝတ္ထု	Duṭṭhagāmaṇi maṅ'" krī" vatthu

SPECIAL CHARACTERS AND CHARACTER MODIFIERS IN ROMANIZATION

Special character	Name	USMARC hexadecimal code
*	asterisk	42
′	soft sign (prime)	A7
'	alif	AE
'	ayn	B0
″	hard sign (double prime)	B7

Character modifiers	Name	USMARC hexadecimal code
õ	tilde	E4
ō	macron	E5
ȯ	dot above	E7
ọ	dot below	F2

Chinese

ROMANIZATION, CAPITALIZATION, AND PUNCTUATION

1. Romanization

a)   The Wade-Giles system of romanization, as employed in Herbert A. Giles' *A Chinese-English Dictionary* (2nd edition, London, 1912), is used with the following modifications and rules of application:

1)   Omit the diacritic marks *breve* (̆) and *circumflex* (̂);
2)   The phonetically obsolete final *-io* (syllabic *yo*) and the phonetically redundant syllabic *yi* and *ê* are eliminated;
3)   The national or Kuo-yü (Peking) standard pronunciation is followed in the reading of characters and in making necessary semantic distinctions between multiple readings of single characters, according to the usage of *Kuo yü tz'u tien (Gwoyeu tsyrdean)* Shanghai, 1937 (reprinted in Taipei, 1959), the romanized orthography of the latter being modified to conform to Wade-Giles[1]
4)   colloquial reading are normally preferred to "literary" ones, and those designated by *Kuo yü tz'u tien* as "another reading" (又 讀) are not used, except as required by usage in special compounds. A list of modifications is appended.

b)   Titles of works written in classical Chinese by Japanese or Korean authors (i.e., in *Kambun* or *Hanmun*) are romanized as Japanese or Korean, respectively; titles of Japanese or Korean editions of works written in Chinese by Chinese authors are romanized as Chinese if "reading marks" or textual matter in Japanese or Korean have not been added. Reference is made from the alternative romanization when such titles are traced as added entries.

2.   Capitalization

a)   The first word of a corporate name is capitalized. The first word of the name of a corporate subdivision appearing in conjunction with the name of the larger body is capitalized only when used in headings.
b)   Geographical names and the names of dynasties are capitalized.
c)   The first word of the title of a book, periodical, or series is capitalized.
d)   Only the first syllable of hyphenated surnames and given names or courtesy names in two syllables (two characters) is capitalized.

3.   Punctuation

a)   A centered point (·) indicating co-ordinate words is transcribed as a comma.
b)   Brackets (「 ... 」) used in the manner of quotation marks (" ... ") are transcribed as the latter.

---

[1]Cf. *Concise Dictionary of Spoken Chinese*, by Yuen Ren Chao and Lien Sheng Yang (Harvard University Press, 1947) p. 279-282 (Concordance of Wade-Giles and National Romanization) and p. 255-278 (Index Proper) and *Chinese Character Indexes*, by Ching-yi Dougherty, Sydney M. Lamb, and Samuel E. Martin (University of California Press, 1963) v. 1, p. xxii-xxix.

4.   Word Division

Each character is romanized as a separate word.

Exceptions:

1) The romanized parts of multicharacter surnames and given names are hyphenated.
2) The romanized parts of multicharacter geographic names are hyphenated when these names appear in titles or as part of corporate names (except for geographical generics, which appear as separate words).

Chung-kuo wen hsüeh chia lieh chuan	中國文學家列傳
Shang-hai shih chih nan	上海市指南
Shih nien lai chih T'ai-wan ta hsüeh	十年來之臺灣大學
Wo so jen shih ti Chiang Chieh-shih	我所認識的蔣介石

Table of Modifications to Romanizations

Number	Giles' Romanization, Character, and Number	Reading and page in Kuo yü tz'u tien	ALA-LC Romanization
1	ch'a 查 193	a) Ja (渣) 2595 b) char (叉) 2793	a) Cha (as a surname) b) ch'a
2	chao 糕 482	jwo (卓) 2726	cho
3	chao 晃 493	chaur (抄) 2814	ch'ao
4	chêng 偵 699	a) jen (眞) 2649 b) jeng (正) 又讀 2681	chen
5	ch'êng 乘 770 (read *shêng* or *chêng* as a numerative of vehicles and temples or annals)	a) cherng (稱) 2892 b) sheng (生) 3185	a) ch'eng b) sheng (in the compounds 大乘 in the Buddhist sense of *vehicle* and 史乘 to mean *annals*)
6	chi 劇 905	a) jyi (鶏) 又讀 1781 b) jiuh (居) 1997	chü
7	ch'i 谿 1007	a) chi (欺) 又讀 2032 b) shi (希) 同溪 2232	hsi
8	ch'i 溪 1009 (also read *hsi*)	a) chi (欺) 又讀 2032 b) shi (希) 2232	hsi

Number	Giles' Romanization, Character, and Number			Reading and page in *Kuo yü tz'u tien*				ALA-LC Romanization
9	ch'i (also read *chi*)	畿	1066	a) ji b) chyi	（鷄） （欺）又讀		1761 2051	chi
10	ch'i (also read *chieh*)	詰	1098	jye	（皆）		1833	chieh
11	ch'i	技	1104	jih	（鷄）		1786	chi
12	ch'i	隙	1119	shih	（希）		2259	hsi
13	ch'iai (also pronounced *k'ai*)	楷	1203	a) kae b) jie	（開） （皆）又讀		1474 1822	k'ai
14	chiang	襁	1240	cheang	（腔）		2141	ch'iang
15	chiang	港	1245	gaang	（剛）		1313	kang
16	chiao	酵	1353	a) jiaw b) shiaw	（交）又讀 （曉）		1866 2333	hsiao
17	ch'iao	雀	1387	a) chiau b) cheau c) chiueh	（橋） （橋） （缺）		2077 2086 2194	a) ch'iao (in the compounds 斑雀 , 家雀） b) ch'üeh
18	chieh	俠	1446	a) jya b) shya	（加）與夾通 （蝦）		1812 2263	hsia
19	chieh	絜	1493	a) jye b) shye	（皆） （寫）		1836 2288	a) chieh (in the sense of *pure, clean*) b) hsieh (in the sense of *to regulate, to adjust*)
20	chieh	憨	1551	chih	（欺）		2068	ch'i
21	ch'ieh	鍇	1576	kae	（開）		1475	k'ai
22	chien	歉	1633	chiann	（牽）		2123	ch'ien
23	chien (as a surname: *Chüan*)	雋	1648	a) jiuann b) jiunn	（損） （均）		2014 2026	a) Chüan (as a surname) b) chün
24	chien	鎸	1649	jiuan	（損）		2010	chüan

Number	Giles' Romanization, Character, and Number			Reading and page in *Kuo yü tzʻu tien*				ALA-LC Romanization
25	chih	砥	1886	a) dii b) jyy	(低) (之) 又讀		622 2579	ti
26	chʻih	幟	1963	jyh	(之)		2592	chih
27	chʻih	杕	2011	shyh	(師)		47	shih
28	chʻin (read *chʻien*: *to engrave*)	錢	2085	a) chiin b) chian	(鈊) 又讀 (銎)		2132 2108	chʻien
29	chʻin	浸	2090	jinn	(金)		1935	chin
30	ching (read *ying*: *a shadow*)	景	2143	a) jiing b) yiing	(京) (英) 同影		1968 4164	a) ching b) ying (in the compound 景印)
31	ching	津	2163	chin	(金)		1911	chin²
32	chʻing	鯨	2202	a) jing b) chyng	(京) (輕) 又讀		1952 2168	ching
33	chʻiung	炯	2377	jeong	(迥)		2027	chiung
34	chʻiung	迥	2380	jeong	(扃)		2028	chiung
35	chu	澍	2612	shuh	(書)		3215	shu
36	chʻu	姝	2625	shu	(書)		3190	shu
37	chʻu	樗	2627	shu	(書)		3199	shu
38	chʻu	徂	2628	tswu	(粗)		3518	tsʻu
39	chʻu (also read *hsü*, and used with 蓄 4744)	畜	2669	a) shiuh b) chuh	(虛) (初)		2493 2914	a) hsü b) chʻu (in the com- pounds 畜生 , 畜類 , 家畜)
40	chuang	奘	2758	a) joang b) tzanq	(莊) (臧)		2743 3411	a) chuang b) tsang (used in the name of the Bud- dhist priest 玄奘)
41	chui	捶	2807	chwei	(吹)		2924	chʻui

---

²The U.S. Board on Geographic Names lists the name   天津   as *Tʻien-ching*, because it follows Giles' romanization.

Number	Giles' Romanization, Character, and Number	Reading and page in Kuo yü tz'u tien	ALA-LC Romanization
42	ch'ui 椎 2823	a) chwei （吹）又讀 2924 b) juei （追） 2728	chui
43	ch'uo 擉 2938	chuh （初） 46	ch'u
44	ch'uo 焯 2943 (also read *ch'ao*)	jwo （卓） 2723	cho
45	chüeh 榷 3243	chiueh （缺） 2196	ch'üeh
46	fang 彷 3439	a) parng （滂） 221 b) faang （方） 472	a) p'ang (in the compounds 彷徨, 彷徉) b) fang (in the compound 彷彿)
47	fou 浮 3600	a) four （否）又讀 432 b) fwu （夫） 498	fu
48	fou 蜉 3602	fwu （夫） 502	fu
49	fou 阜 3607	fuh （夫） 522	fu
50	fou 埠 3608	buh （布） 172	pu
51	hao 鶴 3888 (also read *ho*)	a) heh （河） 1566 b) haur （蒿）語音 1586	ho
52	ho 和 3945	a) her （河） 1543 b) han （寒） 1618 c) hwo （火） 1677 　 huoh （火） 1682	a) ho b) huo (in the compounds 和麵, 暖和, 和藥)
53	ho 燬 3957	huoh （火） 1682	huo
54	ho 郝 3968 (read *Hao* in Peking as a surname)	a) heh （河）讀音 1564 b) hao （蒿）語音 1586	hao
55	ho 霍 3979	huoh （火） 1679	huo
56	hsi 鸙 4117	ji （鶻） 1751	chi
57	hsia 劼 4224	jye （皆） 1830	chieh
58	hsiao 橚 4319 (also read *su*)	suh （蘇） 3691	su

Number	Giles' Romanization, Character, and Number		Reading and page in Kuo yü tz'u tien				ALA-LC Romanization
59	hsiao 肴	4332	a) shyau b) yau	(曉) (腰)	又讀	2308 4009	yao
60	hsiao 餚	4333	a) shyau b) yau	(曉) (腰)	又讀	2308 4009	yao
61	hsieh 薛	4371	shiue	(靴)		2497	hsüeh
62	hsieh 骸	4381	hair	(孩)		1569	hai
63	hsien 軒	4474	shiuan	(喧)		2514	hsüan
64	hsien 檻 (also read k'an)	4510	a) kaan b) jiann	(堪) (堅)		1488 1908	a) k'an (in the compound 門檻) b) chien
65	hsien 艦	4511	jiann	(堅)		1909	chien
66	hsin 莘 (read Shen, name of a place)	4565	a) shin b) shen	(欣) (深)	又讀	2386 3127	a) hsin (in the compound 細莘 [folk medicine] or as a geographic name 莘莊 [in Shanghai] b) shen
67	hsing 馨	4616	a) shin b) shing	(欣) (興)	又讀	2399 2454	hsin
68	hsü 嶼	4762	yeu	(迂)		4372	yü
69	hsüan 壎	4830	a) shiuan b) shiun	(喧) (薰)	又讀	2515 2532	hsün
70	hsün 峻	4897	jiunn	(均)		2023	chün
71	hsün 鵕	4899	jiunn	(均)		2025	chün
72	huan 皖	5062	a) hoan b) woan	(欸) (彎)		1709 4281	wan
73	huang 況 (interchanged with 況 6412 [k'uang])	5146	kuanq	(筐)		1525	k'uang

Number	Giles' Romanization, Character, and Number	Reading and page in *Kuo yü tz'u tien*			ALA-LC Romanization
74	hui 會 5184 (read *kuei*: to calculate; a district of) Chekiang)	a) hoei b) guey c) kuay	(灰) (歸) (快)	1696/99 1388 1509	a) hui b) kuei (in the geographic name 會稽) c) k'uai (in the compound 會計 and surname)
75	hui 潰 5206	a) kuey b) huey	(虧) (灰) 又讀	1514 1703	k'uei
76	hui 瞶 5207	a) guey b) kuey	(歸) (虧)	1387 1514	k'uei
77	hun 焜 5240	kuen	(昆)	1520	k'un
78	hung 嶸 5287	a) horng b) rong	(紅) 又讀 (戎)	1749 3345	jung
79	i 錡 5361	chyi	(欺)	2046	ch'i
80	i 擬 5426 (also read *ni*)	nii	(泥)	909	ni
81	i 霓 5434 (also read *ni*)	ni	(泥)	908	ni
82	i 液 5509	a) yih b) yeh	(衣) 讀音 (耶)	3961 3997	yeh
83	jao 橈 5579	a) rau b) nau	(饒) 又讀 (膒)	3267 881	nao
84	jê 偌 5590	ruoh	(弱)	3324	jo
85	jo 若 5644	a) ruoh b) ree	(弱) (惹)	3324 3263	a) jo b) je (in the compounds 般若 , 蘭若 , etc.)
86	jo 惹 5645	ree	(熱)	3264	je
87	jo 熱 5649	reh	(惹)	3264	je
88	jung 瑩 5742 (also read *ying*)	yng	(英)	4160	ying
89	jung 縈 5743	yng	(英)	4160	ying
90	jung 焭 5744 (also read *ying*)	yng	(英)	4160	ying
91	ko 柯 6039 (read *k'o* in Peking)	ke	(科)	1453	k'o

Number	Giles' Romanization, Character, and Number	Reading and page in *Kuo yü tz'u tien*			ALA-LC Romanization
92	ko 蛤 6058	a) ger b) har	(哥) (哈)	1254 1540	a) ko b) ha (in the compound 蛤蟆)
93	k'uei 恢 6481 (also read *hui*)	huei	(灰)	1687	hui
94	kun 鯤 6525	kuen	(昆)	1520	k'un
95	kung 肩 6584 (also read *chiung*)	jiong	(迥)	2027	chiung
96	kung 駉 6585	jiong	(迥)	2027	chiung
97	kung 礦 6588 (read *k'uang* in Peking)	a) goong b) kuanq	(公) 又讀 (筐)	1441 1527	k'uang
98	li 履 6952 (also read *lü*)	a) lii b) leu	(黎) 又讀 (驢)	1059 1236	lü
99	liao 了 7073	a) le b) leau	(聊) (勒)	973 1086	a) le (when used as a suffix in the sense of completed action or change of status, e.g., 不要了) b) liao
100	lieh 捋 7094	leh	(勒)	970	le
101	lieh 捋 7095	a) leh b) leu c) lhuo	(勒) (驢) (羅)	970 1237 1192	a) le b) lü (in the sense of 捋鬍鬚) c) luo (in the sense of 捋胳膊)
102	lo 勒 7316 (also read *lei*)	a) leh b) lhei	(仂) (雷)	968 980	a) le b) lei (in the sense of *to tighten up with string or rope*)
103	lo 樂 7331 (read *yao: to find pleasure in*) (read *yüeh: music*)	a) leh b) law c) yao d) yueh	(勒) (勞) (腰) (約)	970 1008 4022 4417	a) le b) lao (in the geographical name 樂亭) c) yao (in the sentences 仁者樂山，智者樂水) d) yüeh (to mean *music*, or used as surname)
104	lung 弄 7507 (also read *nung*, *nou*, and *nêng*)	a) now b) neng c) nonq d) long	(撈) 又讀 (能) 又讀 (農) (龍) 又讀	887 903 945 1230	nung

Number	Giles' Romanization, Character, and Number	Reading and page in *Kuo yü tz'u tien*			ALA-LC Romanization
105	mêng 氓 7790	a) mang	（忙）	343	a) mang (in the compound 流氓)
		b) meng	（萌）	348	b) meng
106	miu 繆 7965 (also read *niu*, etc.)	a) mou	（謀） 繆篆	329	Miao (as a surname)
		b) Miaw	（苗） 姓	365	
		c) miow	（謬） 與謬通	366	
		d) muh	（母） 與穆通	401	
107	mo 邈 7998	meau	（苗）	363	miao
108	mo 沒 8016 (also read *mu*; a negation of 有 in which sense also read *mei*)	a) moh	（歿）	297	a) mo
		b) mei	（煤）	310	b) mei (as a negation in colloquial usage)
109	mou 愁 8043	a) maw	（毛）	327	mao
		b) mou	（謀） 又讀	329	
110	mou 畝 8050 (also read *mu*)	a) moou	（謀） 又讀	329	
		b) muu	（母）	390	mu
111	mu 摹 8064 (also read *mo*)	mo	（摩）	286	mo
112	mu 模 8066	a) mo	（摩） 又讀	286	a) mo (in the compounds 模範，模糊)
		b) mu	（母）	390	b) mu
113	mu 鶩 8085 (also read *wu*)	a) muh	（母） 又讀	401	wu
		b) wuh	（烏）	4221	
114	nio 虐 8343	niueh	（謔）	951	nüeh
115	no 吶 8371 (read *na: to blurt out*)	nah	（拿）	867	na
116	pan 般 8591	a) ban	（班）	89	a) pan
		b) parn	（潘）	213	b) p'an (in the compounds 般樂，般桓)
		c) bo	（玻）	22	c) po (in the compound 般若)
117	pan 畔 8606 (also read *p'an*)	pann	（潘）	217	p'an
118	pao 曝 8726 (also read *p'u*)	puh	（鋪）	273	p'u

Number	Giles' Romanization, Character, and Number			Reading and page in *Kuo yü tz'u tien*				ALA-LC Romanization
119	pei (used for 坡 9408)	陂	8770	a) pyi b) po	(批) (坡)		234 193	a) p'i (in 陂塘, 陂池) b) p'o (in 陂陀, or when used for 坡)
120	p'ei	丕	8818	pi	(批)		230	p'i
121	pêng	派	8875	a) bang b) bin	(邦) (賓)		105 150	a) pang b) pin (when used as short form of 濱)
122	pi	泌	8928	a) bih b) mih	(比) (米)		115 357	a) pi (in the geographic name 泌陽) b) mi
123	pi	秘	8932	a) bih b) mih	(比) (米)	又讀	115 357	a) pi (in the geographic name 秘魯 *Peru*) b) mi
124	ping	拼	9290	pin	(品)		249	p'in
125	p'ing	聘	9326	a) pinn b) pinq	(拼) (平)		253 264	a) p'in b) p'ing (in the compound 聘姑娘)
126	po (also read *p'o*)	迫	9345	poh	(坡)		196	p'o
127	po (read *pa* in Peking)	跋	9386	bar	(巴)		14	pa
128	po	鏷	9407	pwu	(鋪)		269	p'u
129	p'o	朴	9416	a) poh b) pwu	(坡) (鋪)	與樸通	197 268	a) p'o (in the compounds 厚朴, 朴硝) b) p'u
130	p'o	勃	9425	bor	(玻)		35	po
131	p'o (also read *p'u*)	璞	9443	pwu	(鋪)		269	p'u
132	pu	圃	9458	puu	(鋪)		270	p'u
133	p'u	都	9518	buh	(布)		172	pu
134	shan	闡	9704	chaan	(產)		2839	ch'an

Number	Giles' Romanization, Character, and Number	Reading and page in *Kuo yü tz'u tien*			ALA-LC Romanization
135	shang 裳 9734	a) charng	(昌)	2871	a) ch'ang (in the sense of *brightness*)
		b) shang	(商) 又讀	3149	b) shang (in the compound 衣裳)
136	shao 灼 9769	jwo	(卓)	2722	cho
137	shên 槮 9828	chin	(欽)	2126	ch'in
138	shên 諗 9844	chern	(陳)	2854	ch'en
139	shên 忱 9848	chern	(陳)	2851	ch'en
140	shih 匙 9941	a) shy	(師)	3040	a) shih (in the compound 鑰匙)
		b) chyr	(痴)	2778	b) ch'ih (to mean *spoon* or when used as a surname)
141	shih 碩 9967	a) shyr	(師)	3000	shuo
		b) shuoh	(朔) 語音	3227	
142	shu 銖 10038	ju	(朱)	2701	chu
143	shun 淳 10139 (also read *ch'un*)	chwen	(春)	2943	ch'un
144	shun 鶉 10142	chwen	(春)	2945	ch'un
145	shun 蹲 10148	chwen	(春)	2945	ch'un
146	shun 純 10149	chwen	(春)	2941	ch'un
147	shun 蒓 10150	chwen	(春)	2943	ch'un
148	shun 隼 10162	joen	(準)	2738	chun
149	sou 漱 10247 (read *shu* colloquially)	a) shuh	(書) 語音	3213	shu
		b) sow	(搜) 古音	3614	
150	su 疏 10321 (read *shu* or *su; to set forth, to explain as a running commentary*)	a) shu	(書)	3197	shu
		b) su	(蘇) 又讀	3671	
151	su 蔬 10322	a) shu	(書)	3198	shu
		b) su	(蘇) 又讀	3671	

Number	Giles' Romanization, Character, and Number			Reading and page in *Kuo yü tz'u tien*				ALA-LC Romanization
152	sui	粹	10417	tsuey	（崔）		3530	ts'ui
153	sun	巽	10441	a) shiunn b) suenn	（燕） （孫）	又讀	2545 3727	hsün
154	tao	燾	10798	a) daw b) taur	（刀） （涛）	又讀	588 730	t'ao
155	tieh	凸	11142	a) dye b) twu	（爹） （土）	又讀	635 818	t'u
156	t'o	拓	11400	a) tah	（他）	与搨通	707	a) t'a (in the compounds 拓本，拓片)
				b) tuoh c) jyr	（拖） （之）		832 2564	b) t'o c) chih（同撫）
157	ts'ang	瑲	11594	chiang	（脍）		2134	ch'iang
158	ts'ao	懆	11649	a) tzaw b) tsao	（糟） （操）	又讀	3398 3502	tsao
159	tsu	祚	11851	tzuoh	（坐）		3431	tso
160	tsun	儁	11964	jiunn	（均）		2026	chün
161	t'un	潡	12241	duenn	（敦）		694	tun
162	t'ung	僮	12300	torng	（通）		857	a) t'ung b) chuang (in the compound 僮族)
163	tzŭ	姊	12359	a) jiee b) tzyy	（皆） （資）	讀音	1837 3358	a) chieh b) tzu (in the compounds 姊妹篇，姊妹花)
164	wai	葳	12448	uei	（威）		4247	wei
165	wai	膸	12449	kuey	（皹）		1514	k'uei
166	wei 尉 (read *Wei*: Wei-ch'ih as a surname) (read *yü*: as a military official)		12621	a) wei b) Yuh	（威） （迂）	 複姓	4268 4398	a) wei b) Yü-ch'ih (as a double surname)

Number	Giles' Romanization, Character, and Number			Reading and page in Kuo yü tz'u tien				ALA-LC Romanization
167	wei	薈	12632	huey	（灰）		1702	hui
168	wu	握	12742	woh	（窩）		4235	wo
169	wu	沃	12793	a) wuh b) woh	（烏） （窩）	又讀	4226 4234	 wo
170	yai	涯	12838	ya	（鴉）		3975	ya
171	yao （also read *nio*)	瘧	12960	a) niueh b) yaw	（虐） （腰）		951 4023	a) nüeh b) yao (in the compound 瘧子）
172	yeh （also read *chieh* and *hsieh*)	擷	12979	a) jye b) shye	（拮） （寫）	又讀	1833 2288	a) chieh (in the compound 擷英） b) hsieh
173	yo （also read *yüeh* and [Peking] *yao*; *to weigh*)	約	13349	iue	（曰）		4402	yüeh
174	yo	籥	13362	yueh	（約）		4419	yüeh
175	yo	岳	13366	yueh	（約）		4414	yüeh
176	yo	嶽	13367	yueh	（約）		4420	yüeh
177	yo	躍	13371	yueh	（約）		4420	yüeh
178	yüan （read *wan*: *pleasant, genial, kind*, used with 12479 娩 [*wan*])	婉	13721	woan	（彎）		4279	wan
179	yüan	琬	13724	woan	（彎）		4280	wan

SPECIAL CHARACTERS AND CHARACTER MODIFIERS IN ROMANIZATION

Special character	*Name*	*USMARC hexadecimal code*
'	ayn	B0

Character modifiers	*Name*	*USMARC hexadecimal code*
◌̈	umlaut (dieresis)	E8

Church Slavic

Vernacular	Romanization	Vernacular	Romanization	Numeric Value
Upper case letters		*Lower case letters*		
А	A	а	a	1
Б	B	б	b	
В	V	в	v	2
Г	G	г	g	3
Д	D	д	d	4
Є	E	є	e	5
Є	Ē	є	ē	
Ѥ	ÎE	ѥ	îe	
Ж	Zh	ж	zh	
Ѕ	Ż	ѕ	ż	6
З	Z	з	z	7
И	I	и	i	8
Й	Ĭ	й	ĭ	
І	Ī	i	ī	10
К	K	к	k	20
Л	L	л	l	30
М	M	м	m	40
Н	N	н	n	50
О	O	о	o	70
П	P	п	p	80
Р	R	р	r	100
С	S	с	s	200
Т	T	т	t	300
ОУ	U	оу	u	400
Ȣ	Ū	ȣ	ū	400
Ф	F	ф	f	500
Х	Kh	х	kh	600
Ѿ	ÔT	ѿ	ôt	800
Ѡ	Ō	ѡ	ō	800
Ц	T̂S	ц	t̂s	900
Ч	Ch	ч	ch	90
Ш	Sh	ш	sh	
Щ	Sht	щ	sht	
Ъ	″ (hard sign)	ъ	″ (hard sign) (see Note 4)	
Ы	Ȳ	ы	ȳ	
Ꙑ	Y	ꙑ	y	
Ь	′ (soft sign)	ь	′ (soft sign)	
Ѣ	Ě	ѣ	ě	

Vernacular	Romanization	Vernacular	Romanization	Numeric Value
Upper case letters		*Lower case letters*		
Ю	$\widehat{\text{IU}}$	ю	$\widehat{\text{iu}}$	
Ѩ	$\widehat{\text{IA}}$	ꙗ	$\widehat{\text{ia}}$	
Ѧ	Ę	ѧ	ę	900
Ѯ	$\widehat{\text{KS}}$	ѯ	$\widehat{\text{ks}}$	60
Ѱ	$\widehat{\text{PS}}$	ѱ	$\widehat{\text{ps}}$	700
Ѳ	Ḟ	ѡ	ḟ	9
Ѵ̈	Ẏ	ѵ̈, y	ẏ (v̇ if used without dia- critical marks)	400
Ҳ	Q	ҳ	Q	
Ѩ	$\widehat{\text{IĘ}}$	ѩ	$\widehat{\text{ię}}$	
Ѭ	$\widehat{\text{IǪ}}$	ѭ	$\widehat{\text{iǫ}}$	
Ћ	Ǵ	ћ	ǵ	

Notes

1. Diacritical signs

   Accents and aspiration marks are ignored in romanization. Marks ignored in romanization include the acute accent ($\acute{\square}$), the grave accent ($\grave{\square}$), the aspiration mark ($\overset{\smallfrown}{\square}$), or combinations thereof ($\overset{\smallfrown}{\square}\acute{} $) or ($\overset{\smallfrown}{\square}\grave{} $).

   The letters ï and ѵ̈ are sometimes printed with two dots (or marks), as shown. In the first case, the two dots are used whenever no other accent appears, and thus they have no particular significance and are ignored in romanization. In the second case, the use of the two dots (or other diacritical marks) indicates that the letter is a vowel, and the letter is romanized ẏ, as provided for in the table.

   The symbol indicating a short i ($\breve{\square}$) is taken into account in romanization, as indicated in the table, resulting in the romanization ĭ.

2. Abbreviations

   Abbreviated words are transcribed in full, without the use of brackets. The most common symbol for abbreviation is $\overline{\square}$. Sometimes, omitted letters are placed above other letters in the word in Church Slavic texts (e.g., ѿ, е́, в), the letter added being sometimes given with a special symbol (e.g., гⷣь). The symbol ⁀ above a letter indicates the omission of ъ or ь.

3. Numerals

   Numerals are represented in Church Slavic by letters (as shown in the romanization table) with the addition of the signs ҂ ◯ ⸏ and ⸎. The addition of an abbreviation sign ($\overline{\square}$) indicates merely the representation of a basic numeral; thus ж represents 2.

Higher numerals are shown as follows:

҂в̄	2,000
Ⓑ	20,000
⁚в̇⁚	200,000
⁏в̇⁏	2,000,000

Thus, the figure 1913 is written ҂аці͞г.

4. Hard sign

   The hard sign (ъ Ъ) is disregarded in romanization when it is found at the end of a word.

5. Dates

   While Church Slavic books are usually dated in the Christian Era, they are in some cases dated by the year of the Mundane Era of Constantinople. To convert to the western calendar, subtract 5508. However, prior to 1700 A.D., the mundane year in Russia began on September 1st, so that two years must be given, obtained by subtracting 5509 and 5008, respectively. Thus, 7203 in the Mundane Era is 1694/95 in the Christian Era. In such cases, if the month of publication is known, the year may be determined by subtracting 5509 for September through December, and 5508 for January through August.

SPECIAL CHARACTERS AND CHARACTER MODIFIERS IN ROMANIZATION

Special Characters	Name	USMARC hexadecimal code
′	soft sign (prime)	A7
″	hard sign	B7

Character Modifiers	Name	USMARC hexadecimal code
́	acute	E2
̄	macron	E5
̆	breve	E6
̇	dot above	E7
̌	hachek (caron)	E9
͡	ligature, 1st half	EB
͡	ligature, 2nd half	EC
̧	right hook	F1

Divehi

Letters of the Alphabet

Consonants

◌	h	◌	t (see Note 4)
◌	ś or ẖ (see Note 1)	◌	l
◌	n (see Note 2)	◌	g
◌	r	◌	ñ
◌	b	◌	s
◌	ḷ	◌	ḍ
◌	k	◌	j
◌	' or ẖ or omit (see Note 3)	◌	c
◌	v	◌	z
◌	m	◌	ṭ
◌	f	◌	p
◌	d	◌	y

Vowels (see Note 5)

◌	a	◌	e
◌	ā	◌	ē
◌	i	◌	o
◌	ī	◌	ō
◌	u	◌	omit (see Note 6)
◌	ū		

Divehi Equivalents to represent Arabic Letters

◌	(ث)	th	◌	(ض)	ḍ
◌	(ح)	ḥ	◌	(ط)	ṭ
◌	(خ)	kh	◌	(ظ)	ẓ
◌	(ذ)	dh	◌	(ع)	' (ayn)
◌	(ش)	sh	◌	(غ)	gh
◌	(ص)	ṣ	◌	(ق)	q

Divehi

Notes

1. Romanize ﻉ as ḥ, when it doubles the following consonant, or is used as a glottal stop.

        aḥvana

        maśaḥ

2. When used in medial position without ˚ (*sukūn*), romanize as ṁ.

        aṁga

        haṁdu

3. Romanization of ﺍ .

    (a) When used in the initial position with any vowel sign, do not romanize.

        ata

        idu

        umuru

        egahugi

    (b) When used in the medial position with any vowel sign, romanize as '.

        ha'hūnu

        fa'isa

        k'īn

    (c) When a consonant follows ﺍ in a medial position, double it in romanization.

        cappalu

        appacci

    (d) When used in the final position with ˚ (*sukūn*), romanize as ẖ.

        boẖ

        biheẖ

4. Romanize ﺕ followed by another ﺕ as ṭ.

        aṭṭeri

5. Only the vowel forms that appear at the beginning of a syllable are listed. When the vowels follow a consonant, ﺍ is not used and the vowel signs are added to the consonant forms. Do not distinguish between the two in romanization.

6. ̥ (called *sukūn*), generally indicates omission of an inherent vowel associated with a consonant. For its other uses, see Notes 1, 3, and 4.

SPECIAL CHARACTERS AND CHARACTER MODIFIERS IN ROMANIZATION

Special Characters	Name	USMARC hexadecimal code
‘	ayn	B0

Character Modifiers	Name	USMARC hexadecimal code
́	acute	E2
̃	tilde	E4
̄	macron	E5
̣	dot below	F2
̤	double dot below	F3
̲	underscore	F6
̮	upadhmaniya	F9

Georgian

Values are shown for the older Khutsuri and the modern Mkhedruli alphabets. There are no upper case letters in Mkhedruli.

Upper case letters		*Lower case letters*		
Khutsuri	*Romanization*	*Khutsuri*	*Mkhedruli*	*Romanization*
Ⴀ	A	ⴀ	ა	a
Ⴁ	B	ⴁ	ბ	b
Ⴂ	G	ⴂ	გ	g
Ⴃ	D	ⴃ	დ	d
Ⴄ	E	ⴄ	ე	e
Ⴅ	V	ⴅ	ვ	v
Ⴆ	Z	ⴆ	ზ	z
Ⴇ	T‘	ⴇ	თ	t‘
Ⴈ	I	ⴈ	ი	i
Ⴉ	K	ⴉ	კ	k
Ⴊ	L	ⴊ	ლ	l
Ⴋ	M	ⴋ	მ	m
Ⴌ	N	ⴌ	ნ	n
Ⴍ	O	ⴍ	ო	o
Ⴎ	P	ⴎ	პ	p
Ⴏ	Ž	ⴏ	ჟ	ž
Ⴐ	R	ⴐ	რ	r
Ⴑ	S	ⴑ	ს	s
Ⴒ	T	ⴒ	ტ	t
Ⴓ	U	ⴓ	უ	u
Ⴔ	P‘	ⴔ	ფ	p‘
Ⴕ	K‘	ⴕ	ქ	k‘
Ⴖ	Ġ	ⴖ	ღ	ġ
Ⴗ	Q	ⴗ	ყ	q
Ⴘ	Š	ⴘ	შ	š
Ⴙ	Č‘	ⴙ	ჩ	č‘
Ⴚ	C‘	ⴚ	ც	c‘
Ⴛ	Ż	ⴛ	ძ	ż
Ⴜ	C	ⴜ	წ	c
Ⴝ	Č	ⴝ	ჭ	č
Ⴞ	X	ⴞ	ხ	x
Ⴟ	J	ⴟ	ჯ	j
Ⴠ	H	ⴠ	ჰ	h

Non-Current or Rarely Used Letters

Upper case letters			*Lower case letters*		
Khutsuri	*Romanization*		*Khutsuri*	*Mkhedruli*	*Romanization*
Ⴡ	Ē		ⴡ	ჱ	ē
Ⴢ	Y		ⴢ	ჲ	y
Ⴤ	Ẋ		ⴤ	ჴ	ẋ
Ⴥ	Ō		ⴥ	ჵ	ō
Ⴣ	W		ⴣ	ჳ	w
				ჶ ჶ	f
				ჸ	ĕ
				ჺ ჸ	' (ayn)
				ჹ ჷ	ŭ

SPECIAL CHARACTERS AND CHARACTER MODIFIERS IN ROMANIZATION

Special Characters	*Name*	*USMARC hexadecimal code*
'	ayn	B0

Character Modifiers	*Name*	*USMARC hexadecimal code*
́	acute	E2
̄	macron	E5
̆	breve	E6
̇	dot above	E7
̌	hachek	E9
̣	dot below	F2

Greek
(Also for Coptic)

Vernacular	Romanization	Vernacular	Romanization
Upper case letters		*Lower case letters*	
A	A	α	a
B	B	β	b
	(V in Modern Greek; see Note 1)		(v in Modern Greek; see Note 1)
Γ	G	γ	g (n before medial γ, κ, ξ, χ)
Δ	D	δ	d
E	E	ε	e
Z	Z	ζ	z
H	Ē	η	ē
Θ	Th	ϑ	th
I	I	ι	i
K	K	κ	k
Λ	L	λ	l
M	M	μ	m
Mπ	B	μπ	b
(initial only)		(initial only)	
N	N	ν	n
Nτ	<u>D</u>	ντ	<u>d</u>
(initial only)		(initial only)	
Ξ	X	ξ	x
O	O	ο	o
Π	P	π	p
P	R	ρ	r
ʽP	Rh (see Note 2)	ʽρ	rh (see Note 2)
Σ	S	σ (final ς)	s
T	T	τ	t
Y	Y	υ	y (u in diphthongs)
Φ	Ph	φ	ph
X	Ch	χ	ch
Ψ	Ps	ψ	ps
Ω	Ō	ω	ō

Breathing Marks (see Note 3)

Mark	Name	Romanization
ʾ	soft breathing	[omit]
ʽ	rough breathing	h

Notes

1. The era of the Modern Greek language begins with texts written after 1453. Texts written before 1454 are considered Classical Greek.

2. Diacritical marks such as accents and the dieresis, and the iota subscript (ͺ) are omitted in romanization. As the result of a presidental decree in Greece in 1982, monosyllabic words are now written without accents; polysyllabic words are written with the acute accent (́) only.

3. The romanization for rough breathing is supplied whether or not the mark appears in the Greek vernacular text.

Numerals

Characters	Value		Characters	Value
α′	1		ρ′	100
β′	2		σ′	200
γ′	3		τ′	300
δ′	4		υ′	400
ε′	5		φ′	500
ς′ or στ	6		χ′	600
ζ′	7		ψ′	700
η′	8		ω′	800
ϑ′	9		ϡ′	900
ι′	10			
ια′	11		͵α	1000
et cetera			͵αα	1001
			͵αβ	1002
κ′	20		et cetera	
κα′	21			
κβ′	22		͵β	2000
et cetera			͵γ	3000
			͵δ	4000
λ′	30		͵ε	5000
μ′	40		et cetera	
ν′	50			
ξ′	60			
ο′	70			
π′	80			
ϟ′	90			

CHARACTER MODIFIERS IN ROMANIZATION

Characters	Name	USMARC hexadecimal code
◌̄	macron	E5
◌̲	underscore	F6

Gujarati

Vowels and Diphthongs (see Note 1)

અ	a		ઋ	ṛ
આ	ā		એ	e
ઇ	i		ઍ	ê
ઈ	ī		ઐ	ai
ઉ	u		ઓ	o
ઊ	ū		ઑ	ô
			ઔ	au

Consonants (see Note 2)

Gutturals		Palatals		Cerebrals		Dentals	
ક	ka	ચ	ca	ટ	ṭa	ત	ta
ખ	kha	છ	cha	ઠ	ṭha	થ	tha
ગ	ga	જ	ja	ડ	ḍa	દ	da
ઘ	gha	ઝ	jha	ઢ	ḍha	ધ	dha
ઙ	ṅa	ઞ	ña	ણ	ṇa	ન	na

Labials		Semivowels		Sibilants		Aspirate	
પ	pa	ય	ya	શ	śa	હ	ha
ફ	pha	ર	ra	ષ	sha		
બ	ba	લ	la	સ	sa		
ભ	bha	ળ	ḷa				
મ	ma	વ	va				

Anusvāra (see Note 3)		*Visarga*		*Avagraha* (see Note 4)	
ં̇	ṃ	:	ḥ	ઽ	' (apostrophe)

Notes

1. Only the vowel forms that appear at the beginning of a syllable are listed; the forms used for vowels following a consonant can be found in grammars; no distinction between the two is made in transliteration.

2. The vowel *a* is implicit after all consonants and consonant clusters and is supplied in transliteration, with the following exceptions:

   (a) when another vowel is indicated by its appropriate sign; and

   (b) when the absence of any vowel is indicated by the subscript sign (◌) called *halanta* or *virāma*.

3. Exception: *anusvāra* is transliterated by:

   ṅ before gutturals,

   ñ before palatals,

   ṇ before cerebrals,

   n before dentals, and

   m before labials.

4. When doubled, *avagraha* is transliterated by two apostrophes (ˮ).

SPECIAL CHARACTERS AND CHARACTER MODIFIERS IN ROMANIZATION

Special character	*Name*	*USMARC hexadecimal code*
ʾ	apostrophe	27

Character modifiers	*Name*	*USMARC hexadecimal code*
́◌	acute	E2
̂◌	circumflex	E3
̃◌	tilde	E4
̄◌	macron	E5
̇◌	dot above	E7
◌̣	dot below	F2
◌̥	circle below	F4

Hebrew and Yiddish

The following romanization table attempts to represent the sound of Hebrew or Yiddish words but is applicable to all Hebraic languages. For Hebrew, it approximates the modern Israeli, primarily Sephardic, pronunciation. For Yiddish, the table follows the standardized, principally Lithuanian, pronunciation. In romanizing Yiddish, the etymology of the word is ignored.

Consonants

Vernacular	Romanization	Vernacular	Romanization
א	' (alif) or disregarded	ל	l
ב	b	מ (final ם)	m
ב	v (in Yiddish, b)	נ (final ן)	n
ג	g	ס	s
ד	d	ע	' (ayn)
ה	h	פ (final ף)	p
ו	v̇ (only if a consonant)	פ (final ף)	f
וו	v̇ (only if a consonant)	צ (final ץ)	ts
ז	z	ק	ḳ
ח	ḥ	ר	r
ט	ṭ	שׁ	sh
י	y (only if a consonant)	שׂ	ś
כ (final ך)	k	תּ	t
כ (final ך)	kh	ת	t (in Yiddish, s̀)

Vowels

In Hebrew	Romanization	In Yiddish	Romanization
◌	a		
◌	a or o	א	a or o
◌	e		
◌	e	ו , אוּ	u
◌	i		
◌	o	וי , אוֹי	oy
◌	u		
◌	e	י , אִי	i
◌	ai		
◌	e	ע	e
◌	i		
וֹ	o	יי , אײַ	ay (if pronounced ai as in *aisle*, or)
וּ	u		
◌	e or disregarded	יי , אײ	ey (if pronounced ei as in *weigh*)
◌	a		
◌	e		
◌	o		

A single prime (′) is placed between two letters representing two distinct consonantal sounds when the combination might otherwise be read as a digraph.

his′hid   הסהיד

RULES OF APPLICATION

In romanizing Hebrew, it is often necessary to consult dictionaries and other sources as an appendage to the romanization table presented here, primarily for the purpose of supplying vowels. The principle dictionary used is *ha-Milon he-ḥadash* (Jerusalem: Ḳiryat-sefer, 1966-1970) by Avraham Even-Shoshan. More detailed instructions on romanization of Hebrew and Yiddish, including cataloging guidelines, can be found in *Hebraica Cataloging* (Washington, D.C.: Library of Congress, Cataloging Distribution Service, 1987) by Paul Maher.

SPECIAL CHARACTERS AND CHARACTER MODIFIERS IN ROMANIZATION

Special Characters	*Name*	*USMARC hexadecimal code*
′	soft sign (prime)	A7
’	alif	AE
‘	ayn	B0

Character Modifiers	*Name*	*USMARC hexadecimal code*
ȁ	grave	E1
á	acute	E2
ọ	dot below	F2

Hindi

Vowels and Diphthongs (see Note 1)

Traditional Style	New Style	Romanization
अ	अ	a
आ	आ	ā
इ	बि	i
ई	बी	ī
उ	बु	u
ऊ	बू	ū
ऋ	बृ	r̥
ॠ	बॄ	r̥̄
ऌ		l̥
ऎ	बॆ	ĕ
ए	बे	e
ऐ	बॅ	ê
ऐ	बैं	ăi
ऐ	बै	ai
ओ	बॉ	ŏ
ओ	बो	o
आँ	आँ	ô
औ	औ	ău
औ	औ	au

Consonants (see Notes 2 and 3)

Gutturals		Palatals		Cerebrals		Dentals	
क	ka	च	ca	ट	ṭa	त	ta
[क़³	qa]	छ	cha	[ट़³	ṭa]	थ	tha
ख	kha	ज	ja	ठ	ṭha	द	da
[ख़³	k̲ha]	[ज़³	za]	ड	ḍa	ध	dha
ग	ga	झ	jha	ड़	ṛa	न	na
[ग़³	g̲ha]	ञ	ña	ढ	ḍha		
घ	gha			ढ़	ṛha		
[घ़³	g̲ha]			ण	ṇa		
ङ	ṅa						

Labials		Semivowels		Sibilants		Aspirate	
प	pa	य	ya	श	śa	ह	ha
फ	pha	र	ra	ष	sha	[हॢ³	ḥa]
[फ़³	fa]	ल	la	स	sa		
ब	ba	व	va	[सॢ³	ṣa]		
भ	bha						
म	ma						

Anusvāra (see Note 4)		*Anunāsika* (see Note 5)		*Visarga*		*Avagraha* (see Note 6)	
◌ं	ṃ	◌ँ	ṅ, m̐	:	ḥ	ऽ	' (apostrophe)

Notes

1. Only the vowel forms that appear at the beginning of a syllable are listed; the forms used for vowels following a consonant can be found in grammars; no distinction between the two is made in transliteration.

2. The vowel *a* is implicit after all consonants and consonant clusters and is supplied in transliteration, with the following exceptions:
    (a) when another vowel is indicated by its appropriate sign; and
    (b) when the absence of any vowel is indicated by the subscript sign (्) called *halanta* or *virāma*.

3. The dotted letters, shown in brackets in the table, are used in Urdu words.

4. Exception: *Anusvāra* is transliterated by:
    ṅ before gutturals,
    ñ before palatals,
    ṇ before cerebrals,
    n before dentals, and
    m before labials.

5. *Anunāsika* before guttural, palatal, cerebral, and dental occlusives is transliterated ṅ. Before labials, sibilants, semivowels, aspirates, vowels, and in final position it is transliterated m̐.

6. When doubled, *avagraha* is transliterated by two apostrophes ('').

SPECIAL CHARACTERS AND CHARACTER MODIFIERS IN ROMANIZATION

Special character	Name	USMARC hexadecimal code
,	apostrophe	27

Character modifiers	Name	USMARC hexadecimal code
á	acute	E2
â	circumflex	E3
ã	tilde	E4
ā	macron	E5
ă	breve	E6
ȧ	dot above	E7
a̐	candrabindu	EF
ạ	dot below	F2
a̤	double dot below	F3
ḁ	circle below	F4
a̲	double underscore	F5
a̱	underscore	F6

Japanese

Romanization System

The modified Hepburn system of romanization as employed in *Kenkyusha's New Japanese-English Dictionary* (3rd and later editions) is used. For the syllabic nasal, *n* is always used preceding *b*, *m*, and *p*. Romanization for words of foreign (i.e., non-Japanese) origin follows the American National Standard system for the romanization of Japanese; e.g., ベトナム (Betonamu); ヴェトナム (Vetonamu).

Word Reading

The reading of Japanese words follows standard Japanese language usage, insofar as this can be determined from standard Japanese dictionaries. A current modern reading is preferred to an obsolete one, except where the usage of standard authorities has established a particular reading for a particular name or book title. The characters 日本 are romanized as *Nihon* unless the usage of standard authorities has established a particular reading; e.g., Dai *Nippon* Teikoku, *Nippon*'ichi, *Nippon* eitaigura, etc. If there are various readings, the reading that appears most frequently in dictionaries is used.

Capitalization

1. *Personal Names:*
    (a) Capitalize each word of a personal name, except the particle *no*.
         Sugawara no Takasue no Musume   菅原孝標女

    (b) Capitalize title and terms of address, except when consisting of a single character or kana for *san, sama, chan, kun*, etc., that is hyphenated following a personal name.
         Kōbō Daishi   弘法大師
         but   Okiku-san   お菊さん

2. *Place Names:* Capitalize each separately written word of a geographic name.
    Yokohama   横浜
    Nihon Rettō   日本列島
    Yūraku-chō   有楽町
    Taiheiyō   大平洋
    Bōsō Hantō   房総半島
    Tōyō   東洋

3. *Corporate Names:* Capitalize each separately written word of a corporate name, except particles and conjunctions.

    Sensō o Kirokusuru Kai   戦 争 を 記 録 す る 会

    Nihon Rikugun   日 本 陸 軍

4. *Documents and Publications:*
    (a)   Capitalize the first word of the title of a publication (book, periodical, series, etc.).

        Tsurezuregusa   徒 然 草

        Chūō kōron   中 央 公 論

    (b)   Capitalize the first word of the name of a document (law, regulation, etc.).

        Rōdō kumiaihō   労 働 組 合 法

        Rōdō iinkai kisoku   労 働 委 員 会 規 則

5. *Historical Events and Periods:*
    (a)   Capitalize each word of the name of a historical event.

        Dainiji Sekai Taisen   第 二 次 世 界 大 戦

        Niniroku Jiken   二 ・ 二 六 事 件

        Meiji Ishin shi   明 治 維 新 史

    (b)   Capitalize the first word of the name of a historical period.

        Jōmon jidai   縄 文 時 代

        Rikuchō jidai   六 朝 時 代

        Heianchō   平 安 朝

        Shōwaki   昭 和 期

6. *Peoples and Languages:* Capitalize names of peoples and languages.

    Nihonjin   日 本 人

    Amerikajin   ア メ リ カ 人

    Nihongo   日 本 語

    Eigo   英 語

7. *Religions and Sects:* Capitalize names of religions and sects.

    Bukkyō   佛 教

    Kirisutokyō   キ リ ス ト 教

    Shintō   神 道

    Zenshū   禅 宗

8. *Derivatives of Proper Names:* Lowercase words derived from names of places or religions, when the derived words are no longer considered to be proper names. When the derivative is formed by the suffix of a single character following a proper name, the proper name is capitalized and the suffix is lowercased and follows a hyphen. (See **Word Division**, 4. *Proper Names, Exceptions*)

    nihontō   日 本 刀

	nihonshu	日本酒
	nihonga	日本画
	butsuga	佛画
	washitsu	和室
	wafuku	和服
	yōshu	洋酒
	kutaniyaki	九谷焼
	kokutani	古九谷
	kanji	漢字
	kanpō	漢方
	kan'yaku	漢薬
	zendera	禅寺
	zensō	禅僧
	kirisutosha	キリスト者
but	Taiwan-sei	台湾製

Punctuation

1. Transcribe a centered point (・) used for dividing words as a comma if it makes the meaning of romanized words clear.

Chūgoku Shikoku no mingei	中国・四国の民芸
Pōru Kurōderu	ポール・クローデル
Matsumoto Seichō, Yamamoto Shūgorō shū	松本清張・山本周五郎集

   For such a center point appearing between numbers, see **Word Division, 5.** *Numerals.*

2. Transcribe brackets (「 ... 」) used in the manner of quotation marks (" ... ") as quotation marks.

Word Division

1. *Sino-Japanese (on) Compounds:* A compound means a word consisting of two or more Chinese characters (kanji), or of Chinese characters and kana, or of kana alone, whether established by dictionary usage or not.

   (a) Write binary compounds as single words.

ichigen ikkō	一言一行
Rikuchō jidai	六朝時代
Nihon kokusei jiten	日本国政事典
kokumin shugi	国民主義
Indo tetsugaku shiyō	印度哲学史要
Tōyō Gakkai	東洋学会
Keiō Gijuku Daigaku Keizai Gakubu	慶応義塾大学経済学部
Tōkyō Daigaku Kyōyō Gakubu	東京大学教養学部

(b)   Trinary, derived, and other compounds.

(1)   Write trinary and derived compounds as single words as long as they contain no more than one binary or trinary compound.

keizaiteki	経済的
seibutsugaku	生物学
jinseikan	人生観
yuibutsuron	唯物論
kenkōhō	健康法
daijinbutsu	大人物
daiōjō	大往生
jibika	耳鼻科
koseibutsugaku	古生物学
hōshakaigaku	法社会学

For a word beginning with such characters as　新 , 旧 , etc., consult any current dictionary to determine whether it is part of a word or is a prefix to the following word or words (see **Word Division**, 3. *Prefixes, Suffixes, etc.* (a)). If it is appropriate, apply the provisions of (2) below.

shinkansen	新幹線
kyūtaisei	旧体制

(2)   Write trinary pseudo-compounds formed by the addition of a single character as single words.

gōshisō	業思想
kakusensō	核戦争
kakukazoku	核家族
ryōseikatsu	寮生活
shinkenchiku	新建築
daijiten	大辞典
daihatsumei	大発明

If, however, a single character is enclosed within brackets used as a quotation marks, transcribe the brackets as quotation marks.

"jin" shisō	「 仁 」思想
"kaku" ronsō	「 核 」論争

(c)   Write single characters in succession constituting a pseudo-compound as one word.

todōfuken	都道府県
shikuchōson	市区町村
shichōson	市町村
shinōkōshō	士農工商
ishokujū	衣食住

(d) Hyphenate grouped compounds involving phonetic changes.

jochū-bōkō	女中奉公
bungei-dokuhon	文芸読本
gōshi-gaisha	合資会社
kabushiki-gaisha	株式会社

but In proper names, romanize as *Kabushiki Kaisha* (e.g., Nissan Jidōsha Kabushiki Kaisha).

(e) Hyphenate one or more single-character modifiers having a common substantive.

shō-chūgakkō	小・中学校
shō-chū-kōtō gakkō	小・中・高等学校
shō-chūkibo kigyō	小・中規模企業
jō-gesuidō	上・下水道
nō-san-gyoson	農山漁村
nō-kō-kōgyō	農・工・鉱業
bun-shi-tetsugaku	文・史・哲学
Meiji sanjūshichi-hachinen	明治三十七・八年

When single character modifiers form a binary or trinary compound, however, follow 1(a) or 1(b) above.

chūshō kigyō	中小企業
Bunri Gakubu	文理学部
rikagaku jiten	理化学辞典
dōshokubutsu jikken	動植物実験

2. *Native Japanese (kun and jūbakoyomi or yutōyomi) compounds.*

(a) Nouns.

(1) Write compound nouns as single words.

wareware	我々
wagahai	我輩
kirisame	霧雨
teashi	手足
yamatodamashii	大和魂
mizusakazuki	水盃
ukiyoe	浮世絵
chanoma	茶の間
chanoyu	茶の湯
kokoroarigao	心有顔
iyagarase	嫌がらせ
kogirei	小綺麗
rikutsudōri	理屈通り

Write separately modifiers which are not part of compounds.

waga hokori	我が誇り
waga musuko	わが息子
waga machi	我が町
waga kyōdo	我が郷土

In case of doubt, prefer the separate form.

waga kuni	我国（わが国）
waga ko	我が子
waga tomo	我友（わが友）
chichi haha	父母
ani imōto	兄妹
are kore	あれこれ

(2) Write separately a *kun* single character word modifying a compound.

onna ekaki	女絵かき
aji jiman	味自慢
koto gassō	琴合奏
mizu shigen	水資源
kome sōdō	米騒動
otoko aite	男相手

(b) <u>Verbs</u>.
(1) Write simple and compound inflected verbs, with their auxiliaries, as single words.

shihaisuru	支配する
doraibusuru	ドライブする
yomiuru	読み得る
nashienai	なし得ない
kansuru	関する
omoidasu	思い出す

(2) Write verbs separately from adverbs or inflected adjectives and verbs.

dō kangaeru	どう考える
aa shitai	ああしたい
sō suru	そうする
kō naru	こうなる
tsuyoku naru	強くなる
utsukushiku naritai	美しくなりたい
ikite ita	生きていた
kaette kuru	帰って来る
yatte miyō	やって見よう
itadaite ikimasu	載いていきます

(3) Write honorific auxiliaries or potential auxiliaries, *dekiru* and *dekinai*, separately from other parts of the verb.

ookuri itashimashō	お送り致しましょう
odekake asobashimasu ka	お出掛け遊ばしますか
gaman dekiru ka	我慢出来るか
gaman dekimasen	我慢出来ません

(c) <u>Adjectives</u>. Write compound inflected adjectives as single words.

bimyōnaru	微妙なる
ikanaru	如何なる
miryokuaru	魅力ある
teikōnaki	抵抗なき
dōdōtaru	堂々たる
osorubeki	恐るべき
ayamatta sahō, ayamariyasui sahō	誤った作法・誤り易い作法

(d) <u>Adverbs and conjunctions</u>. Write compound adverbs and conjunctions as single words.

tokuni	特に
narabini	並に
tomoni	共に
tsuini	遂に
ikani	如何に
suguni	直ぐに
matawa	又は
aruiwa	或いは

(e) <u>Particles</u>. Write particles separately from other words and from each other.

kōfuku *e no* michi	幸福への道
E *wa* dare *ni de mo* kakeru	絵は誰にでも描ける
Sō iu hon *o* yomu *no ga* tanoshii	そういう本を読むのが楽しい
anata *to* watashi *to*	あなたとわたしと
kumo *no* ue *ni*	雲の上に
anata *no* tame *ni*	あなたの為に
nonki *na* ojisan nonki *ni* kamaeru	呑気な小父さん呑気に構える
yunīku *na* sonzai	ユニークな存在

3. *Prefixes, Suffixes, etc.*

(a) Write separately a single-character prefix modifying *on* or *kun* compounds following it.

zen shushō enzetsushū	前首相演説集
ko shachō kaikoroku	故社長懐古録
shin okurigana	新送りがな
shin shokuminchi shugi	新植民地主義
kyū dōtokuritsu	旧道徳律
kyū dojin shakai	旧土人社会

Dai jinmei jiten	大人名事典
sho̅ bungaku jiten	小文学辞典
cho̅ senshinkoku	超先進国
cho̅ genjitsu shugi	超現実主義
han senso̅ undo̅	反戦争運動
han senso̅ron	反戦争論
kaku jidai	各時代
kaku todo̅fuken	各都道府県
kaku musan seito̅	各無産政党
hi bunkateki	非文化的
hi sabetsu shakai	非差別社会
ichi toshokan'in	一図書館員
ichi kinen shashin	一記念写真

(b) Hyphenate a single character modifying, or modified by, foreign words generally written in katakana.

sho̅-enerugī	省エネルギー
kaku-enerugī	核エネルギー
datsu-enerugī	脱エネルギー
sho̅-ene	省エネ
enerugī-gen	エネルギー源
karorī-hyo̅	カロリー表
irasutore̅shon-teki	イラストレーション的

If the foreign word in katakana together with a single character is a long-established word or a corporate name, however, romanize it as one word.

Amerikajin	アメリカ人
kirisutosha	キリスト者
Saiensusha	サイエンス社
sa̅bisugyo̅	サービス業

(c) Write the suffix *to̅* or *nado* (等，など), *hen* (編，篇) used for sections of books, and *sho̅* (抄，鈔) for excepts or commentaries, *ko̅* (考，稿) for treaties or drafts, and *ten* (展) for exhibitions, separately from the word preceding them unless they form Sino-Japanese compounds, e.g., 前編，私考，草稿，特別展

kyo̅do̅ kiken ko̅i *to̅* no kinshi ihan	共同危険行為等の禁止違反
kyo̅ konogoro omoidasu koto *nado*	今日この頃思い出すことなど
senzen sengo *hen*	戦前戦後編
Nihon shokunikushi *sho̅*	日本食肉史抄
Nihon insho *ko̅*	日本印書考
Shina shoshigaku *ko̅*	支那書誌学稿
To̅zai bijutsu ko̅ryū 300-nen *ten*	東西美術交流300年展

(d) Write single-character substantives modified by *on* or *kun* compounds as part of the word preceding it.

Ochiboshū	落穂集
Kokinshū	古今集
Kokin wakashū	古今和歌集
Bunka jinmeiroku	文化人名錄
Nihon seifu gyōsei kikōzu	日本政府行政機構図
Nihon-Ro gaikō jūnenshi	日露外交十年史
Gakkō toshokanhō	学校図書館法
Kokubunji shryō chōsa hōkokusho	国分寺資料調査報告書
Meiji Taishō bungakushi	明治大正文学史
Kagoshima-ken fūbutsushi	鹿児島県風物誌
shizan kagakusha	自然科学者
jibi inkōka	耳鼻咽喉科
kyōdai shimaitachi	兄弟姉妹達
Rōdō Kijunkyoku	労働基準局
Asahi Shinbunsha	朝日新聞社
Nihon Bungaku Kenkyūkai	日本文学研究会

If the word romanized together with a single-character substantive becomes meaningless, hyphenate it with the word preceding it.

Nihon gunkoku-shugika	日本軍国主義下
hatten-tojōkoku	発展途上国

4. *Proper Names.*

(a) Write proper names and titles of books separately from modifiers or words modified by them.

Rinkān den	リンカーン伝
Niwa Fumio shū	丹羽文雄集
Genji monogatari shō	源氏物語抄
Shin jidai	清時代
Min Shin jidai	明清時代
To shi shō	杜詩抄
Nihon shi	日本史
Beikoku shi	米国史
Tōyō shiron	東洋史論

Exceptions:

(1) For proper names, including corporate names, that contain other proper names, follow 1(a)-1(b), 2(a), and 3(d) above.

Edojō	江戸城
Shijōgawara	四條河原
Sohōkai	蘇峰会

Onogumi	小野組
Gendai Nihonshi Kenkyūkai	現代日本史研究会

(2) Write names of historical periods with single-character generic terms as single words.

Shinchō	清朝
Meijiki	明治期

(3) For names of ships, write such prefixes as *maru* or *go* separately from the preceding word.

Asama Maru	浅間丸
Hayabusa Gō	はやぶさ (隼)号
Purejidento Wiruson Gō	プレジデント・ウィルソン号

(4) Hyphenate single characters which can be suffixed to any proper names; e.g., 的 , 型 , 式 , 流 , 産 , 製 , 派 , 系 , 本 , 版

Nihon-teki	日本的
Honkon-gata	香港型
Tanaka Chiyo-shiki	田中千代式
Hōshō-ryū	宝生流
Hokkaidō-san	北海道産
Taiwan-sei	台湾製
Tanaka-ha	田中派
Nakasone-kei	中曽根系
Kanda-bon	神田本
Kanazawa Bunko-ban	金沢文庫版

(5) Hyphenate an auxiliary to a proper name, which results in a double consonant.

Kyashī-tte yonde	キャシーってよんで

(b) Write titles and terms of address separately from personal names.

(1) Write separately a title that precedes a personal name.

Sei Sabieru	聖サビエル

(2) If a title or a term of address following a personal name consists of a binary or trinary compound, write it separately from the personal name.

Meiji Tennō	明治天皇
Taiken Mon'in	待賢門院
Kitashirakawa no Miyasama	北白川の宮様
Nichiren Shōninsama	日蓮上人様
Takezawa Sensei	竹沢先生

(3) Hyphenate a title or a term of address when it consists of a single character or kana for *san, sama, chan, kun*, etc., and follows a personal name.

Bashō-ō	芭蕉翁
Kakushin-ni	覚信尼
Gotoba-in	後鳥羽院

Okiku-san	お菊さん
Nakamura-kun	中村君
Tarō-chan	太郎ちゃん
Non-chan kumo ni noru	ノンちゃん雲に乗る
Sa-shi	左氏

(c) Geographic names
(1) Hyphenate generic terms used as part of the name of jurisdictions or streets.

Tōkyō-to	東京都
Chiyoda-ku	千代田区
Yūraku-chō	有楽町
Yamaguchi-ken	山口県
Yokohama-shi	横浜市
Ogawa-machi	小川町
Ogasawara-mura	小笠原村

Exceptions:

(1) Write generic terms separately if they form Sino-Japanese compounds.

Ogasawara sonchō	小笠原村長
Ogawa chōshi	小川町史
Chiyoda Kuritsu	千代田区立
Yokohama shisei	横浜市政
Tōkyō tomin	東京都民
Yamaguchi kenpō	山口県報

(2) Write *koku* as part of the name of a country.

Nihonkoku	日本国
Manshūkoku	満洲国
Kankoku	韓国

(3) Write *Kuni* separately if preceded by *no* in the name of a province.

| Musashi no Kuni | 武蔵国（武蔵の国） |

(2) Write modifiers differentiating places of the same name as part of the name, if they are part of the name of a jurisdiction.

| Higashiizu-chō | 東伊豆町 |
| Kamikitayama-mura | 上北山村 |

If the modifiers are not part of the name of a jurisdiction, write them separately.

| Minami Yamashiro | 南山城 |
| Tōnan Ajia | 東南アジア |

(3) Write compound names designating merged places or containing a larger place name as single words.

Ujiyamada-shi	宇治山田市
Aizuwakamatsu-shi	会津若松市

(4) Hyphenate generic terms for stations and harbors following place names.

Tōkyō-eki	東京駅
Yokohama-kō	横浜港

If the generic terms form Sino-Japanese compounds, write them separately.

Tōkyō ekichō	東京駅長
Yokohama kōwan	横浜港湾

(5) Write generic terms for geographic features as part of the name.

Sumidagawa	隅田川
Asamayama	浅間山
Biwako	琵琶湖
Shinanoji	信濃路
Saipantō	サイパン島

If the generic terms for Sino-Japanese compounds, write them separately.

Biwa kohan	琵琶湖畔
Asama sanroku	浅間山麓

(d) Abbreviated Forms
(1) Write words consisting of or containing abbreviated proper names as single words.

Nōbi Heiya	濃尾平野
Keihin kōgyō chitai	京浜工業地帯
Meishin kōsoku dōro	名神高速道路
Shin'etsusen	信越線
Ōbeijin	欧米人
ryūō gakusei	留欧学生
Eishibun	英詩文
tainichi bōeki	対日貿易
Kiki kayō	記紀歌謡

Hyphenate, however, a compound consisting of abbreviated names of countries or languages, except when the compound is normally elided.

Nichi-Ro gaikō jūnenshi	日露外交十年史
Nichi-Ei-Doku igo shōjiten	日英独医語小辞典
Sen-Man sōsho	鮮満叢書
Nikka daijiten	日華大辞典
Nitchū kankei	日中関係

(2) Write contracted compound proper names as single words.

Chūkyō jūyō bunkenshū	中共重要文献集
Mantetsu chihō gyōseishi	満鉄地方行政史
Soren no Nihon kenkyū	ソ連の日本研究
Hokushi Jiken no keika	北支事件の経過
Saō monogatari	沙翁物語
Fukuō hyakuwa	福翁百話

5. *Numerals*

(a) Write cardinal numbers under 100, and the numbers 100, 1,000, 10,000, and 100,000, etc., as single words, if spelled out. Separate by hyphens the hundreds, thousands, tens of thousands, etc., in numbers over 100.

sen-kyūhyaku-hachijūsannen	千九百八十三年

(b) Write the ordinal prefix *dai*, numerators, and other suffixes as part of the numbers they precede or follow, if spelled out. Write them separate from the words they modify.

daisan seiryoku	第三勢力
Dainiji Sekai Taisen kaikoroku	第二次世界大戦回顧録

(c) Transcribe a center point between numbers as a period, with no space following it. If, however, the number is spelled out in romanization as a word, then the center point is not represented by a Roman value (cf. *Library of Congress Rule Interpretations, Appendix C.4C*).

	8.15 zengo : sensō to watakushitachi	8・15前後 ：戦争と私たち
	3.14 futō hanketsu	三・一四不当判決
	20.5-seiki no ongaku	20・5世紀の音楽
but	Niniroku Jiken	二・二六事件

(d) Hyphenate numbers joined to modify a common substantive.

3-4-jigen	3・4次元
Shōwa 58-59-nendo	昭和五八・五九年度

SPECIAL CHARACTERS AND CHARACTER MODIFIERS IN ROMANIZATION

Special character	*Name*	*USMARC hexadecimal code*
’	apostrophe	27

Character modifiers	*Name*	*USMARC hexadecimal code*
ō	macron	E5

Javanese, Sundanese, and Madurese

1. Principal consonants[1]

ᬷ	ᬷ	(h)a[2]		ᬷ	ᬷ	pa
ᬷ	ᬷ	na		ᬷ	ᬷ	dha
ᬷ	ᬷ	ca		ᬷ	ᬷ	ja
ᬷ	ᬷ	ra		ᬷ	ᬷ	ya
ᬷ	ᬷ	ka		ᬷ	ᬷ	nya[3]
ᬷ	ᬷ	da		ᬷ	ᬷ	ma
ᬷ	ᬷ	ta		ᬷ	ᬷ	ga
ᬷ	ᬷ	sa		ᬷ	ᬷ	ba
ᬷ	ᬷ	wa		ᬷ	ᬷ	tha
ᬷ	ᬷ	la		ᬷ	ᬷ	nga

2. Other consonant forms[4]

				ᬷ		nya	(jña)
ᬷ		na	(ṇa)	ᬷ		ga	(gha)
	ᬷ	ca	(cha)	ᬷ		ba	(bha)
ᬷ		ra		ᬷ	ᬷ	ha	
ᬷ		ka	(kha)	ᬷ	ᬷ	kha	
ᬷ	ᬷ	ta	(tha)	ᬷ	ᬷ	fa	
ᬷ		sa	(śa)	ᬷ	ᬷ	za	
ᬷ		sa	(ṣa)	ᬷ	ᬷ	gha	
ᬷ		pa	(pha)	ᬷ	ᬷ	'a	

3. Vowels and other agglutinating signs[5]

Vowels				Other	
	ꦲ[6]	ꦄꦄ[7]	a	ꦲ	h
ꦲ	ꦲ	ꦟ	e	ꦱ	r
ꦲ	ꦲ[2]		ĕ	ꦭ	ra
ꦲ	ꦲ	ꦲ	i	ꦉ	rĕ
ꦲ	ꦲ[2]	ꦲ[2]	ꦲ[8]	ꦊ	lĕ
ꦲ	ꦲ	ꦲ	u	ꦪ	ya[9]
					ng

4. Numerals

꧑	1	꧒	2	꧓	3	꧔	4	꧕	5
꧖	6	꧗	7	꧘	8	꧙	9	꧐	0

Notes

1. Each consonant has two forms, the regular and the appended, shown on the left and right respectively in the romanization table. The vowel *a* is implicit after all consonants and consonant clusters and should be supplied in transliteration, unless:
    (a) another vowel is indicated by the appropriate sign; or
    (b) the absence of any vowel is indicated by the use of a *paten* or *pangkon* sign (꧀).

2. This character often serves as a neutral seat for a vowel, in which case the *h* is not transcribed. Generally speaking, *ha* in word-initial or vowel-medial position in a root word, is romanized without the *h*. Root word-final *ha* followed by suffixal vowels, on the other hand, is always romanized with *h*. When questions arise as to whether the *h* should be represented, consult a standard dictionary of Javanese in Latin script, especially Pigeaud, Poerwodarminto, or Horne.

3. The letter nya before the letters ja and ca should be romanized as *n* not *ny*, as in the words *panca*, *prenjak*, and so forth.

4. "Other consonant forms" refers to *aksara murda* ("on the left") and *aksara rekan* ("on the right"). The former are similar to capital letters and have an honorific effect which is not preserved in standard romanization. The *aksara rekan* are used to indicate phonemes alien to Javanese, particularly in words or Arabic and Dutch origin. Nonce forms or idiosyncratic usages may also be encountered. These are best romanized in accordance with the spelling of the foreign word intended. In words of Old Javanese origin, the same characters represent aspirated or other consonants and should be romanized with the alternative equivalents provided in parentheses.

5. Vowels are almost always indicated by one of a class of agglutinating signs (*sandangan*) added above, below, before, or after the consonant or consonant cluster which they affect. Other signs are used to indicate the semi-vowels *r*, *l*, and *y*, as well as the consonants *h* and *ng*, when they occur in certain positions within a syllable. Free standing vowels (shown to the right in romanization table) are rare, usually occurring in the initial position in words of foreign origin. No difference between vowels indicated by free standing characters and those represented by agglutinating signs is preserved in romanization.

6. The various *dirga* marks, which in Old Javanese represented long vowels, are used as colometric devices in New Javanese. They are not represented by macrons in romanization.

7. Sometimes this character, the *a-kara*, is used as a neutral seat that, when marked with the appropriate sign, can also be transliterated as *i*, *u*, etc. Thus ᬕ᭄ is romanized *i*, and so forth.

8. Penultimate *o* in an open syllable, when the final syllable is also open, is romanized as *a*, as in the words *panca*, *angka*, *rangga* and so forth.

9. This character, the *ya-pengkal*, is used in consonant clusters within words. Consonant clusters between words formed when the second word begins with *y* use the ordinary appended form of *ya*. In romanization these two forms are not distinguished.

SPECIAL CHARACTERS AND CHARACTER MODIFIERS IN ROMANIZATION

Special character	*Name*	*USMARC hexadecimal code*
'	apostrophe	27

Character modifiers	*Name*	*USMARC hexadecimal code*
́	acute	E2
̃	tilde	E4
̆	breve	E6
̣	dot below	F2

BLANK PAGE

Kannada

Vowels and Diphthongs (see Note 1)

ಅ	a		ೠ	ḷ̥
ಆ	ā		ಎ	e
ಇ	i		ಏ	ē
ಈ	ī		ಐ	ai
ಉ	u		ಒ	o
ಊ	ū		ಓ	ō
ಋ	r̥		ಔ	au
ೠ	r̥̄			

Consonants (see Note 2)

Gutturals		Palatals		Cerebrals		Dentals	
ಕ	ka	ಚ	ca	ಟ	ṭa	ತ	ta
ಖ	kha	ಛ	cha	ಠ	ṭha	ಥ	tha
ಗ	ga	ಜ	ja	ಡ	ḍa	ದ	da
ಘ	gha	ಝ	jha	ಢ	ḍha	ಧ	dha
ಙ	ṅa	ಞ	ña	ಣ	ṇa	ನ	na

Labials		Semivowels		Sibilants		Aspirate	
ಪ	pa	ಯ	ya	ಶ	śa	ಹ	ha
ಫ	pha	ರ	ra	ಷ	ṣa		
ಬ	ba	ಱ	ṟa	ಸ	sa		
ಭ	bha	ಲ	la				
ಮ	ma	ಳ	ḷa				
		ೞ	ḻa				
		ವ	va				

Anusvāra (Bindu or *Sonne)* (see Note 3)			*Visarga*	
ಂ	ṃ		ಃ	ḥ

Notes

1. Only the vowel forms that appear at the beginning of a syllable are listed; the forms used for vowels following a consonant can be found in grammars; no distinction between the two is made in transliteration.

2. The vowel *a* is implicit after all consonants and consonant clusters and is supplied in transliteration, with the following exceptions:
    (a) when another vowel is indicated by its appropriate sign; and
    (b) when the absence of any vowel is indicated by the superscript sign (ɤ)

3. Exception: *Anusvāra* is transliterated by:

    ṅ before gutturals,

    ñ before palatals,

    ṇ before cerebrals,

    n before dentals, and

    m before labials.

CHARACTER MODIFIERS IN ROMANIZATION

Character modifiers	Name	USMARC hexadecimal code
Ó	acute	E2
Õ	tilde	E4
Ō	macron	E5
Ȯ	dot above	E7
Ọ	dot below	F2
Ọ̤	double dot below	F3
Ọ̥	circle below	F4
O̲	underscore	F6

Kashmiri
(in Perso-Arabic Script)

Letters of the Alphabet

Consonants

Initial	Medial	Final	Alone	Romanization
بـ	ـبـ	ـب	ب	b
پـ	ـپـ	ـپ	پ	p
تـ	ـتـ	ـت	ت	t
ٹـ	ـٹـ	ـٹ	ٹ	ṭ
ثـ	ـثـ	ـث	ث	s̲
جـ	ـجـ	ـج	ج	j
چـ	ـچـ	ـچ	چ	c
حـ	ـحـ	ـح	ح	ḥ
خـ	ـخـ	ـخ	خ	kh
دـ	ـد	ـد	د	d
ڈـ	ـڈ	ـڈ	ڈ	ḍ
ذـ	ـذ	ـذ	ذ	z̲
رـ	ـر	ـر	ر	r
ڑـ	ـڑ	ـڑ	ڑ	ṛ
زـ	ـز	ـز	ز	z
ژـ	ـژ	ـژ	ژ	ts
سـ	ـسـ	ـس	س	s
شـ	ـشـ	ـش	ش	ś
صـ	ـصـ	ـص	ص	ṣ
ضـ	ـضـ	ـض	ض	z̤
طـ	ـطـ	ـط	ط	t̤
ظـ	ـظـ	ـظ	ظ	z̤
عـ	ـمـ	ـع	ع	' (ayn)
غـ	ـغـ	ـغ	غ	gh
فـ	ـفـ	ـف	ف	f
قـ	ـقـ	ـق	ق	q
کـ	ـکـ	ـک	ك ، ک	k
گـ	ـگـ	ـگ	گ	g
لـ	ـلـ	ـل	ل	l
مـ	ـمـ	ـم	م	m
نـ	ـنـ	ـن	ن	n
وـ	ـو	ـو	و	v
ھـ	ـھـ	ه ، ہ	ه	h
یـ	ـیـ	ـی	ی	y

Vowels

Initial	Medial	Final	Alone	Romanization
اَ	◌َ	◌َ	اَ	a
آ	◌ا	◌ا	آ	ā
اٚ	◌ٚ	◌ٚ	اٚ	ạ
اٲ	◌ٲ	◌ٲ	اٲ	ā̤
اِ	◌ِ	◌ِ	اِ	i
اٟ	◌ٟ	◌ی	ای	ī
اٖ	◌ٖ	◌ٖ	اٖ	u'
اُٟ	◌ُٟ	◌ُٟ	اُٟ	ū'
اُ	◌ُ	◌ُ	اُ	u
اوٗ	◌وٗ	◌وٗ	اوٗ	ū
اوٟ	◌وٟ	◌وٟ	اوٟ	o
او	◌و	◌و	او	ō
او	◌و	◌و	او	ọ
-	-	وآ	اوآ	ọ̄
اؠ	◌ؠ	◌ؠ	اؠ	e
اؠ	◌ؠ	◌ؠ	اؠ	ē
-	◌ؠ	◌ی	اؠ	ẏ (see Note 1)

Digraphs Representing Kashmiri Aspirates

ph	پھ
th	تھ
ṭh	ٹھ
ch	چھ
kha	کھ
tsh	ژھ

Notes

1. This sign palatalizes the preceding consonant and in the medial position is at times followed by another vowel, e.g. *a* (◌َ) or *e* (◌ؠ).

   apẏar

   When the short vowel *e* (◌ؠ) follows a palatalized consonant, replace it by ◌ِ .

   khẏen كِهؠن

RULES OF APPLICATION

Letters Which May Be Romanized in Different Ways Depending on Their Context

1. Romanize the Arabic article ال as follows:

    (a) When the article is prefixed to a word beginning with a "moon letter" (ع ، خ ، ح ، ج ، ب ، ا ، غ ، ف ، ق ، ك ، م ، و ، ه ، ى), romanize it as *al*.

    al-Qurān   القران

    (b) When the article is prefixed to a word beginning with a "sun letter" (ت ، ث ، د ، ذ ، ر ، ز ، س ، ش ، ص ، ض ، ط ، ظ ، ل ، ن), replace the *l* of the normal Roman value with a repetition of the letter of digraph that begins the romanization of the word to which the article is prefixed.

    an-nūr   النّور

    (c) When the article precedes the second noun of a gentive phrase (*iḍāfah*), follow the preceding directions for sun and moon letters, but substitute the final short vowel of the Roman value of the first noun for the *a* of the normal Roman value of the article. Romanize such two-word genitive phrases as single words.

    Muḥīuddīn   محى الدّين

2. Represent ◌ّ (*shaddah* or *tashdīd*) by doubling the Roman letter or digraph concerned.

    Muẓaffar   مظفّر

3. ◌ْ (*jazm*) or ◌ْ (*sukūn*) indicate the absence of a vowel following the letter over which it is written. It is not represented in romanization.

    roṇg   روْنگ

4. The vowel sign ◌َ is often omitted in writing, but supply its Roman value *a* in romanization.

Romanization of Foreign Words

Foreign words in a Kashmiri context are romanized according to the present table and accompanying rules. This principle covers all languages, including those also written in the Perso-Arabic script (e.g., Persian or Urdu). The following are specific guidelines, necessarily derived from or related in some way to this principle.

1. Romanize ◌َوْ and ◌َىْ (*or* ◌ے) as *au* and *ai*, respectively, when they are pronounced as diphthongs.

2. Romanize ى (*alif maqṣūrah*) as *a* when it is used in place of ا to represent the long vowel.

    'Īsá   عىسى
    Mūsá   موسى

3. Romanize *tanwīn* (written ً- , ٌ- (ﺍً), or ٍ-) as *un, an,* and *in,* respectively, when it occurs in a word or expression borrowed from Arabic. Otherwise, do not romanize it.

andāzan   انـدازًا

'amalan   عملًا

4. Regardless of pronounciation, romanize ٮ (undotted form of the letter ن) as *n.*

Jammū<u>n</u>   جموّں

jahā<u>n</u>   جهاں

5. Romanize ء (*hamzah*) as ' (*alif*) when medial or final.

aśśahadā'   الشـهداء

ā'īnah   آئنه

mu'min   مؤمن

6. When ء (*hamzah*) represents the connective syllable joining a *mufaz* to what follows, it is romanized *-yi.*

Idārah-yi Haft ...   ادارةۀهفت

7. Izafat.

(a) When the *muzaf* (the first of two words in a grammatical relationship called *izafat*) ends in a consonant, add *-i* to it in romanization.

Tārīkh-i Hindūstān   تاریخ هندوستان

(b) When the *muzaf* ends in a vowel or a silent ه , add *-yi.*

daryā-yi śor   دریای شور

Malikah-yi Inglistān   ملکه انگلستان

SPECIAL CHARACTERS AND CHARACTER MODIFIERS IN ROMANIZATION

Special Characters	*Name*	*USMARC hexadecimal code*
′	soft sign (prime)	A7
'	alif	AE
'	ayn	B0

Character Modifiers	*Name*	*USMARC hexadecimal code*
́	acute	E2
̄	macron	E5
̇	dot above	E7
̣	dot below	F2
̤	double dot below	F3
̲	underscore	F6

Khmer

Consonants

Full Form	Subscript	Romanization	Full Form	Subscript	Romanization
ក	◌	k	ឌ	◌	d
ខ	◌	kh	ឍ	◌	dh
គ	◌	g	ណ	◌	n
ឃ	◌	gh	ប	◌	p
ង	◌	ṅ	ផ	◌	ph
ច	◌	c	ព	◌	b
ឆ	◌	ch	ភ	◌	bh
ជ	◌	j	ម	◌	m
ឈ	◌	jh	យ	◌	y
ញ	◌ or ◌	ñ	រ	◌	r
ដ	◌	ṭ	ល	◌	l
ឋ	◌	ṭh	វ	◌	v
ឌ	◌	ḍ	ឝ	◌	ś
ឍ	◌	ḍh	ឞ	◌	ṣ
ណ	◌	ṇ	ស	◌	s
ត	◌	t	ហ	◌	h
ថ	◌	th	ឡ	-	ḷ
			អ	◌	q

Vowels

Independent	Romanization	Independent	Romanization
ឥ	i	ឱ or ឲ	o
ឦ	ī	ឳ or ឱ	au
ឧ	u	ឫ	r̥
ឩ or ឩ	ū	ឬ	r̥̄
ឯ	e	ឭ	l̥
ឰ	ai	ឮ	l̥̄

Vowels

Dependent	Romanization	Dependent	Romanization
□	□a	□	□ua
□□	□a□	ເໃ	□oe
□́	□á□	ເ□	□ẏa
□̆	□ă□	ເ□	□ia
□ា	□ā	ເ□	□e
□ា́	□â□	ໄ□	□ae
□	□i	ໃ□	□ai
□	□ī	ເ□ា	□o
□	□ẏ	ເ□ៅ	□au
□	□ȳ	○	□aṃ
□	□u	□ះ	□aḥ
□	□ū	□:	□à

Diacritical Marks

Vernacular	Alternative	Romanization
□	□	″ (hard sign)
□	□	′ (soft sign (prime))
□		r□
□		□° (circle above)
□		□' (alif)
□		□' (ayn)
□		□˙ (dot above)

Notes

1. In the consonant portion of this romanization table, the special character □ shows the position of a Khmer script character below which a subscript character is written. A subscript character is always romanized after a full form character, without an intervening vowel, as in ក្រខ្វាក់ (*krakhvák*).

2. When ញ (*ñ*) occurs with a subscript character, the lower element is omitted, as in ញ្ជ (*ñj*). When ញ occurs as its own subscript, it takes the full form ញ, as in កញ្ញា (*kaññā*). Otherwise, the subscript has the form of the lower element alone, as in ខ្ញ (*khñ*).

3. The consonant ប (*p*), followed by the vowel ា (*ā*), takes the special form ពា.

4. In the vowel columns, □ shows the position of the consonant relative to the vowel. This applies to both the Khmer vernacular and to the romanization columns. It should be noted that □ in the Khmer vernacular column can also represent a final consonant with no vowel following, in which case it is romanized simply as □ , as in ដ៏ (*dăb*).

5. The consonants ° (*ṃ*), and ៈ (*ḥ*) are always preceded by a vowel, but, being finals, never themselves bear a vowel. Vowels other than *a* may precede them, as in ទុំ (*ṭuṃ*), សេៈ (*seḥ*).

6. The diacritics ˝ and ˜ are romanized by ʺ and ʹ respectively, immediately following the consonant they modify. They have the alternative form when they co-occur with one of the superscript vowels ˳, ˷, ˮ, and ˵ . When ◌ co-occurs with one of the superscript vowels and with one of the consonants ឌ, ញ, ម, យ, រ, ល, or វ, it is romanized as ʺ , as in ប៊ី (*pʺī*). When ◌ co-occurs with one of the superscript vowels and with one of the consonants ស, ហ, or អ, it is romanized ʹ , as in ស៊ី (*sʹī*). Otherwise, ◌ represents the vowel *u*, as in មុន (*mun*).

7. The diacritics □°, □ʼ, □ʽ, and □˙ in the romanization column are placed after the last letter of the word in which they occur, as in ក្សត្រិយ៍ (*ksatriy°*); ចាះ (*cāḥʼ*); ត៎ (*taʽ*); អាត្មន៍ (*qātman˙*).

8. Conventional signs are: ៗ , romanized by repeating the preceding word or phrase; ។ល។ romanized as *.l.* ; ។ប។ , romanized as *.p.* ; ‑ , romanized by means of a hyphen (-); ៈ , romanized by means of a colon (:), and ។ and ៕ , romanized by means of a period (.). The signs ៙ and ៚ are omitted in romanization.

9. The numerals are: ០ (0), ១ (1), ២ (2), ៣ (3), ៤ (4), ៥ (5), ៦ (6), ៧ (7), ៨ (8), and ៩ (9).

10. Khmer words are not written separately and spacing occurs only after longer phrases. When romanizing, the shortest written form which can stand alone as a word is treated as such. This applies also to Pali and Sanskrit loan-words. Other loan-words are divided as the original language.

SPECIAL CHARACTERS AND CHARACTER MODIFIERS IN ROMANIZATION

Special Characters	Name	USMARC hexadecimal code
ʹ	soft sign (prime)	A7
ʼ	alif	AE
ʽ	ayn	B0
ʺ	hard sign (double prime)	B7

Character Modifiers	Name	USMARC hexadecimal code
◌̀	grave	E1
◌́	acute	E2
◌̂	circumflex	E3
◌̃	tilde	E4
◌̄	macron	E5
◌̆	breve	E6
◌̇	dot above	E7
◌̊	circle above	EA
◌̣	dot below	F2
◌̥	circle below	F4

Korean

Romanization

1. The Library of Congress will continue to follow the McCune-Reischauer system to romanize Korean. See: *Romanization of the Korean Language: Based upon its Phonetic Structure* by G.M. McCune and E.O. Reischauer ([S.l. : s.n., 1939?]), reprinted from the *Transactions of the Korea Branch of the Royal Asiatic Society*.

2. The Library of Congress will designate certain standard dictionaries as final authorities to resolve questions of contemporary pronunciation. A word will be considered to be pronounced as indicated in those dictionaries, and romanized in such a way as to represent its pronunciation most accurately.

3. When romanization rules conflict with the pronunciation of word, prefer to represent the pronunciation. Do not romanize silent syllabic finals.

chouŏn	좋은
yori	료 리 (or 요 리)
namunnip	나 뭇 잎
kap	값
ŏpta	없 다

4. *Sai siot.* Follow McCune-Reischauer directions on romanization of medial (*sai*) *siot*, with these revisions:

    Romanize as *nn* when a syllabic final before *i* and yotized vowels.

yenniyagi	옛 이 야 기
hŏnnil	헛 일

    Romanize as *d* when a syllabic final before all other vowels.

mŏdŏpta	멋 없 다
udot	웃 옷

5. Represent a reinforced medial consonant as it is pronounced, regardless of written form. (NOTE: Some dictionaries represent a reinforced medial consonant with a double consonant: 의 과 [─ 꽈] However, the romanization would not necessarily show a double consonant: ŭikwa)

	Hancha	한 자 (漢字)
but	hanja (*a measure*)	한 자
	silssi	實施
	p'yŏngka	평 가
	munpŏp	文法

6. Words written with double final consonants are to be romanized as they are pronounced.

hŭk	흙
sam	삶
tak	닭
Maksŭ	막 스
Marksŭ	맑 스

7. Initial *niŭn* (ㄴ) and *liŭl* (ㄹ). Follow McCune-Reischauer rules governing initial *niŭn* and *liŭl*, with the following exceptions. The surname 李 is always romanized *Yi*, no matter how it is written (李 , 이 , 리).

nodong	로 동	(or 노 동)
yŏksa	력 사	(or 역 사)
Yi Sŭng-man	리 승 만	(or 이 승 만)

Exception 1) When medial *niŭn* is followed by medial *liŭl*, they are generally romanized *ll*. However, when syllables beginning with 류 or 려 (i.e. 률 , 렬 , 련) follow a vowel or medial *niŭn*, the sound of *liŭl* is generally dropped. In such cases, *liŭl* is not romanized.

	mullihak	文理學
	nayŏl	羅列
	punyŏl	分裂
but	Koryŏ	高麗

Exception 2) To accommodate *Word Division Rule 1*, particles beginning with the letter *liŭl* are to be separated from other words, and are to be romanized beginning with the letter *r* in all cases.

sae yŏksa rŭl wihayŏ	새 歷史 를 위하여
charip kyŏngje ro ŭi tojŏn	自立 經濟 로 의 挑戰
Kim Mari ranŭn puin	金 마리 라는 夫人

8. Following hyphens:
(a) When sounds would normally change, according to McCune-Reischauer rules, sound change is indicated following a hyphen in the following instances:

(1) As second syllable of a forename.

Exception: When the second part of a given name follows a vowel sound and begins with a yotized initial *liŭl* (ㄹ), the medial *r* is omitted (unless there is convincing evidence that the medial *r* is intended to be pronounced.)

	Song, Si-yŏl	宋 時烈
	Yi, Ki-yŏn	리 기 련
but	Kim, Ch'ŏr-wŏn	金 哲源
	An Ung-nyŏl	安 應烈

(2) For all generic terms used as jurisdictions, except the term *pukto*:

Kangwŏn-do 江原道

Wando-gun 완도군

(b) When sounds would normally change, according to McCune-Reischauer rules, sound change **is not** indicated following a hyphen in the following instances:

(1) In a spelled-out cardinal number:

ilch'ŏn-kubaek-yuksipp'al 一九六八

(2) Between a numeral and volume designation:

che 3-chip 第 3輯

4-kwŏn 4卷

(3) Between a year, written in numerals, and a suffix or modifier:

10-chunyŏn 10週年

1900-yŏn 1900年

(4) Between abbreviated forms combined coordinately:

chung-kodŭng hakkyo 中高等 學校

(5) For the generic jurisdiction term *pukto*:

Ch'ungch'ŏng-pukto 忠清北道

(6) When a word of Western origin is modified by a single character modifier, affix, or substantive of Korean or Sino-Korean origin:

esei-chip 에세이집

9. *Words of Western Origin*

(a) The letters that can be used in romanizing words of Western origin are limited to those allowed by the McCune-Reischauer romanization rules. Therefore, while there may be a choice between letters that may be used to represent a consonant, there can be no variation in the representation of vowels. The letters that may be used to represent consonants are:

ㄱ	k, g, ng
ㄴ	n, l
ㄷ	t, ch, j, d
ㄹ	l, r, n
ㅁ	m
ㅂ	p, b
ㅅ	s, sh, n, t, d, p, k
ㅇ	ng
ㅈ	ch, j
ㅊ	ch'
ㅋ	k'
ㅌ	t', ch
ㅍ	p'
ㅎ	h

(b)   When one or more of the prescribed letters corresponds exactly to its counterpart in the Western word being romanized, that letter will always be used.

      dijain (from the word *design*)   디 자 인

      Lenin   레 닌

(c)   When none of the prescribed letters corresponds exactly to its counterpart in the Western word being romanized, apply the romanization system strictly, without approximation of sounds.

      Pet'ŭnam   베 트 남

      (from the word *Vietnam*; the romanization system does not permit the use of the letter *v*)

      chero   제 로

      (from the word *zero*; the romanization system does not permit the use of the letter *z*)

(d)   When the original Western word cannot be ascertained, apply the romanization system strictly.

Word Division

Basic Principles:

1.   Each word or lexical unit (including particles) is to be separated from other words.

      k'alla TV rŭl chungsim ŭro   칼 라   TV 를 中心 으 로

2.   The Library of Congress will designate certain standard dictionaries as final authorities to resolve questions of word division. A word found in these sources will be considered to be a lexical unit, and written as a unit. Words or parts of speech not appearing in these authorities will be separated or connected according to these guidelines. Then, when in doubt, prefer to separate.

3.   A compound word is considered a combination of binary words. (A binary word is a compound consisting of two Chinese characters (*Hancha*) or two syllables of *Han'gul*.)

4.   A compound word is divided into binary components according to euphony.

Specific Rules:

1.   Write a particle (토) as a word separate from the word stem, except as noted in (a) through (d) below.

      na nŭn nae kil e   나 는 내 길 에

      noin kwa pada   老人 과 바 다

      ch'owŏn ŭi kkum ŭl kŭdae ege   草原 의 꿈 을 그 대 에 게

      sae ya sae ya p'arang sae ya   새 야 새 야 파 랑 새 야

1A. Add a particle as a suffix to a verb stem, adverb, or a simple inflection of the verb stem or adverb.

sarang pannŭn anae 사 랑 받 는 아 내

chago mŏktŏni 자 고 먹 더 니

kanan ŭl iginŭn pŏp 가 난 을 이 기 는 法

1B. Write coordinated or multisyllabic particles together as a word. However, always separate the particle 의 (*ŭi*) from other particles.

na mando anida 나 만 도 아 니 다

Han'guk kojŏn e ŭi ch'odae 韓 國 古 典 에 의 招 待

iltŭng egenŭn so rŭl sang ŭro 一 等 에 게 는 소 를 상 으 로

hangmun ŭrosŏ ŭi sahak 學 門 으 로 서 의 史 學

1C. Write independent contracted particles (such as 엔, 엘) separately from the preceding word.

yejŏn en mich'ŏ mollassŏyo 예 전 엔 미 처 몰 랐 어 요

kohyang el kanda 고 향 엘 간 다

1D. When particles are contracted to nouns or pronouns, connect them to those words.

chigŭm ŭn nugun'ga wasŏ 지 금 은 누 군 가 와 서

nan molla 난 몰 라

kŭgŏn na to molla 그 건 나 도 몰 라

2. Write a simple inflected verb, adjective, or adverb as a separate word or as a suffix joined to a word, according to the dictionary that serves as authority or the sense of the element(s) involved.

mŏndong i t'ŭl ttae 먼 동 이 틀 때

pam e ssŭn insaengnon 밤 에 쓴 人 生 論

choguk ŭl chik'in yongsa 조 국 을 지 킨 용 사

nugu rŭl wihayŏ chong ŭn ullina 누 구 를 위 하 여 鍾 은 울 리 나

simni to mot kasŏ palpyŏng nanda 十 里 도 못 가 서 발 병 난 다

irŏbŏrin kaŭl 잃 어 버 린 가 을

mongmarŭn hujo 목 마 른 후 조

2A. Separate an auxiliary verb, adjective, or adverb and its inflection from the word stem.

kago sip'ŭn nae kohyang 가 고 싶 은 내 고 향

ttŏna on kŭ chari e 떠 나 온 그 자 리 에

nae chan i nŏmch'i naida 네 蓋 이 넘 치 나 이 다

2B. Separate the auxiliary 하다 (*hada*), the copula 이다 (*ida*), and inflections of the same from the word stem when they consist of two or more syllables.

sin ŭn ch'angjoja ida 神 은 創 造 者 이 다

sarang iranŭn pyŏng 사 랑 이 라 는 病

2C. Separate a gerund form from the word stem.

p'urŭn pyŏl ŭn sara issŏtta 푸 른 별 은 살 아 있 었 다

3.   Write an imperfect noun as a separate word, except as noted in A-B below.

morankkot p'il muryŏp   모란꽃 필 무렵

ssirŭm ŭn tano ppun anirao   씨름 은 단오 뿐 아니라오

3A. Write a single syllable, imperfect noun as a word joined to an attributive adjective or to a simple inflected verb.

halsu ŏmnŭn saramdŭl   할수 없는 사람들

sinsa sungnyŏ yŏrŏbun   紳士 淑女 여러분

nugu rŭl wihan kŏsin'ga   누구 를 위한 것인가

i choguk ŏdiro kalkŏt in'ga   이 조국 어디로 갈것 인가

3B. Connect a prefix (接頭辭 *chŏptusa*), such as the native Korean prefixes 갓 (*kat*), 홀 (*hol*), 핫 (*hat*), and 풋 (*p'ut*) to the words that follow them.

kassŭmul   갓 스물

tŏtchŏgori   덧 저고리

p'ussarang   풋 사랑

3C. Write a single syllable attributive adjective or prefix as joined to a personal pronoun or imperfect noun.

kŭbun i sŏnsaeng ida   그 분 이 先生 이다

igŏt i chinsang ida   이 것 이 眞相 이다

4.   Write a derived word formed by the addition of a single character modifier, affix, or substantive as a single word, whether the word be of pure Korean or Chinese origin.

Han'guk kwa Han'gugin   韓國 과 韓國人

pudongsan p'yŏngka   不動産 評價

taedosi ŭi inyŏm kwa Han'guk   大都市 의 理念 과 韓國

Hanbando ŭi p'yŏnghwa wa anbo   韓半島 의 平和 와 安保

kyŏngje ch'odaeguk ŭi hyŏngsŏng   經濟 超大國 의 形成

hwangmuji ka changmikkot kach'i   황무지 가 장미꽃 같이

4A. In a Sino-Korean phrase, write a simple inflection of the auxiliary 하다(*hada*) and 되다(*toeda*), and the copula 이 다(*ida*) joined to the word stem.

kodokhal ttae sayŏn ŭl   孤獨할 때 사연 을

yŏngwŏnhan saengmyŏng   永遠한 生命

haengbokhan Miguk saenghwal   행복한 미국 생활

chomyŏnghae pon uri choguk   照明해 본 우리 祖國

4B. Connect a single character modifier, affix, or substantive of Western origin with a hyphen to a word of Korean or Sino-Korean origin. Connect a single character modifier of Korean or Sino-Korean origin with a hyphen to a word of Western origin.

Pak Mog-wŏl taep'yo esei-chip   朴 木月 代表 에세이集

kukche maak'et'ing-non   國際 마아케팅論

4C.　Write an attributive adjective or a pre-formative character separately from the word it modifies.

　　　sin hŏnpŏp　　　　　　　　　　　　新　憲法

　　　chŏ hanŭl edo sŭlpʻŭm i　　　　　저　하늘　에　도　슬픔　이

　　　Hanʻguk sinhak nonmun chʻong saegin　韓國　神学　論文　總　索引

　　　kŭndaesa ŭi chae chomyŏng　　　近代史　의　再　照明

　　　kwanhan il yŏnʻgu　　　　　　　관한　일　연구

4D.　Write two coordinated characters, affixes, or substantives together as an integral part of the word.

　　　suchʻurip chŏlchʻa　　　　　　　輸出入　節次

　　　kungnaeoe sajŏng　　　　　　　國内外　事情

　　　Hanʻguk sŏhwaga inbo　　　　　韓國　書画家　印譜

　　　chʻŏngsonyŏn ege tŭrinŭn Hanŏl　청소년　에게　드리는　한얼

4E.　Write a single character suffix together with the word stem.

　　　kongsanchʻŭk ŭi chujang　　　　共産側　의　主張

　　　arŭmdaun tongmuldŭl　　　　　아름다운　동물들

4F.　Add the binary主義(*chuŭi*; used chiefly as a formative element) to its modifier as a suffix.

　　　minjujuŭi　　　　　　　　　　民主主義

　　　Marŭkʻŭsŭ-chuŭi wa Kidokkyo　마르크스主義　와　基督教

5.　　Write any binary component of a compound as a single word, when possible.

　　　tʻoji kaeryang chohap　　　　　土地　改良　組合

5A.　Write a single character substantive as part of the preceding binary element of a compound. Write a single character substantive or an additional modifier together as part of the binary element.

　　　kukse kibonpŏp　　　　　　　　國税　基本法

　　　chijŏng tʻonggye chosapʻyo　　　指定　統計　調査表

　　　Hanʻguk chŏntʻong mokcho kŏnmulto　韓國　傳統　木造　建物図

　　　kyeryang kyŏngjehakchŏk yŏnʻgu　計量　経済学的　研究

5B.　If two single character substantives appear in succession, write the second one as a separate word.

　　　kukse kibonpŏp non　　　　　　國税　基本法　論

　　　chijŏng tʻonggye chosapʻyo chip　指定　統計　調査表　集

　　　hyŏndae chakka samsipsamin chip　現代　作家　三十三人　集

　　　Chungguk kojŏn Hansiin sŏn　　中國　古典　漢詩人　選

　　　kwijokche sŏl kwa kwallyoje non　貴族制　説　과　官僚制　論

5C.　Write a single character noun as a separate word.

　　　hyŏn haengjŏng ha e che kisul　現　行政　下　에　諸　技術

　　　Moktanʻgang haeng yŏlchʻa　　牧丹江　行　列車

　　　Hanʻguk Chunggong kan ŭi kyoyŏk　韓國　中共　間　의　交易

5D. *Borrowed (Western) words or terms:* When it can be determined that a word or words in Korean consisted of more than one word in the original language, apply the following guidelines.

If they appear separately, write them separately.

syeip'ŭ ŏp	세 이 프　업
t'eibŭl maenŏ	테 이 블　매 너

If they appear without spaces, write them as a single word. (It is useful to also provide an access point in which the word or words are separated in the same manner as in the original language.)

syeip'ŭŏp (originally *shape up*)	세 이 프 업
(and another access point from *syeip'ŭ ŏp*)	
t'eibŭlmaenŏ (originally *table manners*)	테 이 블 매 너
(and another access point from *t'eibŭl maenŏ*)	

If they appear with a center dot (·), write them separately.

syeip'ŭ ŏp	세 이 프 · 업
t'eibŭl maenŏ	테 이 블 · 매 너

6. *Personal Names*

6A. Write a family name consisting of two characters as a single word. Hyphenate a given name in two characters or a courtesy name (in place of a given name), and capitalize only the first letter of the first syllable.

Ch'oe Ch'i-wŏn	崔　致遠
Yi Kwang-su	이　광 수
Kim So-wŏl	金　素月
Namgung Kak	南宮　珏
Sŏnu Chong-wŏn	鮮于　宗源

6B. Write a pseudonym or other assumed name as one word.

Kim Sakkat	김　삿 갓
Ch'ungmugong	忠武公

6C. Write a Buddhist priestly or posthumous name as one word.

Iryŏn	一然
Sŏk Myŏngjŏng	釋　明正

6D. Write a reign title, temple name, or title of nobility as one word without a hyphen.

T'aejo	太祖
Yi Sejong	李　世宗
Kwanggaet'o Wang	廣開土　王
Hyegyŏnggung Hong Ssi	惠慶宮　洪　氏
Chang Hŭibin	張　禧嬪
Hyŏnu Haengja	賢愚　行者

7. *Corporate Names, Geographical Names, Names in Publication Titles, etc.*

7A. Treat a corporate name also as a binary compound when possible. Write separately as binary elements general terms such as 學會(*Hakhoe*), 學科(*Hakkwa*), 敎會(*Kyohoe*), etc.

Han'guksa Hakhoe	韓國史 學會
(*Society of Korean History*)	
Han'guk Sahakhoe	韓國 史學會
(*World History Society of Korea*)	
Nasŏng Hanin Changno Kyohoe	라성 한인 장로 교회
Kugŏ Kungmun Hakkwa	國語 國文 學科
Nodong Kijun Chosaguk	勞動 基準 調査局
Han'guk Hyumŏnisŭt'ŭ-hoe	韓国 휴머니스트 · 会

7B. Write a proper name, term of address, or publication title separately from its modifier and also separately from the word it modifies.

Wŏllam Yi Sang-jae Ong	月南 李 商在 翁
Nanjung ilgi ch'o	乱中 日記 抄
Hŭngsŏn Kun	興宣 君
Kwibong chip	龜峯 集
Wŏnye Hakkwa chi	園芸 学科 誌
Taegu Maeil Sinmunsa sa	大邱 每日 新聞社 史

7C. Hyphenate a generic term used as part of the name of a jurisdiction, and indicate phonetic changes, except in the case of the term 北道(*pukto*).

Kangwŏn-do	江原道
Kyŏngsang-pukto	慶尚北道
Taegu-si	大邱市
Kahoe-dong	嘉會洞

7D. Write a generic term for a type of topographic feature, architectural construction, or a corporate entity used as a part of a proper name, together with its name.

Hallasan	漢拏山
Naktonggang	洛東江
Tongnimmun	獨立門
Tonga Ilbosa	東亞 日報社
Yurisŏng	유리城

7E. Treat a generic term for a topographical feature or a jurisdiction also as a binary element when combined with another word.

T'aebaek sanmaek	太白 山脈
Anju Kunminhoe	安州 君民會
Wŏnju kunji	原州 君誌
Sŏjangdae Manwŏl Sanjŏng	西壯台 滿月 山頂

8. *Abbreviated Forms:*

8A. Write contractions which include proper names as a single word.

Yŏngamsaji   靈巖寺址 （靈巖寺 ＋ 寺址）

Sŏul T'ŭkpyŏlsirip Namsan Tosŏgwan   서울 特別市立 南山 圖書館
（서울 特別市 ＋ 市立 ...）

8B. Write an abbreviated or contracted proper name, Korean or foreign, as a single word.

onŭl ŭi Pukhan   오늘 의 北韓

Chŏn'gyŏngnyŏn   全経聯

Chunggongkwŏn ŭi changnae   中共圈 의 將来

8C. Hyphenate abbreviated forms combined coordinately. Do not indicate phonetical changes. Write a single character substantive as part of the final element in that combination.

ch'oesin Pul-Han sajŏn   最新 佛韓 辞典

Sŏul Chung-Kodŭng Hakkyo   서울 中高等 學校

sinyŏk Sin-Kuyak chŏnsŏ   新訳 新旧約 全書

chung-tanp'yŏn sosŏl   中短篇 小說

Paekhwabon Tang-Song sanmunsŏn   白話本 唐宋 散文選

Myŏng-Ch'ŏng p'ilgi kosa sŏnyŏk   명청 필기 고사 선역

9. *Numerals:*

9A. In romanizing numbers and adjacent words, create binaries whenever possible. Write the pre-formative element 第 (che) joined to the following number to form a binary.

che-1   第1

cheil   第一

che-3 segye   第3 世界

chesam segye   第三 世界

However, prefer to join a number to a suffix or generic term that follows it with a hyphen (for example; 次 (ch'a), 回 (hoe), 번 (pŏn), 年 (yŏn)). Do not indicate phonetical changes after the hyphen. In such cases, when 第 (che) precedes the number, separate it from the number.

che 1-ch'a   第 1次

che ilch'a   第 一次

che 3-chip   第 3輯

In more complex situations, still attempt to create binaries when possible.

cheil, i Konghwaguk   第一・二 共和國

che-1, 2 Konghwaguk   第1・2 共和國

9B. Write a spelled-out cardinal number as one word. In a number over one hundred, separate by hyphens, without phonetic changes, each unit of ten (十 sip), hundred (百 paek), thousand (千 ch'on), etc.

ilch'ŏn-kubaek-yuksipp'allyŏn   一九六八年

9C.　Treat a contracted form of a cardinal number or calendar year as one word.

    yuksibinyŏn saŏp kyehoek　　六十二年　事業　計劃

    62-yŏn saŏp kyehoek　　62年　事業　計劃

    tosi ch'ilsibil　　都市　七十一

    tosi 71　　都市　71

9D.　In case of certain contracted numerals that have been firmly established through common usage, prefer that form.

    sa-ilgu haksaeng ŭigŏ　　四・一九　學生　義擧

    o-illyuk kunsa hyŏngmyŏng　　五・一六　軍事　革命

    samil undong　　三一　運動

9E.　In writing native Korean numbers, also attempt to create binaries when possible.

    se pŏntchae　　세 번째

    ch'aek nekwŏn　　책 네권

    som han'gŭn　　솜 한근

    so yŏl mari　　소 열 마리

Capitalization

1.　Each separately written word of a corporate name (except particles), or an abbreviation thereof, is capitalized.

    Han'guk Ilbosa　　韓國　日報社

    Taehan Sanggong Hoeŭiso　　大韓　商工　會議所

2.　Each separate word of a personal name is capitalized.

    Yi Kwang-su　　李　光洙

    Chŏng Yŏn-hŭi　　鄭　然喜

3.　Titles and terms of address are capitalized.

    Pak Taet'ongnyŏng　　朴　大統領

    Cho Yong-gi Moksa　　조 용기 목사

4.　Each separately written word of a geographic name is capitalized. An abbreviated geographical name is capitalized. An abbreviated geographical name is capitalized in coordinate compounds and at the beginning of other compound words.

    Sŏul T'ŭkpyŏlsi　　서울　특별시

    Kyŏngbuk Sup'il Tonginhoe　　경북　수필　동인회

5.　The first word of the title of a book, periodical, or series is capitalized.

    Hyŏndae kukchepŏp　　現代　國際法

    Silch'ŏn munhak ŭi sijip　　실천 문학 의 시집

6. Names of dynasties are capitalized.
    Yijo obaengnyŏn   李朝　五百年
    Myŏng-Ch'ŏng sidae   明清　時代

7. A word derived from a proper name is capitalized only if the name retains its full, original meaning.
    Yangmyŏnghak yŏn'gu   陽明學　研究
    Hyŏndae wa K'ŭrisŭch'yan ŭi sinang   현대　와　크리스챤　의　신앙

8. Abbreviated forms combined coordinately are capitalized if called for by these guidelines.
    Sin-Kuyak Sŏngsŏ   新旧約　聖書
    Siryong Pul-Han sajŏn   실용　불한　사전

9. In all other cases, follow the directions found in the officially designated style manual.

Punctuation

1. A centered point (·) indicating coordinate words is generally transcribed as a comma, except where the rules require a hyphen.
    Chung-Kodŭng Hakkyo   中·高等　學校
    Nam-Pukhan kyŏngje hyŏmnyŏk 南·北韓　經濟　協力

    In other instances, it may be transcribed or not transcribed, depending on the context.
    sa-ilgu ŭi minjungsa   四·一九　의　民衆史
    Chang Tae-uk chŏ   張　大郁·著
    Iryŏp, Iltang sihwajip   一葉·日堂　詩畫集

2. Brackets (「 ... 」) used in the manner of quotation marks (" ... ") are transcribed as the latter.
    "Munhak kwa chisŏng" siinsŏn 「文學　과　知性」　詩人選
    "Si wa haebang" tongin sijip   「詩　와　解放」　동인　시집

Dictionaries to be Used as Authorities in Korean

To determine standard contemporary pronunciation in South Korea and North Korea:

Nam, Kwang-u. *Han'gugŏ p'yojun parŭm sajŏn.* (Kyŏnggi-do Sŏngnam-si: Han'guk Chŏngsin
    Munhwa Yŏn'guwŏn, 1984)
南　廣祐.　韓國語　標準　發音　辭典.

Hyŏndae Chosŏnmal sajŏn. Che 2-p'an. ([P'yŏngyang]: Kwahak, Paekkwa, Sajŏn Ch'ulp'ansa, 1981)
현대　조선말　사전.

As the basis for word division decisions for contemporary publications from South Korea and North Korea:

Sinp'yŏn kugŏ taesajŏn. (Sŏul T'ŭkpyŏlsi: Taeyŏng Ch'ulp'ansa, 1976)
신 편 국 어 대 사 전 .

Hyŏndae Chosŏnmal sajŏn. (1981)
현 대 조 선 말 사 전 .

Supplementary source for word division decisions for classical Korean publications:

Ko pŏpchŏn yongŏjip. ([Seoul]: Pŏpchech'ŏ, 1979)
古 法 典 用 語 集 .

To determine reading and pronunciation of Chinese characters:

Chang, Sam-sik. *Tae Han-Han sajŏn.* (Sŏul T'ŭkpyŏlsi: Sŏngmunsa, 1964)
張 三 植 . 大 漢 韓 辭 典 .

Sin chajŏn. ([Seoul]: Sinmun'gwan, 1915; Reprint: [Seoul]: Cho Yong-sŭng, 1973)
新 字 典 .

SPECIAL CHARACTERS AND CHARACTER MODIFIERS IN ROMANIZATION

Special Characters	Name	USMARC hexadecimal code
'	alif	AE
'	ayn	B0

Character Modifiers	Name	USMARC hexadecimal code
ŏ	breve	E6

Flowchart for Applying Korean Word Division and Romanization

Word Division

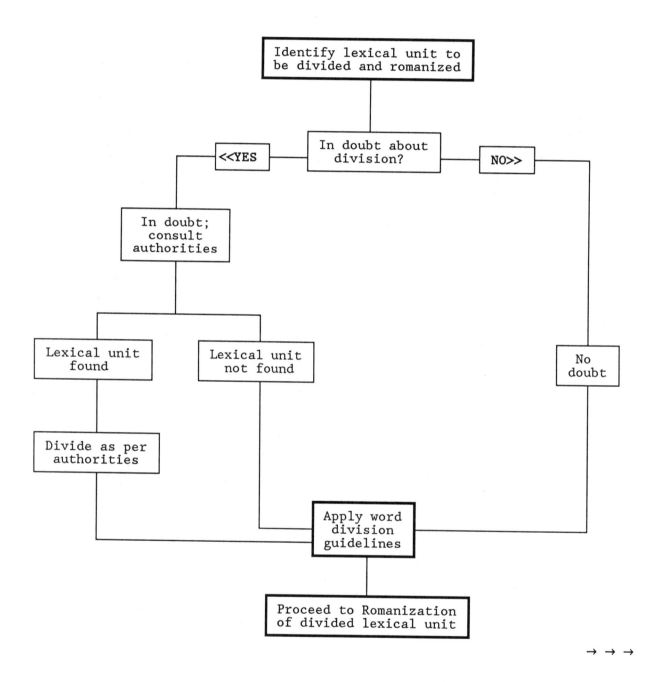

→ → →

Romanization

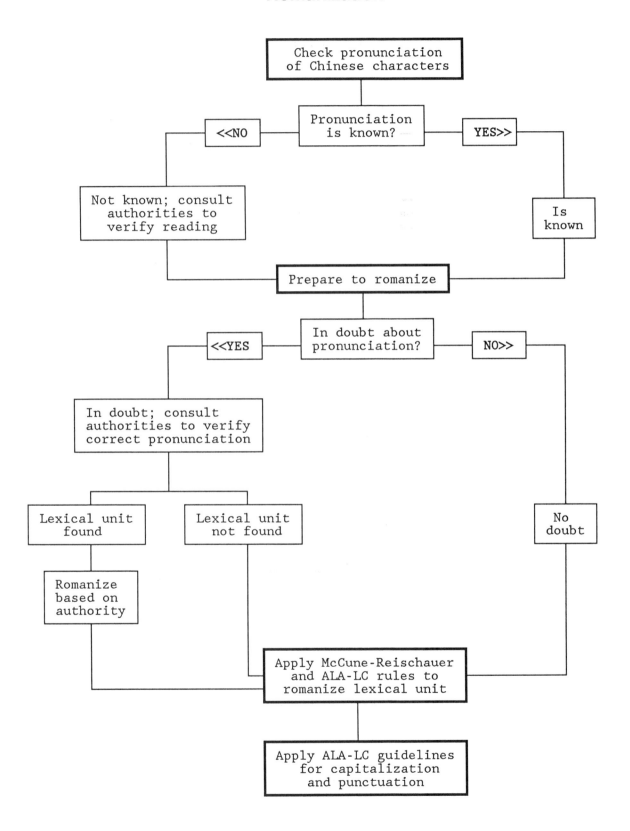

Kurdish
(in Perso-Arabic Script)

Letters of the Alphabet

Consonants

Initial	Medial	Final	Alone	Romanization
ء	ء	ء	ء	' (alif)
بـ	ـبـ	ـب	ب	b
پـ	ـپـ	ـپ	پ	p
تـ	ـتـ	ـت	ت	t
جـ	ـجـ	ـج	ج	j
چـ	ـچـ	ـچ	چ	ch
حـ	ـحـ	ـح	ح	ḥ
خـ	ـخـ	ـخ	خ	kh
د	ـد	ـد	د	d
ر	ـر	ـر	ر	r
ز	ـز	ـز	ز	z
ژ	ـژ	ـژ	ژ	zh
سـ	ـسـ	ـس	س	s
شـ	ـشـ	ـش	ش	sh
صـ	ـصـ	ـص	ص	ṣ
عـ	ـعـ	ـع	ع	' (ayn)
غـ	ـغـ	ـغ	غ	gh
فـ	ـفـ	ـف	ف	f
ڤـ	ـڤـ	ـڤ	ڤ	v
قـ	ـقـ	ـق	ق	q
کـ	ـکـ	ـک	ک	k
گـ	ـگـ	ـگ	گ	g
لـ	ـلـ	ـل	ل	l
مـ	ـمـ	ـم	م	m
نـ	ـنـ	ـن	ن	n
و	ـو	ـو	و	w
هـ	ـهـ	ـه	ه	h
یـ	ـیـ	ـی	ی	y

<u>Vowels</u>

Initial	Medial	Final	Alone	Romanization
ه	ـه	ـه	ه	a
ا	ـا	ـا	ا	ā
و	ـو	ـو	و	u
وو	ـوو	ـوو	وو	ū
-	-	-	-	i
یـیـ	ـیـیـ	ـیی	یی	ī

RULES OF APPLICATION

1. When ى represents the *iḍafah*, romanize it as *-i* following a consonant and as *-y* following a vowel. Attach this romanization to that of the preceding word.

2. Romanize the conjunction و as *wa*.

3. Romanize the particles ب and ل as *ba-* and *la-*. Attach this romanization to that of the following word.

4. Romanize the *zhēr* (unwritten vowel) as *i*.

5. Use the single prime (ʹ) in the following situations:

    (a) To separate two letters representing two distinct consonantal sounds, when the combination might otherwise be read as a digraph;

    (b) To mark the use of a letter in its final form when it occurs in the middle of a word.

6. For the romanization of Kurdish dialectical variants bearing diacritics (e.g., ز), use the romanization of the letter without the diacritic.

7. Romanize foreign words occurring in a Kurdish context and written in Kurdish letters according to the present tables and rules.

SPECIAL CHARACTERS AND CHARACTER MODIFIERS IN ROMANIZATION

Special character	*Name*	*USMARC hexadecimal code*
ʹ	soft sign (prime)	A7
ʼ	alif	AE
ʻ	ayn	B0

Character modifiers	*Name*	*USMARC hexadecimal code*
◌̄	macron	E5
◌̣	dot below	F2

Lao

Consonants (See Note 1)

Vernacular	Romanization When Initial		Romanization When Final
ກ	k		k
ຂ	kh		(k)
ຄ	kh		(k)
ງ	ng		ng
ຈ	ch		(t)
ສ	s		(t)
ຊ	s		(t)
ຍ	ny	(See Note 2)	-
ດ	d		t
ຕ	t		(t)
ຖ	th		(t)
ທ	th		(t)
ນ	n		n
ບ	b		p
ປ	p		(p)
ຜ	ph		(p)
ຝ	f		(p)
ພ	ph		(p)
ຟ	f		(p)
ມ	m		m
ຢ	y		-
ຣ	r		(n)
ລ	l	(See Note 3)	(n)
ວ	v	(See Note 4)	-
ຫ	h	(See Note 5)	-
ອ	' (ayn)	(See Note 6)	-
ຮ	h		-

Obsolete Consonants

Vernacular	Romanization
ຌ	s
ຎ	t
ຏ	t
ຐ	tsa
ຬ	l

Vowels (See Note 7)

Vernacular	Romanization	Vernacular	Romanization
□ະ, ◌̆	a	ເ□ະ, ◌̆ອ	ǫ
□າ	ā	◌̊, □ອ	ǭ
◌̊	i	ເ◌̊ະ, ເ◌̊	œ
◌̂	ī	ເ◌̂	œ̄
◌̂	ư	ເ◌̃ຈະ, ◌̃ຈ	ia
◌̂	ư̄	ເ◌̃ຈ, ◌ຈ	īa
ຸ	u	ເ◌̊ະ, ເ◌̊ອ	ưa
ຸ, ◌̥	ū	ເ◌̊ອ	ư̄a
ເ□ະ, ເ◌̂	e	◌̂ອະ, ◌̆ອ	ua
ເ□	ē	◌̂ອ, □ອ	ūa
ແ□ະ, ແ◌̆	æ	ໄ□, ໃ□, ◌̆ຍ	ai
ແ□	ǣ	□າຍ, □າ ʃ	āi
ໂ□ະ, ◌̂	o	ເ◌̂າ	ao
ໂ□	ō	◌̊າ	am

Special Symbols

Vernacular	Romanization
ໆ	...
ຯ	(syllable repeated)
ໆລໆ	la

Notes

1. Some consonants do not occur as finals, except in loan-words. The romanization for these consonants is enclosed in parentheses in the table.

2. In final position, ຍ follows as vowel, closing the diphthong, and is romanized as *i*. See the vowel table (*ai* and *āi*). In non-initial position, ຍ is often written in a secondary form, ʃ. See the vowel table (*ia* and *īa*).

3. The combining-form of ລ is ◌ . It is not romanized except when subscript to ຫ , thus: ຄຶ ສຽບ (*khitsatīan*), ຫຼຂບ (*lāi*).

4. In initial position, ວ is romanized as *v*, thus: ວັດ (*vat*).

   When medial ວ is followed by a vowel, it forms a cluster with the initial consonant, and is romanized as *w*, thus: ຂວາ (*khwā*), ແຂວງ (*khwǣng*).

   When medial ວ is followed by a final consonant, it is romanized *ūa*, thus: ບວກ (*būak*), ດ້ວຍ (*dūai*).

   When ວ is in final position following a vowel, it is romanized as *o*, thus: ນາວ (*nāo*), ແກ້ວ (*kǣo*). See also the vowel table (*ua* and *ūa*). The forms ◌ິວ and ◌ີວ are romanized as *iu* and *īu*, and the forms ◌ຽວ and ເ◌ຽວ are romanized as *īeo*.

5. ຫ is not romanized before ຍ (*ny*), ນ (*n*), ມ (*m*), ຣ (*r*), ລ (*l*), and ວ (*v*), thus: ຫຍ້າ (*nyā*). ຫນ and ຫມ are often written as ligatures, thus: ໜ (*n*) and ໝ (*m*).

6. ອ is used in initial position for syllables beginning with a vowel, thus ອິກ (*ʿīk*). When not in initial position, ອ is a vowel. See the vowel table (*ọ*, *ǭ*, *ưa*, *ūra*).

7. In the vowel columns, □ shows the position of the consonant relative to the vowel. In all cases the romanization of the vowel is intended to follow the romanization of the consonant even though parts of the vernacular representation of the vowel may be written before the consonant.

8. The numerals are: ໐ (0), ໑ (1), ໒ (2), ໓ (3), ໔ (4), ໕ (5), ໖ (6), ໗ (7), ໘ (8), and ໙ (9).

9. In Lao, words are not written separately. In romanization, however, the shortest written form which can stand alone as a word is treated as such. This applies also to Pali and Sanskrit loan-words. Other loan-words have the same division as the original language. Tonal marks (◌̀, ◌̂, ◌̃, ◌̌) are not romanized.

10. When the pronunciation requires one consonant to serve a double function, at the end of one syllable and at the beginning of the next syllable, it is romanized twice according to the respective values, thus: ຄຶ ສຽບ (*khitsatīan*).

SPECIAL CHARACTERS AND CHARACTER MODIFIERS IN ROMANIZATION

Special Characters	*Name*	*USMARC hexadecimal code*
Æ	digraph AE (upper case)	A5
Œ	digraph OE (upper case)	A6
U'	U-hook (upper case)	AC
'	ayn	B0
æ	digraph ae(lower case)	B5
œ	digraph oe (lower case)	B6
u'	u-hook (lower case)	BD

Character Modifiers	*Name*	*USMARC hexadecimal code*
ō	macron	E5
ꞯ	right cedilla	F8

Lepcha

Vowels and Diphthongs (see Note 1)

𐒡	a (see Note 2)	𐒡3	ū
𐒡(	ā	𐒡	e
S𐒡	i	(𐒡	o
S𐒡	ī	(𐒡	ŏ
𐒡)	u	𐒡	ă

Consonants (see Note 3)

Gutturals		**Palatals**		**Cerebrals**		**Dentals**	
ɛ	ka	ꙮ	ca	ꙮ	ṭa	ꙮ	ta
ʊ	kha	ʊ	tsa	ꙮ	ṭha	ꙮ	tha
ω	ga	ꙮ	cha	ꙮ	ḍa	ꙮ	da
ɣ	ṅa	ꙮ	tsha	ꙮ	ḍha	ꙮ	na
		ꙮ	ja				
		ꙮ	za				
		ꙮ	ña				

Labials		**Semivowels**		**Sibilants**		**Aspirate**	
ꙮ	pa	ɛ	ya	ꙮ	śa	ꙮ	ha
ꙮ	pha	ɣ	ra	ꙮ	sa		
ꙮ	fa	ꙮ	la				
ꙮ	ba	ꙮ	va				
ꙮ	ma	ꙮ	wa				

Some Consonant Clusters

ꙮ	kla	ꙮ	bla
ꙮ	gla	ꙮ	mla
ꙮ	pla	×	hla
ꙮ	fla		

Notes

1. Only the vowel forms that appear at the beginning of a syllable are listed; the forms used for vowels following a consonant exclude 𐒡 . No distinction between the two is made in romanization.

ɛ(	ka	S ɛ	ki

2. 𐒡 is also used as a glottal stop and ɛ is added to it in a cluster. It is romanized ʻa.

𐒡ꙮ)	ʻayuk

3. The vowel *a* is implicit after all consonants and consonant clusters and is supplied in romanization, except when another vowel is indicated by its appropriate sign.

RULES OF APPLICATION

1. When ε, ⲅ, ⲉ, ⲁ, ⳉ, ⳅ, ⲅ and ⳙ are used in the final position (i.e., preceded by a vowel but not followed by one), they assume different shapes and are used as superscripts above the preceding syllables.

έ	kak	ὲ	kap
'ε	kaṅ	ε̃	kam
ε	kat	ε̣	kar
ε̣	kan	έ	kal

2. When ε is added to another consonant or consonants in a cluster (i.e., without any intervening vowel), it assumes the shape ʋ and is added to the preceding consonant or consonants.

ε̣ʋ	kya	ⳅʋ	mya	ⳅⲅ	klya

3. When ⲅ is added to another consonant or consonant in a cluster (i.e., without any intervening vowel), it assumes the shape ﻝ and is added to the preceding consonant or consonants.

ε̣ﻝ	kra	ω	gra

SPECIAL CHARACTERS AND CHARACTER MODIFIERS IN ROMANIZATION

Special Characters	Name	USMARC hexadecimal code
ʻ	ayn	B0

Character Modifiers	Name	USMARC hexadecimal code
ό	acute	E2
õ	tilde	E4
ō	macron	E5
ŏ	breve	E6
ȯ	dot above	E7
ọ	dot below	F2

Limbu

Vowels and Diphthongs (see Note 1)

अ	a		अ॰	ai
आ	ā		आ॰	o
इ	i		आ॰	au
उ	u		अ	ŏ
ए	e		अ	ĕ

Consonants (see Note 2)

Gutturals		**Palatals**		**Dentals**	
Z	ka	अ	ca	ट	ta
ट	kha	ट	cha	ठ	tha
४	ga	ज	ja	ड	da
५	gha	६	jha	ढ	dha
३॰	ṅa	ॠ	ña	Z	na

Labials		**Semivowels**		**Sibilants**		**Aspirate**	
ω	pa	ई	ya	७	śa	ट	ha
∞	pha	ॠ	ra	ॠ	sa		
७	ba	ॹ	la				
ॐ	bha	ॹ	va				
ॠ	ma						

Notes

1. Only the vowel forms that appear at the beginning of a syllable are listed; the forms used for vowels following a consonant exclude अ. No distinction between the two is made in romanization.

Ẕ	kā		Z॰	ki

2. The vowel *a* is implicit after all consonants and consonant clusters and is supplied in romanization, with the following exceptions:

    (a) when another vowel is indicated by its appropriate sign; and

    (b) when the absence of any vowel is indicated by the subscript sign (_) called *sa-i*.

RULES OF APPLICATION

1. ꞏꞏ (*mukphreṅ*) is used to indicate a slight breathing after a vowel. It is romanized ḥ.

ꯛ,ꯚ	kaḥyo	ꯟ,ꯠ	piḥrĕ
ꯡ,ꯢ	tāḥmā	ꯣ,ꯤ	muḥlā

2. ꞊ (*kemphreṅ*) is used to make a vowel slightly longer than usual. It is romanized '.

ꯥꯦ	yu'mā	ꯧꯨ	thā'bĕ

3. When Z, ꞏꞏ, ꞏꞏ, Z, ꞏꞏ, ꞏꞏ, ꞏꞏ, and ꞏꞏare used in the final position (i.e., preceded by a vowel but not followed by one), they assume different shapes and are used as superscripts above the preceding syllables.

Zꞏ	kak	Zꞏ	kap
Z꞉	kaṅ	Zꞏ	kam
Z	kat	Z	kar
Zꞏ	kan	Zꞏ	kal

4. When ꞏꞏ is added to another consonant or consonants in a cluster (i.e., without any intervening vowel), it assumes the shape ꞏ and is added to the preceding consonant or consonants.

Zꞏ	kya

5. When ꞏꞏ is added to another consonant or consonant in a cluster (i.e., without any intervening vowel), it assumes the shape ꞏ and is added to the preceding consonant or consonants.

Z	kra

6. When ꞏꞏ is added to another consonant or consonants in a cluster (i.e., without any intervening vowel) it assumes the shape ꞏ and is added to the preceding consonant or consonants.

Zꞏ	kva

SPECIAL CHARACTERS AND CHARACTER MODIFIERS IN ROMANIZATION

Special Characters	*Name*	*USMARC hexadecimal code*
'	apostrophe	27

Character Modifiers	*Name*	*USMARC hexadecimal code*
Ó	acute	E2
Õ	tilde	E4
Ō	macron	E5
Ŏ	breve	E6
Ȯ	dot above	E7
Ọ	dot below	F2

Malay
(in Jawi-Arabic Script)

Letters of the Alphabet

Initial	Medial	Final	Alone	Romanization
ا	ـا	ـا	ا	omit (see Note 1)
بـ	ـبـ	ـب	ب	b
تـ	ـتـ	ـت	ت	t
ثـ	ـثـ	ـث	ث	*th, s (see Notes 2)
جـ	ـجـ	ـج	ج	j
چـ	ـچـ	ـچ	چ	c
حـ	ـحـ	ـح	ح	h
خـ	ـخـ	ـخ	خ	kh
د	ـد	ـد	د	d
ذ	ـذ	ـذ	ذ	*dh, z (see Notes 2 and 3)
ر	ـر	ـر	ر	r
ز	ـز	ـز	ز	z (see Note 3)
سـ	ـسـ	ـس	س	s
شـ	ـشـ	ـش	ش	sy (see Note 3)
صـ	ـصـ	ـص	ص	*ṣ, s (see Notes 2 and 3)
ضـ	ـضـ	ـض	ض	*ḍ, d (see Notes 2 and 3)
طـ	ـطـ	ـط	ط	*ṭ, t (see Notes 2 and 3)
ظـ	ـظـ	ـظ	ظ	*ẓ, l, z (see Notes 3 and 4)
عـ	ـعـ	ـع	ع	(omit; see Note 3)
غـ	ـغـ	ـغ	غ	gh (see Note 3)
ڠـ	ـڠـ	ـڠ	ڠ	ng
فـ	ـفـ	ـف	ف	*f, p (see Note 3 and 5)
قـ	ـقـ	ـق	ق	*q, k (see Note 2)
ڤـ	ـڤـ	ـڤ	ڤ	p
كـ	ـكـ	ـك	ك	k
ݢـ	ـݢـ	ـݢ	ݢ	g
لـ	ـلـ	ـل	ل	l
مـ	ـمـ	ـم	م	m
نـ	ـنـ	ـن	ن	n
ڽـ	ـڽـ	ـڽ	ڽ	ny
هـ	ـهـ	ﻩ ، ة	ﻩ ، ة	h
و	ـو	ـو	و	w, u, o, au (see Note 6)
يـ	ـيـ	ـى	ى	y, i, e, ai (see Note 7)

Vowels and Diphthongs

ا	ـَ	a
و	ـُ	u
ي	ـِ	i
-	~	ĕ
ي	ـيْ	e, ai
و	ـوْ	o, au

Notes

1. For the use of *alif* see rules 3-5.
2. Letters in the romanization column marked with an asterisk (*) represent the romanized value of the equivalent Jawi letter when it occurs in Arabic words (not Arabic loan words). The letter not designated with an asterisk represents the proper romanization value for the letter when it occurs in Malay words. The boundary between words that are Arabic loans and those that are foreign Arabic terms used in Malay context is not always easy to draw. Common usage for the types of literature in which such words appear should always be followed.
3. Jawi letters typically found only in Arabic and Arabic loan words.
4. Some words of Arabic origin with the letter ظ have come into the language with the equivalent *l* (e.g., *lahir*); others with the equivalent *z* (e.g., *zalim*).
5. The letter ف is often used as a shorthand way of writing ڤ. When this is clearly the case, the letter ف should be romanized as *p*.
6. On و (*wau*), see rules 6 and 8b.
7. On ي (*yad*), see rules 7 and 8b.

RULES OF APPLICATION

1. Jawi orthography is far from standard, particularly in handwritten documents. Nevertheless, for the purposes of cataloging, it is essential to standardize the romanized form of every lexeme. Two widely accepted standards for writing Malay in the Latin script exist, the Indonesian and the Malaysian. In this table, the Indonesian standard, referred to as *Ejaan Bahasa Indonesia yang Disempurnakan* has been employed.

2. Arabic words (not Arabic loan words) appearing in a Malay text are analogous to French words and expressions in a Russian novel or Latin phrases in a Catholic theology text, and their distinctness should be preserved by transliterating them in accordance with the rules goberning

the romanization of the relevant language, Arabic or Malay. Malay words of Arabic origin whose orthography is the same as the Arabic might therefore be romanized differently at different points in the same text. Thus the word قدوس will be romanized *kudus* when it appears as a Malay word, but *qudūs* when it is used as an Arabic term or in an Arabic phrase.

3. ا (*alif*), و (*wau*), and ي (*yad*) are used to support ء (*hamzah*); when so used these letters are not represented in romanization. See rule 8b.

4. At the beginning of a word, alif represents an initial vowel or diphthong and is romanized accordingly as *a, e, i, u, o* (اُو), *au,* (او), *e,* (ايـ), or *ai* (ايـ). Following a consonant, alif represents the vowel romanized as *a*.

5. The optional *alif gantung* (for example, in the word (for example, in the word تبلُغ), when used, does not change the romanized form of the word.

6. The letter و (*wau*) is used: (a) to represent the consonant romanized as *w*; (b) to represent the vowels and diphthong romanized as *u, o,* and *au*; and (c) to support ء (*hamzah*) (see rule 8b).

7. The letter ي (*yad*) is used: (a) to represent the consonant romanized as *y*; (b) to represent the vowels and diphthong romanized as *i, e* and *ai*; and (c) to support ء (*hamzah*) (see rule 8b).

8. 9 (*hamzah*)

    (a) In Arabic words, and most Arabic loans where it is found, hamzah is romanized according to the rules for Arabic (including use of the non-alphabetic mark ʼ (*alif*).

    (b) Hamzah used to separate contiguous vowels, supported by ا, or و or ي , is not represented in romanization (for example, *lain* لاٸن , *laut* لاؤت , *permintaan* قرمنتاࣱ).

    (c) Hamzah replacing initial alif in vowel-initial words to which the prefix *ke-* or *se-* has been appended is represented by the vowel value that it elided (*keenam* كٸنم , *seindah* سٸنده , *seorang* سٸورڠ).

    (d) A hamzah used after the reduplicating numeral 2 in vowel-final roots followed by the suffixes *-an* or *-i* is not represented in romanization.

    (e) The occasional use of hamzah to represent a word-final glottal stop (for example, تٸداء) is romanized as *k*.

9. Words doubled with the number 2 should be written out in full (for example: *mata-mata* مات۲). When the root word ends in a consonant such that an appended *-an* or *-i* suffix must reduplicate the final consonant, the doubled consonant is not represented in the romanization (for example: *rumput-rumputan* رمڤت۲تن).

10. In cases where the postpositive *itu* or prepositive *yang* are joined to the preceding or following word, they should be romanized as separate words.

11. *Alif maqsūrah, waṣlah, maddah, shaddah,* and *tanwīn* are not commonly used in Jawi script except in Arabic words or phrases. If they do not appear as adornment on Malay words, they are not represented in the romanization. *Ta marbutah*, romanized as *t*, is not properly a Jawi script character either, but sometimes it may be found in Malay texts.

SPECIAL CHARACTERS AND CHARACTER MODIFIERS IN ROMANIZATION

Special Characters	Name	USMARC hexadecimal code
'	alif (hamzah)	AE

Character Modifiers	Name	USMARC hexadecimal code
̆	breve	E6
̣	dot below	F2

Malayalam

Vowels and Diphthongs (see Note 1)

അ	a			ൠ	r̥̄
ആ	ā			ൡ	l̥
ഽ	å	(see Note 2)		എ	e
ഇ	i			ഏ	ē
ഈ	ī			ഐ	ai
ഉ	u			ഒ	o
ഊ	ū			ഓ	ō
ഋ	r̥			ഔ	au

Consonants (see Note 3)

Gutturals		**Palatals**		**Cerebrals**		**Dentals**	
ക	ka	ച	ca	ട	ṭa	ത	ta
ഖ	kha	ഛ	cha	ഠ	ṭha	ഥ	tha
ഗ	ga	ജ	ja	ഡ	ḍa	ദ	da
ഘ	gha	ഝ	jha	ഢ	ḍha	ധ	dha
ങ	ṅa	ഞ	ña	ണ	ṇa	ന	na

Labials		**Semivowels**		**Sibilants**		**Aspirate**	
പ	pa	യ	ya	ശ	śa	ഹ	ha
ഫ	pha	ര	ra	ഷ	ṣa		
ബ	ba	റ	r̠a	സ	sa		
ഭ	bha	ററ	t̠ta (see Note 4)				
മ	ma	ല	la				
		ള	ḷa				
		ഴ	ḻa				
		വ	va				

Anusvāra (see Note 5)		*Visarga*		*Avagraha*	
ം	ṃ	ঃ	ḥ	ഽ	’ (apostrophe)

Notes

1. Only the vowel forms that appear at the beginning of a syllable are listed; the forms used for vowels following a consonant can be found in grammars; no distinction between the two is made in transliteration.

2. When ഉ is used in combination with the vowel *u* (ഉ), the combination is also transliterated by *ă*.

3. The vowel *a* is implicit after all consonants and consonant clusters and is supplied in transliteration, with the following exceptions:
   (a) when another vowel is indicated by its appropriate sign;
   (b) when the absence of any vowel is indicated by the superscript sign ‿ (also used for the vowel *ă*); and
   (c) when the following modified consonantal forms are used:

ൿ	k	ൻ	n	ൿ	l	ർ	r
ൺ	ṇ	ൽ	t	ൾ	ḷ		

4. When ‌ാ appears as a subscript in a cluster, it is transliterated *ṯa*.

5. Exception: *Anusvāra* is transliterated by:
   ṅ before **gutturals**,
   ñ before palatals,
   ṇ before cerebrals,
   n before dentals, and
   m before labials.

CHARACTER MODIFIERS IN ROMANIZATION

Character modifiers	*Name*	*USMARC hexadecimal code*
Ó	acute	E2
Õ	tilde	E4
Ō	macron	E5
Ȯ	dot above	E7
Ọ	dot below	F2
O̲	underscore	F6

Marathi

Vowels and Diphthongs (see Note 1)

Traditional Style	New Style	Romanization
अ	अ	a
आ	आ	ā
इ	ज़ि	i
ई	ज़ी	ī
उ	अॄ	u
ऊ	अॄ	ū
ऋ	अॄ	r̥
ॠ	अॄ	r̥̄
ऌ		l̥
ए	ॲं	e
ऍ	ऍं	ê
ऐ	ऐं	ai
ओ	ओ	o
ऑ	ऑं	ô
औ	औ	au

Consonants (see Note 2)

Gutturals		Palatals		Cerebrals		Dentals	
क	ka	च	ca	ट	ṭa	त	ta
ख	kha	छ	cha	ठ	ṭha	थ	tha
ग	ga	ज	ja	ड	ḍa	द	da
घ	gha	झ	jha	ढ	ḍha	ध	dha
ङ	ṅa	ञ	ña	ण	ṇa	न	na

Labials		Semivowels		Sibilants		Aspirate	
प	pa	य	ya	श	śa	ह	ha
फ	pha	र	ra	ष	sha		
ब	ba	ल	la	स	sa		
भ	bha	ळ	ḷa				
म	ma	व	va				

		Anusvāra (see Note 3)	*Visarga*	*Avagraha* (see Note 4)	
	ṅ̇	ō̃	: ḥ	s	’ (apostrophe)

Notes

1. Only the vowel forms that appear at the beginning of a syllable are listed; the forms used for vowels following a consonant can be found in grammars; no distinction between the two is made in transliteration.

2. The vowel *a* is implicit after all consonants and consonant clusters and is supplied in transliteration, with the following exceptions:
    (a) when another vowel is indicated by its appropriate sign;
    (b) when the absence of any vowel is indicated by the subscript sign (֬) called *halanta* or *virāma*.

3. Exception: *Anusvāra* is transliterated by:
    ṅ before gutturals,
    ñ before palatals,
    ṇ before cerebrals,
    n before dentals, and
    m before labials.

    In other circumstances it is transliterated by a tilde (õ) over the vowel.

4. When doubled, *avagraha* is transliterated by two apostrophes (”).

SPECIAL CHARACTERS AND CHARACTER MODIFIERS IN ROMANIZATION

Special character	*Name*	*USMARC hexadecimal code*
’	apostrophe	27

Character modifiers	*Name*	*USMARC hexadecimal code*
́	acute	E2
̂	circumflex	E3
̃	tilde	E4
̄	macron	E5
̇	dot above	E7
̣	dot below	F2
̥	circle below	F4

Mongolian
(Classical Mongolian in Vertical Script)

Initial	Medial	Final	Romanization
⫡	◂ (see Note 1)	◞ ◝ (see Note 1)	a
◂	◂ (see Note 1)	◞ ◝ (see Note 1)	e
⫡	◠	◠	i
⫢	◖ (see Note 1)	◔ (see Note 1)	o or u
⫣	◖ ◊ (see Note 1)	◔ (see Note 1)	ȯ or u̇
·◂	·◂ ◂	◞	n
	◊	⌡	ng
⊃	◁	⌐	q
·⊃	◁ ◁	·⌐ ⌐	ġ
⊙	⊙	⊋	b
⊍	⊍	⊌	p
⊋	⊋	⊋	f
⊁	⊹	⊁ ⌐	s
⊹⁚	⊹⁚		ś
ℱ (see Note 2)	◠ ◊ (see Note 2)	⌐ (see Note 2)	t or d
↲	↲	↲	l
⊤	⊤	⊿	m
н	н		c
⋏	⋎		j
◁	◂	◠	y
⌒ (see Note 2)	⌒ (see Note 2)	⌡ (see Note 2)	k or g
⌒	⌒		k
⋊	⋊	◠	r
⋀	⋀		v
⫡	◂	⌡	h

Notes

1. Romanize medial and final vowels according to the rules of vocalic harmony.

2. Romanize the dental and velar stops according to the pronunciation given in standard dictionaries.

TRANSCRIPTION OF GALIG LETTERS

Vowels and Diphthongs

	a		r̥̄
	ā		l̥
	i		l̥̄
	ī		e
	u		ai
	ū		o
	r̥		au

Consonants

Gutturals		**Palatals**		**Cerebrals**		**Dentals**	
	ka		ca		ṭa		ta
	kha		cha		ṭha		tha
	ga		ja		ḍa		da
	gha		jha		ḍha		dha
	ṅa		ña		ṇa		na

Labials		**Semivowels**		**Sibilants**		**Aspirate**	
	pa		ya		śa		ha
	pha		ra		ṣa		
	ba		la		sa		
	bha		va				
	ma						

Anusvara		*Visarga*	
◦	ṃ	⁚	ḥ

CHARACTER MODIFIERS IN ROMANIZATION

Character modifiers	*Name*	*USMARC hexadecimal code*
◌́	acute	E2
◌̃	tilde	E4
◌̄	macron	E5
◌̇	dot above	E7
◌̣	dot below	F2
◌̥	circle below	F4

Moplah
(in Arabic Script)

Letters of the Alphabet

	Initial	Medial	Final	Alone	Romanization
Consonants					
Gutturals					
	ڪ ، ک	ک	ک	ک	k
	که	که	که	که	kh
	گ	گ	گ	گ	g
	گه	گه	گه	گه	gh
	ڹ	ڹ	ۼ	ۼ	ṅ
Palatals					
	چ	چ	چ	چ	c
	چه	چه	چه	چه	ch
	ج	ج	ج	ج	j
	جه	جه	جه	جه	jh
	ڃ	ڃ	ڃ	ڃ	ñ
Cerebrals					
	ڎ	ڎ	ڎ	ڎ	ṭ
	ڎه	ڎه	ڎه	ڎه	ṭh
	ڔ	ڔ	ڔ	ڔ	ḍ
	ڔه	ڔه	ڔه	ڔه	ḍh
	ڹ	ڹ	ڹ	ڹ	ṇ
Dentals					
	ت	ت	ت	ت	t
	ته	ته	ته	ته	th
	د	د	د	د	d
	ده	ده	ده	ده	dh
	ن	ن	ن	ن	n
Labials					
	ڀ	ڀ	ڀ	ڀ	p
	ڀه	ڀه	ڀه	ڀه	ph
	ب	ب	ب	ب	b
	به	به	به	به	bh
	م	م	م	م	m

Vowels and Diphthongs (see Note)

Initial	Romanization
اَ	a
آ ، اٰ	ā
اِ	i
اِي	ī
اُ	u
اُو	ū
اٛرْ	ṛ
اٜ	e
اٜے	ē
اَيْ	ai
اٗ	o
اٗوْ	ō
اَوْ	au

NOTE: Only the vowel forms that appear at the beginning of syllables are listed. The forms used for vowels following a consonant exclude ا (*alif*), except in the case of *ā* (آ *or* اٰ). No distinction between the two is made in romanization.

	Initial	Medial	Final	Alone	Romanization
Semivowels					
	يـ	ـيـ	ـي	ي	y
	ڔ	ـڔ	ـڔ	ڔ	r
	لـ	ـلـ	ـل	ل	l
	و	ـو	ـو	و	v
	ر	ـر	ـر	ر	r̲
	رّ	ـرّ	ـرّ	رّ	t̲t̲
	ضـ	ـضـ	ـض	ض	ḷ
	ژ	ـژ	ـژ	ژ	l̲
Silibants					
	شـ	ـشـ	ـش	ش	ś
	ڜـ	ـڜـ	ـڜ	ڜ	ṣ
	سـ	ـسـ	ـس	س	s

	Initial	Medial	Final	Alone	Romanization
Aspirate					
	ഥ	൧	൧ , ഄ	ഥ	h

Arabic Letters Representing Non-Malayalam Consonants

	Initial	Medial	Final	Alone	Romanization
	ﺛ	ﺜ	ﺚ	ﺙ	thh
	ﺣ	ﺤ	ﺢ	ﺡ	ḥ
	ﺧ	ﺨ	ﺦ	ﺥ	kh
	ﺩ	ﺪ	ﺪ	ﺫ	ẕ
	ﺯ	ﺰ	ﺰ	ﺯ	z
	ﺻ	ﺼ	ﺺ	ﺹ	s
	ﺿ	ﻀ	ﺾ	ﺽ	ẓ
	ﻃ	ﻄ	ﻂ	ﻁ	ṭ
	ﻇ	ﻈ	ﻆ	ﻅ	ẓ
	ﻛ	ﻜ	ﻊ	ﻉ	' (ayn)
	ﻏ	ﻐ	ﻎ	ﻍ	gh
	ﻓ	ﻔ	ﻒ	ﻑ	f
	ﻗ	ﻘ	ﻖ	ﻕ	q
	-	-	ﺔ	ﺓ	h

RULES OF APPLICATION

Letters Which May Be Romanized in Different Ways Depending on Their Context

1. ْ , ُ , َ (*jazm*) indicates the absence of any vowel following the letter over which it is written. It is not represented in romanization.

   prākṛtam   ﭘﺮاﻛﺮﺗﻢ

2. When ّ (*shaddah*) appears over any consonant or digraph, represent it in romanization by doubling the consonant or digraph.

   uṇṭākkappeṭṭat   اُﻧْﺪاﻛَّﭙﺪَّﺙ

3. Romanize ى (*alif maqṣūrah*) used in place of اl to represent the long vowel as *á*.

   Mūsá   ﻣﻮُﺳﻲ
   'Īsá   ﻋﻴﺴﻲ

4. When the word ending in ة is in the construct state, romanize ة as *t*.

    Tarjamat al-sirru al-jalīl تَرْجَمَة الْسِّيرُّ الْجَلِيْل

    Sūrat al-Fātiḥah سُوْرَة الْفْاتِحَة

5. When medial or final, romanize ء (*hamzah*) as '.

    Khulafā' خُلَفَآءٌ
    'Ā'iśah عَآئِشَة
    Ẓā'ah ضَائَة

6. Romanize the Arabic article اَلْ (also written ال) as *al-*.

    'alaihi al-salām عَلَيْهِ الْسَّلامْ

SPECIAL CHARACTERS AND CHARACTER MODIFIERS IN ROMANIZATION

Special Characters	Name	USMARC hexadecimal code
'	alif	AE
'	ayn	B0

Character Modifiers	Name	USMARC hexadecimal code
́	acute	E2
̃	tilde	E4
̄	macron	E5
̇	dot above	E7
̣	dot below	F2
̤	double dot below	F3
̲	underscore	F6

Non-Slavic Languages
(in Cyrillic Script)

Non-Slavic languages in the Cyrillic script make use of many letters from the basic Cyrillic alphabet presented below. For those letters, use the romanization shown in the table. For other letters, follow the romanization given in the applicable language section on the pages that follow. Languages are listed in alphabetical order by name. Dates after the name of a language refer to the year the Cyrillic alphabet was introduced or the year an alphabet was modified to accommodate spelling reform.

Upper case letters		*Lower case letters*	
Vernacular	*Romanization*	*Vernacular*	*Romanization*
А	A	а	a
Б	B	б	b
В	V	в	v
Г	G	г	g
Д	D	д	d
Е	E	е	e
Ё	Ë	ё	ë
Ж	Zh	ж	zh
З	Z	з	z
И	I	и	i
Й	Ĭ	й	ĭ
К	K	к	k
Л	L	л	l
М	M	м	m
Н	N	н	n
О	O	о	o
П	P	п	p
Р	R	р	r
С	S	с	s
Т	T	т	t
У	U	у	u
Ф	F	ф	f
Х	Kh	х	kh
Ц	T͡S	ц	t͡s
Ч	Ch	ч	ch
Ш	Sh	ш	sh
Щ	Shch	щ	shch
Ъ	″ (hard sign)	ъ	″ (hard sign)
Ы	Y	ы	y
Ь	′ (soft sign)	ь	′ (soft sign)
Э	Ė	э	ė
Ю	I͡U	ю	i͡u
Я	I͡A	я	i͡a

Upper case letters		Lower case letters	
Vernacular	Romanization	Vernacular	Romanization

Abaza (1938)

| - | - | I | ħ |
| - | - | ъ | ″ (hard sign) |

Abkhaz (1954)

Ҕ	Gh	ҕ	gh
Џ	J	џ	j
Ҽ	Ćh	ҽ	ćh
Ҿ	ĆҞ	ҿ	ćҟ
З	Z	з	z
Ҙ	D͡Z	ҙ	d͡z
Қ	Ҟ̇h	қ (к)	ҟ̇h
Ҡ	Q	ҡ	q
Ҩ	W	ҩ	w
Ҧ	Ph	ҧ	ph
Ҭ	Th	ҭ (т)	th
Х	Ḣ	ҳ (х)	ḣ
Ҵ	T͡S	ҵ	t͡s
Ҷ	Ċh	ҷ (ч)	ċh
Ә	Ẇ	ә	ẇ

Adygei (1938)

| I | Ḣ | I | ħ |
| - | - | ъ | ″ (hard sign) |

Aisor

ԁ	D	d	d
ə	Ǎ	ə	ǎ
J	Ǐ	j	ǐ
L	L	l	l
Q	Q	q	q
S	S	s	s
T	Ṫ	t	ṫ
ħ	Ḣ	ħ	ħ

Altai (1845 & 1922)

J	D́	j	d́
Ҥ (Ḥ)	N͡G	ҥ (ḥ)	n͡g
Ö	Ȯ	ö	ȯ
ÿ	U̇	ÿ	u̇

Upper case letters		Lower case letters	
Vernacular	*Romanization*	*Vernacular*	*Romanization*

Altai (1938)   No additional characters.

Altai (1944)

J	D́	j	d́
Ҥ (н')	N͡G	ҥ (н')	n͡g
Ö	Ȯ	ö	ȯ
ӱ	U̇	ӱ	u̇

Avar (1938)

-	-	I	ḣ
-	-	ъ	″ (hard sign)

Azerbaijani (1940)

Ғ	Gh	ғ	gh
Ə	Ă	ə	ă
Й	Ĭ	й	ĭ
J	Ĭ̆	j	ĭ̆
К	Ġ	к (ҝ)	ġ
Ө	Ȯ	ө	ȯ
Y	U̇	y	u̇
һ	Ḣ	һ	ḣ
Ч	J	ч	j
’	’ (apostrophe)	’	’ (apostrophe)

The letters J , j replaced Й, й in 1959.

Balkar (1936)

’	’ (apostrophe)	’	’ (apostrophe)
-	-	ъ	″ (hard sign)

Balkar (1939)   No additional characters.

Bashkir (1939)

Ғ	Gh	ғ	gh
Ҙ	T͡H	ҙ	t͡h
Ҡ	Q	ҡ (k)	q
Ң	N͡G	ң	n͡g
Ө	Ȯ	ө	ȯ
Ç	Th	ç	th
Y	U̇	y	u̇
һ	Ḣ	һ	ḣ
Ә	Ă	ә	ă

	Upper case letters		Lower case letters	
	Vernacular	*Romanization*	*Vernacular*	*Romanization*

Buryat (1939)

	Upper Vernacular	Upper Romanization	Lower Vernacular	Lower Romanization
	Ө	Ȯ	ө	ȯ
	Y	U̇	y	u̇
	ħ	Ḣ	ħ	ḣ

Chechen (1862)

	Upper Vernacular	Upper Romanization	Lower Vernacular	Lower Romanization
	Ҕ	Gh	ҕ	gh
	Џ	J	џ	j
	ħ	Ḣ	ħ	ḣ
	Ј	Ĭ	ј	ĭ
	Қ	Ḳh	қ	ḳh
	Ҟ	Q̇	ҟ	q̇
	Ӈ	Ṅ	ӈ	ṅ
	Ԥ	Ph	ԥ	ph
	Q	Q	q	q
	Ҕ	Ġh	ҕ	ġh
	Ҭ	Th	ҭ	th
	X̌	K͡H	x̌	k͡h
	Ц̇ (or Ƃ˝)	Ṫs	ц̇ (or Ƃ˝)	ṫs
	Ч̇ (or Ƃ˝)	Ċh	ч̇ (or Ƃ˝)	ċh

Chechen (1908)

	Upper Vernacular	Upper Romanization	Lower Vernacular	Lower Romanization
	Ԫ	Gh	ԫ	gh
	ħ	H	ħ	h
	Ј	Ĭ	ј	ĭ
	Қ	Ḳh	қ	ḳh
	Ҟ	Q̇	ҟ	q̇
	Ӈ	N	ӈ	n
	Ԥ	Ph	ԥ	ph
	Q	Q	q	q
	ħ	Ġh	ħ	ġh
	Ҭ	Th	ҭ	th
	X̌	K͡H	x̌	k͡h
	Ц̆	Ṫs	ц̆	ṫs
	Ч̆	Ċh	ч̆	ċh

Chechen (1938)

	Upper Vernacular	Upper Romanization	Lower Vernacular	Lower Romanization
	I	Ḣ	I	ḣ
	-	-	ъ	″ (hard sign)

Upper case letters		Lower case letters	
Vernacular	Romanization	Vernacular	Romanization

Chukchi (1958)

Ӄ	Q	ӄ	q
Ӈ	N͡G	ӈ	n͡g
-	-	’	’ (apostrophe)

Chuvash (Missionary)   No additional characters.

Chuvash (1872, modified 1923, 1926, 1933)

Ă	Ă	ă	ă
Ĕ	Ĕ	ĕ	ĕ
Љ (Љ)	Ĺ	љ (љ)	ĺ
Ӈ	Ń	ӈ (ӈ ӈ)	ń
Ç	Ś	ç	ś
Т̆	T́	т̆	t́
Ҍ	Ch	ҍ	ch
Ӳ	U̇	ӳ (ÿ)	u̇

Chuvash (1938)

Ă	Ă	ă	ă
Ĕ	Ĕ	ĕ	ĕ
Ç	Ś	ç	ś
Ÿ	U̇	ÿ	u̇

Dargwa (Uslar)

Æ	Æ	æ	æ
W	W	w	w
Ӡ	Gh	ӡ	gh
Г̆	Ǵh	г̆	ǵh
Ҕ	J	ҕ	j
З	D͡Z	з	d͡z
һ	Ḣ	һ	ḣ
ħ	K̊h	ħ	k̊h
ħ̃	H́	ħ̃	ḱ
J	Ĭ	j	ĭ
Ӄ	K̇h	ӄ	k̇h
Ӄ̊	Q	ӄ̊	q
Ӄ̆	Ḱ	ӄ̆	ḱ
П	Ph	п	ph
Q	Q	q	q
Ҕ	Ġh	ҕ	ġh
Т	Th	т	th
б̃	T͡Sh	б̃	t͡sh
Ӄ	Ċh	ӄ	ċh
-	-	’	″ (hard sign)

Upper case letters		Lower case letters	
Vernacular	*Romanization*	*Vernacular*	*Romanization*

Dargwa (1938)

-	-	I	ħ
-	-	ъ	″ (hard sign)

Dungan (1952)

Ә	Ă	ә	ă
Җ	J	җ	j
Ң	N͡G	ң (н)	n͡g
ў	Ŭ	ў	ŭ
Y	U̇	y	u̇

Eskimo--Yuit Dialect

Г'	Gh	г'	gh
К'	Q	к'	q
Л'	Ĺ	л'	ĺ
Н'	N͡G	н'	n͡g
X'	Ḣ	x'	ḣ
ў	W	ў	w

Even (1937)   No additional characters.

Even (1959)

Ӈ	N͡G	ӈ	n͡g
Ө	Ȯ	ө	ȯ
Ӫ	Ō	ӫ	ō

Evenki (1937)   No additional characters.

Evenki (1958)

Ӈ	N͡G	ӈ	n͡g

Gagauz--Bulgaria
    This language is romanized according to the Bulgarian table.

Gagauz--U.S.S.R. (1957)

Ä	Ă	ä	ă
Ö	Ȯ	ö	ȯ
ÿ	U̇	ÿ	u̇

Ingush (1938)

I	Ḣ	I	ħ
-	-	ъ	″ (hard sign)

| Upper case letters | | Lower case letters | |
| Vernacular | Romanization | Vernacular | Romanization |

Kabardian (1936)

| - | - | ' | h̆ |
| - | - | ъ | ʺ (hard sign) |

Kabardian (1938)

| I | Ḣ | I | h̄ |
| - | - | ъ | ʺ (hard sign) |

Kalmyk (1927)   No additional characters.

Kalmyk (1938)

Ä	Ӑ	ä	ӑ
Ö	Ӧ̆	ö	ӧ̆
Ӱ	Ŭ	ӱ	ŭ

Kalmyk (1957)

Ә	Ă	ә	ă
һ	Ḣ	һ	h̄
Җ	J	җ	j
-	-	Ң	n͡g
Ө	Ȯ	ө	ȯ
Y	Ú	ү	ú

Karachay (1938)

| ẏ | W | ẏ | w |
| - | - | ъ | ʺ (hard sign) |

Karachay-Balkar

| ẏ | W | ẏ | w |
| - | - | ъ | ʺ (hard sign) |

Karakalpak (1940)   No additional characters.

| - | - | ъ | ʺ (hard sign) |

Karakalpak (revised ca. 1947)

Ғ	Gh	ғ	gh
Қ	Q	қ (қ)	q
Ҳ	Ḣ	ҳ	h̄

| Upper case letters | | Lower case letters | |
Vernacular	Romanization	Vernacular	Romanization
Karakalpak (1957)			
Ғ	Gh	ғ	gh
Қ	Q	қ	q
-	-	Ң	n͡g
Ѳ	Ȯ	ѳ	ȯ
Y	U̇	y	u̇
ў	W	ў	w
Х	Ḣ	х	ḣ
Ә	Ă	ә	ă
Karelian			
Ä	Ă	ä	ă
Ö	Ȯ	ö	ȯ
ÿ	U̇	ÿ	u̇
Kazakh (1940)			
Ә	Ă	ә	ă
Ғ	Gh	ғ (ғ)	gh
Қ	Q	қ (қ)	q
Ң	N͡G	ң	n͡g
Ѳ	Ȯ	ѳ	ȯ
Ұ	Ū	ұ (ӯ)	ū
Y	U̇	y	u̇
һ	Ḣ	һ	ḣ
I	Ī̇	i	ī̇
Khakass (1893 missionary)			
-	-	н	n͡g
Ö	Ȯ	ö	ȯ
ÿ	U̇	ÿ	u̇
J	J̄	j	j̄
Khakass (1924-1927)			
J	J̄	j	j̄
ÿ	U̇	ÿ	u̇
Ö	Ȯ	ö	ȯ
-	-	н	n͡g
-	-	һ	g͡h

Upper case letters		Lower case letters	
Vernacular	*Romanization*	*Vernacular*	*Romanization*

Khakass (1939)

Upper case letters		Lower case letters	
-	-	Ғ	gh
İ	Ī	і	ī
-	-	Ҥ	n͡g
Ӧ	Ȯ	ӧ	ȯ
Ӱ	U̇	ӱ	u̇
-	-	Ӌ (ч)	j

Khanty (1937)

Upper case letters		Lower case letters	
Л' (Л')	L' (apostrophe)	л' (л')	l' (apostrophe)
Л'ь (Л'ь)	L'′ (apostrophe; soft sign)	л'ь (л'ь)	l'′ (apostrophe; soft sign)

Note: In 1952 the generic Cyrillic-based alphabet for Khanty was replaced by separate alphabets for each of the four individual dialects.

Khanty--Shuryshkary Dialect (1952)

Upper case letters		Lower case letters	
-	-	Ӈ	n͡g

Khanty--Kazym Dialect (1952)

Upper case letters		Lower case letters	
Ä	Ä	ä	ä
Ә	Ă	ә	ă
Ӛ	Ă̈	ӛ	ǎ̈
Л'	L'	л'	l'
-	-	Ӈ	n͡g
Ө	Ȯ	ө	ȯ
Ӫ	Ŏ	ӫ	ŏ

Khanty--Surgut Dialect (1952)

Upper case letters		Lower case letters	
Ä	Ä	ä	ä
Қ	Q	қ	q
-	-	Ӈ	n͡g
Ө	Ō	ө	ō
Ӫ	Ȯ	ӫ	ȯ
Ӱ	U̇	ӱ	u̇
Ә	Ă	ә	ă
-	-	'	' (apostrophe)

| Upper case letters | | Lower case letters | |
Vernacular	Romanization	Vernacular	Romanization
Khanty--Vakh Dialect (1952)			
Ä	Ä	ä	ä
Ӄ	Q	ӄ	q
-	-	ӈ	n͡g
Ö	Ȯ	ö	ȯ
Ѳ	Ō	ѳ	ō
Ӫ	Ŏ̇	ӫ	ŏ̇
ÿ	U̇	ÿ	u̇
Ə	Ă	ə	ă
Ӭ	Ǎ̇	ӭ	ǎ̇
-	-	'	' (apostrophe)
Kirghiz (1940)			
Ҥ	N͡G	ҥ	n͡g
Ѳ	Ȯ	ѳ	ȯ
Y	U̇	y	u̇
Komi (1938)			
-	-	i	ī
Ö	Ȯ	ö	ȯ
Komi (Molodtsov) (1919)			
ԁ	D	ԁ	d
ԃ	D́	ԃ	d́
Җ	D̲z̲h̲	җ	d̲z̲h̲
Ҙ	Ź	ҙ	ź
Ҙ	D͡Z	ҙ	d͡z
Ј	Ĭ̇	ј '	ĭ̇
Ԉ (Љ)	Ĺ	ԉ (љ)	ĺ
Ԋ (Њ)	Ń	ԋ (њ)	ń
Ö	Ȯ	ö	ȯ
Ҁ	Ś	ҁ	ś
Ԏ	T́	ԏ	t́
Komi-Permyak (Missionary)			
Ö	Ȯ	ö	ȯ
Komi-Permyak (1938)			
-	-	i	ī
Ö	Ȯ	ö	ȯ

Upper case letters		Lower case letters	
Vernacular	Romanization	Vernacular	Romanization

Koryak

Ӄ	Q	ӄ	q
Ӈ	N͞G	ӈ	n͞g
-	-	’	’ (apostrophe)

Kumyk (1938)   No additional characters.

| - | - | ъ | ″ (hard sign) |

Kurdish (1946)

Ġ	G’	̓г (г’)	g’
Ə	Ă	ə	ă
Ә̓	Ă’	̓ә (ә ’)	ă’
К̇	K’	̓к (к’)	k’
Ӧ	Ȯ	ӧ	ȯ
П̃	P’	п̃ (п’)	p’
Р̇	R’	̓р (р’)	r’
Т̇	T’	̓т (т’)	t’
ħ	Ḣ	h	ḣ
ħ̓	Ḣ’	̓h (h’)	ḣ’
ч̇	Ch’	ч̇ (ч’)	ch’
Ої (Q)	Q	q	q
W	W	w	w
-	-	’	’ (apostrophe)

Lak (1864)

ꚉ	Gh	ꚉ	gh
ħ	Ḣ	h	ḣ
ħ̊	K̊h	ħ	k̊h
ꞯ	Ḣẇ	ꞯ	ḣẇ
ꚕ	Ḥ́	ꚕ	ḥ́
J	Ĭ	j	ĭ
К̆̈	Ḱ	к̆̈	ḱ
Ӄ	Ḳh	ӄ	ḳh
К̇	Q̇	к	q̇
Q	Q́	q	q́
Ç	Ś	ç	ś
Ꚑ	T̄	ꚑ	t̄
Ꚑ̣	Th	ꚑ̣	th
Х̇	K͞H	х̇	k͞h
Ц̇	Ṫs	ц̇	ṫs
ꞵ″	Ts̄	ꞵ″	ts̄
ч	C̄h	ч	c̄h
ч̇	Ċh	ч̇	ċh
Ш̈	Śh	ш̈	śh

	Upper case letters		*Lower case letters*	
	Vernacular	*Romanization*	*Vernacular*	*Romanization*

Lak (1938)

	-	-	I	ħ
	-	-	ъ	″ (hard sign)

Lapp (Missionary)

	-	-	ŋ	n͡g

Lapp (1937)

	-	-	н'	n͡g

Lezghian (1938)

	-	-	I	ħ
	-	-	ъ	″ (hard sign)

Lezghian (Uslar)

	Æ	Æ	æ	æ
	W	W	w	w
	ҁ	Gh	ҁ	gh
	҃	Ǵh	҃	ǵh
	Ђ	J	ђ	j
	З	D͡Z	з	d͡z
	ħ	Ḣ	ħ	ḣ
	ҳ	Ǩh	ҳ	ǩh
	ҕ	Ĥ	ҕ	ĥ
	J	Ĭ	j	ĭ
	Ḱ	K̄	ḱ	k̄
	Қ	Ḳh	қ	ḳh
	Ҟ	Q̇	к	q̇
	Ҝ	Q́	ҝ	q́
	ń	P̄	ń	p̄
	Ҧ	Ph	ҧ	ph
	Ơ	Q	q	q
	Ҕ	Ġh	ҕ	ġh
	Т	T̄	т	t̄
	Ҭ	Th	ҭ	th
	ẏ	Ú	ẏ	ú
	Ɓ	T͡Sh	ɓ	t͡sh
	Ƃ	T̄s	ƃ	ts̄
	Ҷ	C̄h	ҷ	c̄h
	Ӽ	Ċh	ӽ	ċh
	-	-	'	″ (hard sign)

Upper case letters		Lower case letters	
Vernacular	*Romanization*	*Vernacular*	*Romanization*

Lithuanian

Ж	Ž	ж	ž
Й	J	й	j
Ц	C	ц	c
Ч	Č	ч	č
Ш	Š	ш	š
Ѣ	Ė	ѣ	ė

Mansi (1937)

-	-	н'	n͡g

Mansi (1958)

-	-	ŋ	n͡g

Mari--Meadow Dialect (Missionary)

Ю̂	Ё	ю̂	ё

Mari--Meadow Dialect (1870's and early Soviet)

Ä	Ă	ä	ă
Ҥ	N͡G	ҥ	n͡g
Ö	Ȯ	ö	ȯ
Ӱ	U̇	ӱ	u̇

Mari--Meadow Dialect (1938)

-	-	ҥ	n͡g
Ö	Ȯ	ö	ȯ
Ӱ	U̇	ӱ	u̇

Mari--Mountain Dialect (missionary)

Ю̂	Ё	ю̂	ё

Mari--Mountain Dialect (1870's and early Soviet)

Ä	Ă	ä	ă
Ҥ	N͡G	ҥ	n͡g
Ö	Ȯ	ö	ȯ
Ӱ	U̇	ӱ	u̇
Ы	Ẏ	ы	ẏ

Upper case letters		*Lower case letters*	
Vernacular	*Romanization*	*Vernacular*	*Romanization*

Mari--Mountain Dialect (1938)

Ä	Ă	ä	ă
Ö	Ȯ	ö	ȯ
Ӱ	U̇	ӱ	u̇
Ы̆	Ẏ	ы̆	ẏ

Moldavian (Early and 1924)

-	-	’	’ (apostrophe)

Moldavian (1937)

Ӂ	J	ӂ	j

This letter was added to the Moldavian alphabet in 1958.

Mongolian (1941-1945)

Ө	Ȯ	ө	ȯ
Y	U̇	ү	u̇

Mordvin--Erzya Dialect (Early missionary)

І̂О	Ë	і̂о	ë

Mordvin--Erzya Dialect (Later missionary)

Ҥ	N͡G	ҥ	n͡g

Mordvin--Erzya Dialect (Early Soviet & 1938)   No additional characters.

Mordvin--Moksha Dialect (Missionary)

Æ	Ă	æ	ă

Mordvin--Moksha Dialect (1923)

Ĕ	Ĕ	ĕ	ĕ
Лк	Lk͟h	лк	lk͟h
Ҥ	N͡G	ҥ	n͡g
Ŏ	Ŏ	ŏ	ŏ
Рк	Rk͟h	рк	rk͟h
Ы	Y̆	ы	y̆
Ӭ	Ă	ӭ	ă

Mordvin--Moksha Dialect (1938)   No additional characters.

Nanai   No additional characters.

| Upper case letters | | Lower case letters | |
Vernacular	Romanization	Vernacular	Romanization
Nenets (1937)			
-	-	ʼ	' (apostrophe)
Netets (1958)			
-	-	ŋ	n͡g
Nivkh			
-	-	ʼ	' (apostrophe)
Nogai (1938) No additional characters.			
Ossetic--Digor Dialect (1938)			
Æ	Æ	æ	æ
-	-	ʼ	' (apostrophe)
-	-	ʻ	' (ayn)
-	-	ъ	ʺ (hard sign)
Ossetic--Iron Dialect (1938)			
Æ	Æ	æ	æ
-	-	ъ	ʺ (hard sign)

Note: When used alone, the language name "Ossetic" usually refers to this dialect.

Romany--Bulgaria			
Р̆	Ṛ	р̆	ṛ
Romany--U.S.S.R.			
Г (Ғ)	Gh	г (ғ)	gh
Selkup (1936)			
-	-	ʼ	' (apostrophe)
Shor (Missionary)			
-	-	ÿ	u̇
-	-	ö	ȯ
-	-	ҥ	n͡g
-	-	j	ċh
Shor (1927)			
-	-	ҥ	n͡g
-	-	ö	ȯ
-	-	ÿ	u̇
Shor (1938)			
-	-	ÿ	u̇
-	-	ö	ȯ

Upper case letters		Lower case letters	
Vernacular	*Romanization*	*Vernacular*	*Romanization*

Tabasaran (1938)

-	-	I	ḩ̇
-	-	ъ	″ (hard sign)

Tajik (1940)

Ғ	Gh	ғ	gh
-	-	ӣ	ī
Қ	Q	қ	q
ӯ	Ū	ӯ	ū
Х	Ḣ	х	ḣ
Ҷ	J	ҷ	j
-	-	ъ	″ (hard sign)

Tat

-	-	I	ḣ
-	-	ъ	″ (hard sign)

Tatar (1938)

Ә	Ă	ә	ă
Ө	Ȯ	ө	ȯ
Ү	U̇	ү	u̇
Җ	J	җ (ж)	j
Ң	N͡G	ң (ŋ)	n͡g
һ	Ḣ	һ	ḣ

Tatar--Crimea   No additional characters.

-	-	ъ	″ (hard sign)

Tatar--Kryashen

Ä	Ă	ä	ă
-	-	ҥ	n͡g
Ö	Ȯ	ö	ȯ
ÿ	U̇	ÿ	u̇

Turkmen (1940)

Җ	J	җ	j
Ң	N͡G	ң	n͡g
Ө	Ȯ	ө	ȯ
Ү	U̇	ү	u̇
Ә	Ă	ә	ă

Upper case letters		Lower case letters	
Vernacular	*Romanization*	*Vernacular*	*Romanization*

Tuva

-	-	ң	n͡g
Ө	Ȯ	ө	ȯ
Y	U̇	ү	u̇

Udekhe

-	-	'	' (apostrophe)

Udmurt (missionary)

Ö	Ȯ	ö	ȯ

Udmurt--Early Soviet and 1937 alphabets)

Ӝ	J	ӝ	j
Ӟ	D͡Z	ӟ	d͡z
-	-	й	ĭ
Ö	Ȯ	ö	ȯ
Ӵ	Ċh	ӵ	ċh

Uighur (1947)

Ғ	Gh	ғ	gh
Ә	Ă	ә	ă
Җ	J	җ	j
Қ	Q	қ (ҡ)	q
Ң	N͡G	ң	n͡g
Ө	Ȯ	ө	ȯ
Y	U̇	ү	u̇
һ	Ḣ	һ	ḣ

Uzbek (1940)

Ғ	Gh	ғ	gh
Қ	Q	қ (қ)	q
Ў	Ŭ	ў (ӯ)	ŭ
Х	Ḣ	х (х)	ḣ

Yakut (1819)   No additional characters.

Upper case letters Vernacular	Romanization	Lower case letters Vernacular	Romanization

Yakut (1851 Böhtlingk)

Ä	Ė	ä	ė
Ö	Ȯ	ö	ȯ
Ӱ	U̇	ӱ	u̇
Ҕ	Gh	ҕ	gh
Ҥ	N͡G	ҥ (ʜ)	n͡g
Ц̱	D́	ц̱	d́
Ḣ	Ń	ʼн (н')	ń
J	Ĭ	j	ĭ
Ɉ	I͡N	ɉ	i͡n
L	L	l	l
-	-	h	ḧ
Ā, etc.	AA, etc.	ā, etc.	aa, etc.

Yakut (1939)

Ҕ	Gh	ҕ	gh
Ҥ	N͡G	ҥ	n͡g
Ɵ	Ȯ	ɵ	ȯ
h	Ḧ	h	ḧ
Y	U̇	ү	u̇

SPECIAL CHARACTERS AND CHARACTER MODIFIERS IN ROMANIZATION

Special Characters	Name	USMARC hexadecimal code
ʼ	apostrophe	27
Æ	digraph AE (upper case)	A5
′	soft sign	A7
ʻ	ayn	B0
æ	digraph ae (lower case)	B5
″	hard sign	B7

Character Modifiers	Name	USMARC hexadecimal code
ó	acute	E2
ō	macron	E5
ŏ	breve	E6
ȯ	dot above	E7
ö	umlaut (dieresis)	E8
ǒ	hachek	E9
o̊	circle above (angstrom)	EA
͡	ligature, 1st half	EB
͡	ligature, 2nd half	EC
ŏ	candrabindu	EF
o̧	cedilla	F0
o̩	dot below	F2

Oriya

Vowels and Diphthongs (see Note 1)

ଅ	a		ଋ	ṝ
ଆ	ā		ଌ	l̥
ଇ	i		ଏ	e
ଈ	ī		ଐ	ai
ଉ	u		ଓ	o
ଊ	ū		ଔ	au
ଋ	r̥			

Consonants (see Note 2)

Gutturals		**Palatals**		**Cerebrals**		**Dentals**	
କ	ka	ଚ	ca	ଟ	ṭa	ତ	ta
ଖ	kha	ଛ	cha	ଠ	ṭha	ଥ	tha
ଗ	ga	ଜ	ja	ଡ	ḍa	ଦ	da
ଘ	gha	ଝ	jha	ଢ	ḍha	ଧ	dha
ଙ	ṅa	ଞ	ña	ଣ	ṇa	ନ	na

Labials		**Semivowels**		**Sibilants**		**Aspirate**	
ପ	pa	ୟ	ya	ଶ	śa	ହ	ha
ଫ	pha	ୟ	ẏa	ଷ	sha		
ବ	ba	ର	ra	ସ	sa		
ଭ	bha	ଲ	la				
ମ	ma	ଳ	ḷa				
		ଵ	ba (see Note 3)				

Anusvāra (see Note 4)		*Bisarga*		*Candrabindu* (*anunāsika*) (see Note 5)		*Abagraha* (see Note 6)	
ଂ	ṃ	ଃ	ḥ	ଁ	n̐, m̐	ଽ	' (apostrophe)

Notes

1. Only the vowel forms that appear at the beginning of a syllable are listed; the forms used for vowels following a consonant can be found in grammars; no distinction between the two is made in transliteration.

2. The vowel *a* is implicit after all consonants and consonant clusters and is supplied in transliteration, with the following exceptions:
    (a) when another vowel is indicated by its appropriate sign; and
    (b) when the absence of any vowel is indicated by the subscript sign (੍) called *hasanta*.

3. ଵ is used both as a labial and as a semivowel. When it occurs as the second consonant of a consonant cluster, it is transliterated *va*. When ଵ is doubled, it is transliterated *bba*.

4. Exception: *Anusvāra* is transliterated by:
    ṅ before gutturals,
    ñ before palatals,
    ṇ before cerebrals,
    n before dentals, and
    m before labials.

5. *Candrabindu* before gutteral, palatal, cerebral, and dental occlusives is transliterated *n̆*. Before labials, sibilants, semivowels, the aspirate, vowels, and in final position it is transliterated *m̆*.

6. When doubled, *abagraha* is transliterated by two apostrophes (”).

SPECIAL CHARACTERS AND CHARACTER MODIFIERS IN ROMANIZATION

Special character	Name	USMARC hexadecimal code
’	apostrophe	27

Character modifiers	Name	USMARC hexadecimal code
Ó	acute	E2
Õ	tilde	E4
Ō	macron	E5
Ȯ	dot above	E7
Ŏ	candrabindu	EF
Ọ	dot below	F2
Ǫ	circle below	F4

Ottoman Turkish

RULES OF APPLICATION

1. Ottoman Turkish is meant here to mean the Turkish language as found in written records of the area controlled by the Ottoman Empire (ca. 1300 to 1919) and in use in Turkey from 1919 until the adoption of the Roman alphabet (officially introduced in 1928). Ottoman Turkish covers Turkish written in the Arabic alphabet and in other non-Roman alphabets as well (e.g., Armenian, Cyrillic, Greek, Hebrew). It does not include the other Turkic languages of Eastern Europe, the Near East and Central Asia.

2. In romanizing Ottoman Turkish the principle of *conversion* is applied as far as possible, i.e., the word, phrase, name, or title being romanized is represented, if possible, by the form it has in modern Turkish orthography, even if that means converting some letters to their modern equivalents. Foreign words, or words of non-Turkish origin that have become loan-words in Turkish, are converted like Ottoman Turkish. Modern Turkish usage in capitalization is followed.

3. Some limitations to the applicability of conversion are recognized. When the orthography of the Ottoman Turkish original reveals a conflict with modern Turkish usage, whether in pronunciation, in syntax, or in vocabulary, the letter (letters), word, or expression is romanized according to the table. Conversion as a principle is not applied to word order, which is not changed to conform to modern syntax. Obsolete terms are not replaced by their modern equivalents to reflect current terminology. Paragraphs 5-8 below provide more detailed guidance.

4. Some variations in modern Turkish orthography are found among standard publications. The reference works listed below are recommended for guidance in romanization.

Dictionaries and Spelling Guides

Büyük lûgat ve ansiklopedi ("Meydan Larousse"). 1969-1973.

Hony, H.C. *A Turkish-English dictionary.* 2nd ed. 1957.

Redhouse yeni Türkçe-İngilizce sözlük. 1968.

Türk Dil Kurumu. *Yeni imlâ kılavuzu.* 3rd ed. 1967 (And other editions)

Turkey. Millî Eğitim Bakanlığı. *Türk ilmi transkripsyon kılavuzu.* 1946.

Specialized Works

İslâm ansiklopedisi. 1940-

Istanbul. Üniversite. Kütüphane. *İstanbul Üniversitesi Kütüphanesi Türkçe basmalar alfabe kataloğu (1729-1928).* 1956.

Koray, Enver. *Türkiye tarih yayınları bibliyografyası, 1729/1955-*

Türkiye bibliyografyası. 1934-

Chapman, Harry W. *1939-1948 Türkiye bibliyografyası özad indeski = A First-name index to the Türkiye bibliyografyası, 1939-1948.* 1968.

When the Turkish sources do not agree, the usage which seems predominant is followed. For certain kinds of variation, a uniform treatment is adopted. (See paragraphs 5-8 below.)

Aşık Paşa zade *or* Aşık Paşazade *or* Aşıkpaşazade

Heading: Aşıkpaşazade

When the word or expression being looked for is not found in Turkish sources, it is romanized by analogy with similar words or expressions. References are freely made when they will help to guide a user of the catalog from forms found in published sources to the form that has been adopted for the catalog. Variants from which references are made may be either names or the titles of works. References are especially useful when the title may be interpreted as being in any of several languages. Added entries may be provided instead of references when appropriate.

5. Phonetic considerations contribute to variability and inconsistency in the spelling of certain words and classes of words. For cataloging purposes, the orthography specified below is adopted in the conversion of both words and names.

(a) Final -*p* versus final -*b*: the spelling *p* is adopted for all cases in which *p/b* variation occurs.
tıp *not* tıb
harp *not* harb
Ratip *not* Ratib
but Bab-i Saadet *[no variation]*

(b) Final -*t* versus final -*d*: the spelling *t* is adopted for all cases in which *t/d* variation occurs.
mevcut *not* mevcud
Ahmet *not* Ahmed
but Belgrad *[no variation]*

(c) Final -*k* versus final -*g*: The spelling *k* is adopted for all cases in which *k/g* variation occurs.
renk *not* reng

(d) Final -*ç* versus final -*c*: the spelling *ç* is adopted for all cases in which *ç/c* variation occurs.
burç *not* burc

(e) Medial -*tt*- versus medial -*dd*-: the spelling *dd* is adopted for all cases in which variation occurs.
Bedreddin *not* Bedrettin

(f) Medial -*iy*- versus -*iyy*-: the spelling -*iy*- is adopted for all cases, whether the particular word concerned is variously spelled or not.
harbiye *not* harbiyye
cumhuriyet *not* cumhuriyyet

6.   Other variations require a standardized orthography for cataloging purposes.

(a) *Izafet.* Final *i* or ı preceded by a hyphen, the combination functioning as the sign of izafet, may otherwise be found in the form *i* or ı (sometimes *yi, yı*) added directly to the word being modified. In converting from Ottoman Turkish, *-i* is added to the word being modified when it ends in a consonant, *-yi* when it ends in a vowel. Vowel harmony is disregarded.

Devlet-i Âliye-yi Osmaniye

Izafet is not indicated between the elements of a personal name except when it is expressly indicated in the Ottoman Turkish orthography.

(b) The Arabic article *al*, when romanized in modern Turkish, may take various forms, among them: *al, el, ur, ül, 'l, üs, ed, en,* and *et.* When the article functions as the middle element of a phrase or compound word or name, within a Turkish context, it is converted in accordance with the predominant usage in modern Turkish orthography for the particular word or name. It will usually happen that the component elements are combined as a single word.

alelumum	Abdüssettar
bilhassa	Abdurrahman
maalesef	Ebülgazi
darülfünun	*x-ref from* Ebül Gazi

When the Arabic article occurs in an Arabic title, it is romanized according to the rules for Arabic. (See (9) below.)

(c) *Diacritics.* A dieresis (ˉ̈) is retained if found to be commonly used in Turkish in the particular word concerned, even if it is not used consistently. A circumflex (ˉ̂) is retained where found in modern Turkish usage. It is always placed over the final long *i* of the relative adjective (*nisbe*) and names derived from it.

(d) An apostrophe (') is inserted between a proper noun, or a number, and a suffixed inflection.
Mustafa'nin vakfı
1975'te
1976'de

7.   Non-Turkish titles. Rarely, an Ottoman Turkish work will be found to bear a title that is entirely non-Turkish. "Non-Turkish" should not be taken to refer to any word or phrase that is only foreign in origin but has been accepted as belonging to Turkish. (This caveat is particularly necessary for words and expressions that derive from Arabic, the majority of which have become Turkish.) As already indicated in the present scheme, Turkish lexicographic sources will settle most such questions. In the very rare case when a title is non-Turkish (i.e., the words and phrases used have not been accepted into the Turkish language), then the title may be romanized according to the rules for the language involved.

8.   General notes.

(a) Word divisions follow predominant usage in modern Turkish. Where word division in the original varies decidedly from modern style and it is desirable to reflect the presentation in the publication being cataloged, the Ottoman Turkish word division may be retained.

(b) The Arabic word *ibn*, "son of", occurring in names of the Islamic type, usually appears in modern Turkish orthography as *Ibn* at the beginning of a name and as *bin* (often abbreviated *b.*) in the middle of a name. The Ottoman Turkish form is romanized so as to maintain this distinction uniformly, but the abbreviation *b.* is not used.

9.   When conversion is impractical because the word or words to be romanized are not part of the lexicon of modern Turkish and cannot be documented in Turkish sources in roman orthography, and analogous forms are not available for guidance, the orginal is romanized letter by letter, as prescribed by the rules for romanization of the alphabet concerned. When a title is being romanized and the language of the title is not identifiable with certainty, the title is romanized as from Ottoman Turkish according to the table. It should be noted that letter-by-letter romanization is applied *only* to the word or expression which cannot be converted to modern Turkish orthography. It may only be necessary to transliterate a single letter or group of letters within a word which is otherwise convertible to modern Turkish. The associated words in a context are, as far as possible, romanized according to the principles of conversion.

If the Ottoman Turkish original is written in the Arabic alphabet, the consonants are romanized as in the Ottoman Turkish table presented in this section.

The vowels and orthographic symbols other than vowel signs (*hemze, şedde, medde, tenvin*) are romanized according to the rules for Arabic or Persian, as appropriate. They are supplied if omitted from the Turkish original. (Systematic romanization in these cases promotes reversibility. See the romanization tables for Arabic and Persian.) No attempt is made to represent the Ottoman Turkish pronunciation of vowels beyond what is conveyed by the orthography of the orginal.

10. The romanization table for Ottoman Turkish (presented on the next two pages) is based on the romanization system published by Eleazer Birnbaum in the *Journal of the American Oriental Society*, volume 87 (1967). A few slight modifications have been introduced.

10.   **Romanization Table for Ottoman Turkish**

NOTE: Use table if principle of conversion cannot be applied. See 2. in RULES OF APPLICATION.

Letters of the Alphabet

Initial	Medial	Final	Alone	Romanization
ا	ـا	ـا	ا	omit (see Note 1)
بـ	ـبـ	ـب	ب	b
پـ	ـپـ	ـپ	پ	p
تـ	ـتـ	ـت	ت	t
ثـ	ـثـ	ـث	ث	s̲
جـ	ـجـ	ـج	ج	c
چـ	ـچـ	ـچ	چ	ç
حـ	ـحـ	ـح	ح	ḥ
خـ	ـخـ	ـخ	خ	ḫ
د	ـد	ـد	د	d
ذ	ـذ	ـذ	ذ	ẕ
ر	ـر	ـر	ر	r
ز	ـز	ـز	ز	z
ژ	ـژ	ـژ	ژ	j
سـ	ـسـ	ـس	س	s
شـ	ـشـ	ـش	ش	ş
صـ	ـصـ	ـص	ص	ṣ
ضـ	ـضـ	ـض	ض	ż
طـ	ـطـ	ـط	ط	ṭ
ظـ	ـظـ	ـظ	ظ	ẓ
عـ	ـعـ	ـع	ع	ʻ (ayn)
غـ	ـغـ	ـغ	غ	ġ
فـ	ـفـ	ـف	ف	f
قـ	ـقـ	ـق	ق	ḳ
كـ	ـكـ	ـك	ك	k
گـ	ـگـ	ـگ	گ	g (see Note 2)
ـ	ـڭـ	ـڭ	ڭ	ñ (see Note 3)
لـ	ـلـ	ـل	ل	l
مـ	ـمـ	ـم	م	m
نـ	ـنـ	ـن	ن	n
وـ	ـوـ	ـو	و	v (see Note 4)
هـ	ـهـ	ـه ، ة	ه ، ة	h (see Note 5)
يـ	ـيـ	ـى	ى	y (see Note 6)

Notes

1. For orthographic uses of this letter, see the Arabic and Persian romanization tables.
2. Frequently written without the distinguishing upper strokes.
3. Frequently written without the distinguishing dots.
4. For the uses of this letter other than to represent the consonantal sound *v*, see the Persian romanization table.
5. For the distinction between ٥ and ة see the Arabic romanization table.
6. For the uses of this letter other than to represent the consonantal sound *y*, see the Persian romanization table.

SPECIAL CHARACTERS AND CHARACTER MODIFIERS IN ROMANIZATION

Special Characters	*Name*	*USMARC hexadecimal code*
′	soft sign (prime)	A7
’	alif	AE
‘	ayn	B0
ı	Turkish i (small)	B8

Character Modifiers	*Name*	*USMARC hexadecimal code*
́	acute	E2
̂	circumflex	E3
̃	tilde	E4
̄	macron	E5
̆	breve	E6
̇	dot above	E7
̈	umlaut (dieresis)	E8
̧	cedilla	F0
̣	dot below	F2
̲	underscore	F6
̭	upadhmaniya	F9

Pali
(in Various Scripts)

Notes

1. Only the vowel forms that appear at the beginning of a syllable are listed; the forms used for vowels following a consonant can be found in grammars; no distinction between the two is made in transliteration.

2. The vowel *a* is implicit after all consonants and consonant clusters and is supplied in romanization, except when another vowel is indicated by its appropriate sign.

3. Exception: *Niggahīta* and *saññaka* combinations representing nasals, are romanized by:

    ṅ before gutterals, ñ before palatals,
    ṇ before cerebrals, n before dentals, and
    ṃ before labials.

4. In Bengali script, *ba* and *va* are not differentiated. The romanization should follow the value of the consonant in the particular passage, ascertainable by checking the same passage as printed in other scripts.

Romanization	Bengali	Burmese	Devanagari	Sinhalese	Thai
Vowels (see Note 1)					
a	অ	အ	अ	අ	อ , อํ
ā	আ	အာ	आ	ආ	อา
i	ই ঈ	ဣ ဥ	इ	ඉ	อิ อี
ī	ই ঈ		ई	ඊ	อี
u	উ ঊ	ဥ ဦ	उ	උ	อุ อุ
ū	উ ঊ		ऊ	ඌ	อุ อู
e	এ	ဧ	ए	එ	เอ
o	ও	ဩ	ओ	ඔ	โอ

Consonants (see Note 2)					
Gutturals					
ka	ক	က	क	ක	ก
kha	খ	ခ	ख	ඛ	ข
ga	গ	ဂ	ग	ග	ค
gha	ঘ	ဃ	घ	ඝ	ฆ
ṅa	ঙ	င	ङ	ඞ	ง
Palatals					
ca	চ	စ	च	ච	จ
cha	ছ	ဆ	छ	ඡ	ฉ
ja	জ	ဇ	ज	ජ	ช
jha	ঝ	ဈ	झ	ඣ	ฌ
ña	ঞ	ည	ञ	ඤ	ญ , ฌ

Romanization	Khmer	Lao	Tua Tham/A	Tua Tham/B	Northern Thai

Vowels (Independent) (see Note 1)

Romanization	Khmer	Lao	Tua Tham/A	Tua Tham/B	Northern Thai
a	អ	ອ	ᩋ	ᩋ	–
ā	អា	ອາ	ᩋᩣ	ᩋᩣ	–
i	ឥ	ອິ	ᩍ	ᩍ	ᩍ
ī	ឦ	ອີ	ᩎ	ᩎ	ᩎ
u	ឧ	ອຸ	ᩏ	ᩏ	ᩏ
ū	ឩ, ឨ	ອູ	ᩐ	ᩐ	ᩐ
e	ឯ	ເອ	ᩑ	ᩑ	ᩑ
o	ឱ, ឲ	ໂອ	ᩒ , ᩓ	ᩓ	–

Vowels (Dependent) (see Note 1)

Romanization	Khmer	Lao	Tua Tham/A	Tua Tham/B	Northern Thai
a	□	□	□	□	□
ā	□ា	□າ	□	□	□
i	□ិ	□ິ	□	□	□
ī	□ី	□ີ	□	□	□
u	□ុ	□ຸ	□	□	□
ū	□ូ	□ູ	□	□	□
e	េ□	ເ□	ເ□	ເ□	ເ□
o	េ□ា	ໂ□	ເ□	ເ□	ໂ□

Consonants (see Note 2)

Gutturals

Romanization	Khmer		Lao	Tua Tham/A	Tua Tham/B	Northern Thai
ka	ក	□	ກ	ᨠ	ᨠ	ᨠ
kha	ខ	□	ຂ	ᨡ	ᨡ	ᨡ
ga	គ	□	ຄ	ᨣ	ᨣ	ᨣ
gha	ឃ	□	ฆ	ᨥ	ᨥ	ᨥ
ṅa	ង	□	ງ	ᨦ	ᨦ	ᨦ

Palatals

Romanization	Khmer		Lao	Tua Tham/A	Tua Tham/B	Northern Thai
ca	ច	□	ຈ	ᨧ	ᨧ	ᨧ
cha	ឆ	□	ฉ	ᨨ	ᨨ	ᨨ
ja	ជ	□	ຊ	ᨩ	ᨩ	ᨩ
jha	ឈ	□	ฌ	ᨫ	ᨫ	ᨫ
ña	ញ	□ , □	ຎ	ᨬ	ᨬ	ᨬ

Pali

Romanization	Bengali	Burmese	Devanagari	Sinhalese	Thai
Cerebrals					
ṭa	ট	ဋ	ट	ට	ฏ, ฐ
ṭha	ঠ	ဌ	ठ	ඨ	ฑ
ḍa	ড	ဍ	ड	ඩ	ฒ
ḍha	ঢ	ဎ	ढ	ඪ	ณ
ṇa	ণ	ဏ	ण	ණ	ณ
Dentals					
ta	ত	တ	त	ත	ต
tha	থ	ထ	थ	ථ	ถ
da	দ	ဒ	द	ද	ท
dha	ধ	ဓ	ध	ධ	ธ
na	ন	န	न	න	น
Labials (see Note 4)					
pa	প	ပ	प	ප	ป
pha	ফ	ဖ	फ	ඵ	ผ
ba	ব	ဗ	ब	බ	พ
bha	ভ	ဘ	भ	භ	ภ
ma	ম	မ	म	ම	ม
Semivowels (see Note 4)					
ya	য	ယ	य	ය	ย
ra	র	ရ	र	ර	ร
la	ল	လ	ल	ල	ล
ḷa		ဠ	ळ	ළ	ฬ
va	ব	၀	व	ව	ว
Sibilant					
sa	স	သ	स	ස	ส
Aspirate					
ha	হ	ဟ	ह	හ	ห

Niggahīta (see Note 3) *Visagga*

ँ ṃ   : ḥ

Romanization	Khmer	Lao	Tua Tham/A	Tua Tham/B	Northern Thai
Cerebrals					
ṭa					
ṭha					
ḍa					
ḍha					
ṇa					
Dentals					
ta					
tha					
da					
dha					
na					
Labials					
pa					
pha					
ba					
bha					
ma					
Semivowels					
ya					
ra					
la					
ḷa					
va					
Sibilant					
sa					
Aspirate					
ha					

Niggahīta (see Note 3)   *Visagga*

◌̇ ṃ   : ḥ

SPECIAL CHARACTERS AND CHARACTER MODIFIERS IN ROMANIZATION

Special character	Name	USMARC hexadecimal code
ʼ	apostrophe	27

Character modifiers	Name	USMARC hexadecimal code
ñ	tilde	E4
ō	macron	E5
ṅ	dot above	E7
ṇ	dot below	F2

Panjabi
(in Gurmukhi Script)

Vowels and Diphthongs (see Note 1)

ਅ	a		ਏ	e
ਆ	ā		ਐ	ai
ਇ	i		ਓ	o
ਈ	ī		ਔ	au
ਉ	u			
ਊ	ū			

Consonants (see Notes 2 and 3)

Sibilants		Aspirate		Gutturals		Palatals	
ਸ	sa	ਹ	ha	ਕ	ka	ਚ	ca
ਸ਼	sha			ਖ	kha	ਛ	cha
				ਖ਼	<u>kh</u>a	ਜ	ja
				ਗ	ga	ਜ਼	za
				ਘ	<u>gh</u>a	ਝ	jha
				ਘ	gha	ਞ	ña
				ਙ	ṅa		

Cerebrals		Dentals		Labials		Semivowels	
ਟ	ṭa	ਤ	ta	ਪ	pa	ਯ	ya
ਠ	ṭha	ਥ	tha	ਫ	pha	ਰ	ra
ਡ	ḍa	ਦ	da	ਫ਼	fa	ਲ	la
ਢ	ḍha	ਧ	dha	ਬ	ba	ਲ਼	ḷa
ਣ	ṇa	ਨ	na	ਭ	bha	ਵ	wa
				ਮ	ma	ੜ	ṛa

Bindī (see Note 4)		*Ṭippī* (see Note 5)		*Adhik* (see Note 6)	
ਂ	ṃ	ੰ	m̐	ੱ	*[doubles the following consonant]*

Notes

1. Only the vowel forms that appear at the beginning of a syllable are listed; the forms used for vowels following a consonant can be found in grammars; no distinction between the two is made in transliteration.

2. The vowel *a* is implicit after consonant clusters and may be implicit after consonants except when they are final or when another vowel is indicated by its appropriate sign. The cases in which the vowel *a* is implicit, however, can be determined only from a knowledge of the language or from suitable reference sources. In such cases the *a* is supplied in transliteration.

3. The dotted letters are used in Urdu words.

4. Exception: *Bindī* is transliterated by:
    ṅ before gutturals,
    ñ before palatals,
    ṇ before cerebrals,
    n before dentals, and
    m before labials.

5. Exception: *Ṭippī* is transliterated by:
    ṅ before gutturals,
    ñ before palatals,
    ṇ before cerebrals,
    n before dentals, and
    m before labials.

6. Exception: When *adhik* implies the combination of a non-aspirated and an aspirated consonant, the combination is transliterated as a non-aspirated, followed by an aspirated consonant.

CHARACTER MODIFIERS IN ROMANIZATION

Character modifiers	Name	USMARC hexadecimal code
õ	tilde	E4
ō	macron	E5
ŏ	breve	E6
ȯ	dot above	E7
ọ	dot below	F2
ọ	underscore	F6

Persian

Letters of the Alphabet

Initial	Medial	Final	Alone	Romanization
‍ا	‍ل	‍ل	ا	omit (see Note 1)
ﺑ	ﺒ	ﺐ	ب	b
ﭘ	ﭙ	ﭗ	پ	p
ﺗ	ﺘ	ﺖ	ت	t
ﺛ	ﺜ	ﺚ	ث	s̲
ﺟ	ﺠ	ﺞ	ج	j
ﭼ	ﭽ	ﭻ	چ	ch
ﺣ	ﺤ	ﺢ	ح	ḥ
ﺧ	ﺨ	ﺦ	خ	kh
ﺩ	ﺪ	ﺪ	د	d
ﺫ	ﺬ	ﺬ	ذ	z̲
ﺭ	ﺮ	ﺮ	ر	r
ﺯ	ﺰ	ﺰ	ز	z
ﮊ	ﮋ	ﮋ	ژ	zh
ﺳ	ﺴ	ﺲ	س	s
ﺷ	ﺸ	ﺶ	ش	sh
ﺻ	ﺼ	ﺺ	ص	ṣ
ﺿ	ﻀ	ﺾ	ض	ẓ
ﻃ	ﻄ	ﻂ	ط	ṭ
ﻇ	ﻈ	ﻆ	ظ	z̧
ﻋ	ﻌ	ﻊ	ع	ʻ (ayn)
ﻏ	ﻐ	ﻎ	غ	gh
ﻓ	ﻔ	ﻒ	ف	f
ﻗ	ﻘ	ﻖ	ق	q
ﻛ	ﻜ	ﻚ	ك	k (see Note 2)
ﮔ	ﮕ	ﮓ	گ	g (see Note 3)
ﻟ	ﻠ	ﻞ	ل	l
ﻣ	ﻤ	ﻢ	م	m
ﻧ	ﻨ	ﻦ	ن	n
ﻭ	ﻮ	ﻮ	و	v (see Note 3)
ﻫ	ﻬ	ﺔ ، ﻪ	ة ، ﻩ	h (see Note 4)
ﻳ	ﻴ	ﻰ	ى	y (see Note 3)

Vowels and Diphthongs (see Note 5)

◌َ	a	آ، ◌ٰ	ā (see Note 6)	◌ِی	ī
◌ُ	u	◌َی	á (see Note 7)	◌َوْ	aw
◌ِ	i	◌ُو	ū	◌َیْ	ay

Notes

1. For the use of ا (*alif*) to support ء (*hamzah*) and ◌ٓ (*maddah*) see rule 1(a). For the romanization of ء and ◌ٓ see rules 4 and 5 respectively. For the use of ا to represent the long vowel romanized *ā* see the table of vowels and diphthongs, and rule 1(b).

2. Final ک and گ (often written ك and گ) may have the form ك, without the distinguishing upper stroke or strokes. The two letters are always distinguished in romanization.

3. For other values of و and ی see the table of vowels and diphthongs, and rules 2, 3, and 7.

4. ة (dotted ه) when used as an alternative to ت is romanized *t*.

5. Vowel points are not printed on Library of Congress cards.

6. See rules 1(b) and 5.

7. See rule 3(d).

RULES OF APPLICATION

Letters Which May Be Romanized in Different Ways Depending on Their Context

1. ا (*alif*) is used:

   (a) As a support for ء (*hamzah*) and ◌ٓ (*maddah*). In these cases it is not represented in romanization. See rules 4 and 5.

   (b) To indicate the long vowel romanized *ā*. For the use of ا in *tanvīn* see rule 6.

   dānā   دانا

2. و is used to represent:

   (a) The consonant romanized *v*.

   varzish   ورزش

   davā   دوا

   sarv   سرو

Silent و following خ is retained in romanization.

| khvāstan | خواستن |
| khvud | خود |

(b)   The long *u*-vowel (and short *u*-vowel in some monosyllables) is romanized *ū*.

dūr	دور
chūn	چون
tū	تو

(c)   The diphthong romanized *aw*.

| Firdawsī | فردوسی |

When the diphthong precedes a consonantal و, the combination is romanized *avv*. See rule 7.

و may be used as a support for ء (*hamzah*); in this case it is not represented in romanization. See rule 4.

3.   ی is used to represent:

(a)   The consonant romanized *y*.

yār	یار
siyāh	سیاه
pāy	پای

(b)   The long vowel romanized *ī*.

| Īrān | ایران |
| qālī | قالی |

(c)   The diphthong romanized *ay*.

| ayvān | ایوان |
| ray | ری |

(d)   The final long vowel romanized *á*.

| Muṣṭafá | مصطفیَ |

For the use of ی as a mark of *iz̤āfah* see rule 8(c).

ی in the medial forms ـیـ, ـیـ, without dots, may be used as a support for ء (*hamzah*); in this case ی is not represented in romanization. See rule 4 below.

Orthographic Symbols Other Than Letters and Vowel Signs

The signs listed below are frequently omitted in Persian writting and printing; their presence must then be inferred. They are represented in romanization according to the following rules:

4.   ء (*hamzah*)

    (a)   When initial, ء is not represented in romanization.

    (b)   When medial or final, ء is romanized ' (alif) except as noted in (c) and (d) below.

            mu'a<u>ss</u>ir   مؤثر
            khulafā'   خلفاء
            pā'īn   پائين

    (c)   When used as a mark of *i<u>z</u>āfah*, ء is romanized -'i.

            astānah-'i dar   آستانهٔ در

    (d)   When used to mark the indefinite article, ء is romanized 'i.

            khānah'i   خانهٔ

5.   آ (*maddah*)

    (a)   Initial آ is romanized *ā*

            āb   آب
            Kullīyat al-Ādāb   كلية الآداب

    (b)   Medial آ, when it represents the phonetic combination '*ā*, is so romanized.

            ma'ā<u>s</u>ir   مآثر
            Daryā'ābādī   دریاآبادی

    (c)   آ is otherwise not represented in romanization.

            gardāvarandah   گردآورنده

6.   *Tanvīn* (written ٌ, ٍ, ً, اً), which occurs chiefly in Arabic words, is romanized *un, in, an,* and *an,* respectively.

7.   ّ (*shaddah* or *tashdīd*) is represented by doubling the letter or digraph concerned.

            khurram   خرّم
            avval   اوّل
            bachchah   بچّه
            Khayyām   خیّام

Note the exceptional case where ّ is written over و and ى to represent the combination of long vowel plus consonant.

nashrīyāt	نشرّيات
qūvah	قوّه

Grammatical Structure as It Affects Romanization

8.   *Iẓāfah*. When two words are associated in the relation known as *iẓāfah*, the first (the *muẓāf*) is followed by an additional letter or syllable in romanization. This is added according to the following rules:

    (a)   When the *muẓāf* bears no special mark of *iẓāfah*, it is followed by -*i*.

dar-i bāgh	در باغ
qālī-i Īrān	قالى ايران
khānah-i buzurg	خانه بزرگ

    (b)   When the *muẓāf* is marked by the addition of ء, it is followed by -*'i*.

qālī-'i Īrān	قالئ ايران
khānah-'i buzurg	خانهٔ بزرگ

    (c)   When the *muẓāf* is marked by the addition of ى, it is followed by -*yi*.

rū-yi zamīn	روى زمين
Daryā-yi Khazar	درياى خزر
khānah-yi buzurg	خانه‌ى بزرگ

    (d)   *Iẓāfah* is represented in romanization of personal names only when expressly indicated in the Persian script.

Affixes and Compounds

9.   Affixes.

    (a)   When the affix and the word with which it is connected grammatically are written separately in Persian, the two are separated in romanization by a single prime (ʹ). See also 12(b) below.

	khānah'hā	خانه‌ها
	khānah'am	خانه‌ام
	khānah'ī	خانه‌اى
	mī'ravam	مى روم
but	mīravam	ميروم
	bih'gū	به‌گو
	bar'rasīhā	بررسيها
	Kāẓim'zādah	كاظم زاده
but	Kāẓimzādah	كاظمزاده

(b)   The Arabic article *al* is separated by a hyphen, in romanization, from the word to which it is prefixed.

dār al-muʻallimīn   دار المعلمين

ʻAbd al-Ḥusayn   عبد الحسين

10.   Compounds. When the elements of a compound (except a compound personal name) are written separately in Persian, they are separated in romanization by a single prime (ʹ). See also 12(b) below.

	marīz̤ʹkhānah	مريض خانه
but	marīz̤khānah	مريضخانه
	Shāhʹnāmah	شاه نامه
but	Shāhnāmah	شاهنامه

Note the treatment of compound personal names:

Ghulām ʻAlī   غلام علي *or* غلامعلي

Shāh Jahān   شاه جهان *or* شاهجهان

Ibn Abī Ṭālib   ابن ابي طالب *or* ابن ابيطالب

Orthography of Persian in Romanization

11.   Capitalization.

(a)   Rules for the capitalization of English are followed, except that the Arabic article *al* is lower cased in all positions.

(b)   Diacritics are used with both capital and lower case letters.

12.   The single prime (ʹ) is used:

(a)   To separate two letters representing two distinct consonantal sounds, when the combination might otherwise be read as a digraph.

marzʹhā   مرزها

(b)   To mark the use of a letter in its final form when it occurs in the middle of a word. See also rules 9(a) and 10 above.

rāhʹhā   راهها

Qāyimʹmaqāmī   قايم مقامي

Bihʹāz̲īn   به آذين

13.   Foreign words in a Persian context, including Arabic words, are romanized according to the rules for Persian. For short vowels not indicated in the script, the Persian vowels nearest the original pronunciation of the word are supplied in romanization.

14.   Dictionaries.

In romanizing Persian, the Library of Congress has found it necessary to consult dictionaries as an appendage to the romanization tables, primarily for the purpose of supplying vowels. For Persian, the principle dictionary consulted is:

M. Mu'īn. *Farhang-i Fārsī-i mutavassit.*

SPECIAL CHARACTERS AND CHARACTER MODIFIERS IN ROMANIZATION

Special Characters	Name	USMARC hexadecimal code
′	soft sign (prime)	A7
ʾ	alif	AE
ʿ	ayn	B0

Character Modifiers	Name	USMARC hexadecimal code
́	acute	E2
̄	macron	E5
̣	dot below	F2
̤	double dot below	F3
̲	underscore	F6

Pushto

Letters of the Alphabet

Initial	Medial	Final	Alone	Romanization
ا	ـا	ـا	ا	omit (see Note 1)
بـ	ـبـ	ـب	ب	b
پـ	ـپـ	ـپ	پ	p
تـ	ـتـ	ـت	ت	t
ټـ	ـټـ	ـټ	ټ	ṭ
ثـ	ـثـ	ـث	ث	s̲
جـ	ـجـ	ـج	ج	j
چـ	ـچـ	ـچ	چ	ch
حـ	ـحـ	ـح	ح	ḥ
خـ	ـخـ	ـخ	خ	s̱
خـ	ـخـ	ـخ	خ	ẕ
خـ	ـخـ	ـخ	خ	kh
د	ـد	ـد	د	d
ډ	ـډ	ـډ	ډ	ḍ
ذ	ـذ	ـذ	ذ	z
ر	ـر	ـر	ر	r
ړ	ـړ	ـړ	ړ	ṛ
ز	ـز	ـز	ز	z
ژ	ـژ	ـژ	ژ	zh
ږ	ـږ	ـږ	ږ	ẕh
سـ	ـسـ	ـس	س	s
شـ	ـشـ	ـش	ش	sh
ښـ	ـښـ	ـښ	ښ	ṣh
صـ	ـصـ	ـص	ص	ṣ
ضـ	ـضـ	ـض	ض	ẓ
طـ	ـطـ	ـط	ط	ṭ
ظـ	ـظـ	ـظ	ظ	ẓ
عـ	ـعـ	ـع	ع	ʻ (ayn)
غـ	ـغـ	ـغ	غ	gh
فـ	ـفـ	ـف	ف	f
قـ	ـقـ	ـق	ق	q
كـ	ـكـ	ـك	ك	k
گـ	ـگـ	ـگ	گ	g
ګـ	ـګـ	ـګ	ګ	g
لـ	ـلـ	ـل	ل	l
مـ	ـمـ	ـم	م	m
نـ	ـنـ	ـن	ن	n
ڼـ	ـڼـ	ـڼ	ڼ	ṇ

نـمـ	ـمـمـ	ـمـمـ	نـمـ	ṇ
و	ـو	ـو	و	w (see Note 2)
ھ	ـھ	ھ ، ة	ه ، ة	h
ـيـ	ـيـ	ـى ، ـي	ى ، ي	y (see Note 3)

Vowels and Diphthongs (see Note 4)

Romanization	Initial	Medial	Final
a (see Note 5)	اَ	◌َ	◌َ
u	اُ	◌ُ	◌ُ
i	اِ	◌ِ	◌ِ
ā	آ	◌ا	ا◌
á	-	-	(see Note 6) ى ◌
ū	اُو	◌ُو	◌ُو و
ī	اِيـ	◌ِيـ	◌ِى ، ◌ِي
o	اَو	◌َو	◌َو و
e	اِيـ ، اِبـ	◌ِبـ ، ◌ِيـ	◌ى ، ◌ي ، ◌ـي ، ◌ح
aw	اَوْ	◌َوْ	◌َوْ
ay	اَيْـ	◌َيْـ	◌َى ، ◌َيْ
ạy	-	-	◌ى ، ◌ئ ، ◌ع

Notes

1. For the use of ا (*alif*) see the table of vowels and diphthongs, and rules 1-4.
2. For other uses of و see the table of vowels and diphthongs, and rule 5.
3. For other forms and used of ى see the table of vowels and diphthongs, and rules 6 and 7.
4. Vowel points are rarely found in Pushto writing and printing. Vowels not indicated in the script are supplied in romanization.
5. In addition to the three short vowels recognized by the orthography of all languages using Arabic script, Pushto possesses a short, central vowel for which the sign ◌ (differentiated from ◌) has sometimes been used. Both signs, whether written or inferred, may be romanized *a*. When this central vowel is indicated by ٴ (*hamzah*), the vowel is romanized *ạ*; the *hamzah* in this case is not represented in romanization. See rule 8(c) and (d). When it is desired for any reason to show the presence of a central vowel in a particular word, the romanization *ạ* may be used.
6. See rule 7(a).
7. See rule 7(b).

RULES OF APPLICATION

Letters Which May Be Romanized in Different Ways Depending on Their Context

1.   ‌‌ا (*alif*) is used:

    (a)   To indicate the presence of any of the short vowels *a, u, i.*
        atah   اتة
        ulas   الس
        inʻām   انعام

    (b)   To represent the long vowel romanized *ā*. When so used, ا is usually written with ◌̄ (*maddah*).
        ādam   آدم

    (c)   To represent, in combination with و or ى :

        (1)   The long vowels romanized *ū* and *ī* respectively.
            ūsh   اوش
            Īrān   ايران

        (2)   The long vowels romanized *o* and *e* respectively.
            os   اوس
            eshal   ايښل

        (3)   The diphthongs romanized *aw* and *ay* respectively.
            awwal   اول
            ayyām   ايام

2.   ا (*alif*), when medial or final, is used to represent the long vowel romanized *ā*.
        bābā   بابا

3.   ا (*alif*), when final, sometimes represents the combination romanized *an*. This value is confined to a few words of Arabic origin. See rule 10.

4.   ا (*alif*), when used to support ء (*hamzah*), is not represented in romanization; see rule 8.

5.   و is used to represent:

    (a)   The consonant romanized *w*.
            wror   ورور

        In Persian words, silent و following خ is retained in romanization.
            khwushḥāl   خوشحال

    (b)   The long vowel romanized *ū*. See also rule 1(c1).
            nūm   نوم

    (c)   The long vowel romanized *o*. See also rule 1(c2).
            kor   كور

(d)   The diphthong romanized *aw*. See also rule 1(c3).

        yaw   يو

(e)   The short vowel romanized *u*. Such cases are rare in Pushto orthography.

        u   او

Note: و when used to support ء (*hamzah*) is not represented in romanization. See rule 8.

6.   ي is used to represent:

    (a)   The consonant romanized *y*.

            yaw   يو

    (b)   The long vowel romanized *ī*. See also rule 1(c1)

            mīnah   مينه

    (a)   The long vowel romanized *e*. See also rule 1(c2).

            ḍer   ډير ، ډېر

            dre   دری ، درې ، درے

    (c)   The diphthong romanized *ay*. See also rule 1(c3).

            shay   شی

        Note: Medial ـيـ when used to support ء (*hamzah*) is usually written without dots (ـئـ ، ئ); it is not represented in romanization. See also rule 8(b) and (c)

7.   ى when final has two special uses. It may represent:

    (a)   The long vowel romanized *á*. This use is confined to word of Arabic origin.

            Muṣṭafá   مصطفىٰ

    (b)   The diphthong romanized *ạy*. When used with this value, ى usually has the form ے in Peshawar, ی in Afghanistan. See also rule 8(c).

        ḍoḍay   ډوډی ، ډوډے

Orthographic Symbols Other Than Letters and Vowel Signs

    The signs listed below are often omitted in Pushto writing and printing; their presence must be inferred. They are represented in romanization according to the following rules:

8.   ء (*hamzah*)

    (a)   In initial position, ء is not represented in romanization.

    (b)   In words of Arabic origin, ء when medial or final is romanized ' (*alif*).

            su'āl   سؤال

            dā'imī   دائمى

            mas'alah   مسأله

(c) When written over final ى or ـى, ء indicates the diphthong romanized *ay*. See rule 7(b).
ghwāṟay   غوارئ

(d) In the orthography of Peshawar, ء when written over final ه indicates the short vowel romanized *ạ*. See the table of vowels and diphthongs, footnote 7.
nạh   نـهٔ

9. $\bar{\Box}$ (*maddah*) is written over ه (*alif*) to indicate the long vowel romanized *ā*.
ākhir   آخر

10. *Tanwīn* (written $\overset{\sim}{\Box}$) occurs in words of Arabic origin and represents a final syllable which is romanized *an*. *Tanwīn* is usually associate with ا (*alif*), which is not represented in romanization. See rule 3.
fiṭratan   فطرًا

11. $\overset{\smile}{\Box}$ (*tashdīd*) is represented by doubling the letter or digraph concerned.
awwal   اوّل

Grammatical Structure as It Affects Romanization

12. *Iẕāfah*. When two words are associated in the Persian construction known as *iẕāfah*, the first (the *muẕāf*) is followed by an additional letter or syllable in romanization. This is added according to the following rules:

(a) When the *muẕāf* bears no special mark of *iẕāfah*, it is followed by -*i*.
dars-i ʻibrat   درس عبرت
ṣāḥib-i mubārak   صاحب مبارك

(b) When the *muẕāf* is marked by the addition of ء (*hamzah*), it is followed by -*ʼi*.
(c) When the *muẕāf* is marked by the addition of ى, it is followed by -*yi*.

Affixes and Compounds

13. Affixes.

When the affix and the word with which it is connected grammatically are written separately in Pushto, the two are separated in romanization by a single prime (ʹ).
nāʹashnā   ناآشنا
warʹastawī   وراستوى

Note 1: The particle د (*da*), meaning "of", is always written as a separate word in romanization.
da dạh   د دهٔ

Note 2: The Arabic article *al* is separated from what follows by a hyphen. The *l* of the article is retained in romanization, regardless of whether or not this *l* is assimilated in pronunciation to the sound of the following letter.
ʻAbd al-Rashīd   عبد الرشيد
Faẕl al-Ḥaqq   فضل الحق
Niẕām al-Dīn   نظام الدين

14.   Compounds.

The elements of a compound (except a compound personal name) are separated in romanization by a single prime (*'*).

	kitāb'khānah	كتابخانه
but	marīẕkhānah	كتابخانه

Orthography of Pushto in Romanization

15.   Capitalization.

(a)   Rules for the capitalization of English are followed, except that the Arabic article *al* is lower cased in all positions.

(b)   Diacritics are used with both capital and lower case letters.

16.   Foreign words in a Pushto context, including Arabic, Persian, and Urdu words, are romanized according to the rules for Pushto. For vowels not indicated in the script, the Pushto vowels nearest those in the original pronunciation of the word are supplied in romanization.

Yūnīwarsiṭī Buk Ejạnsī   يونيورسﭤى بك ايجنسى
(*not* University Book Agency)

Dārmastatar   دارمستتر
(*not* Darmesteter)

SPECIAL CHARACTERS AND CHARACTER MODIFIERS IN ROMANIZATION

Special Characters	*Name*	*USMARC hexadecimal code*
'	soft sign (prime)	A7
'	alif	AE
'	ayn	B0

Character Modifiers	*Name*	*USMARC hexadecimal code*
́	acute	E2
̄	macron	E5
̇	dot above	E7
̣	dot below	F2
̤	double dot below	F3
̲	underscore	F6

Russian

Vernacular	Romanization	Vernacular	Romanization
Upper case letters		*Lower case letters*	
А	A	а	a
Б	B	б	b
В	V	в	v
Г	G	г	g
Д	D	д	d
Е	E	е	e
Ё	Ë	ё	ë
Ж	Zh	ж	zh
З	Z	з	z
И	I	и	i
І (see Note 1)	Ī	і (see Note 1)	ī
Й	Ĭ	й	ĭ
К	K	к	k
Л	L	л	l
М	M	м	m
Н	N	н	n
О	O	о	o
П	P	п	p
Р	R	р	r
С	S	с	s
Т	T	т	t
У	U	у	u
Ф	F	ф	f
Х	Kh	х	kh
Ц	T͡S	ц	t͡s
Ч	Ch	ч	ch
Ш	Sh	ш	sh
Щ	Shch	щ	shch
Ъ (see Note 2)	″ (hard sign)	ъ (see Note 2)	″ (hard sign)
Ы	Y	ы	y
Ь (see Note 1)	′ (soft sign)	ь (see Note 1)	′ (soft sign)
Ѣ (see Note 3)	Ī͡E	ѣ (see Note 3)	ī͡e
Э	Ė	э	ė
Ю	I͡U	ю	i͡u
Я	I͡A	я	i͡a
Ѧ (see Note 4)	Ę	ѧ (see Note 4)	ę
Ѳ (see Note 3)	Ḟ	ѳ (see Note 3)	ḟ
Ѵ (see Note 3)	Ẏ	ѵ (see Note 3)	ẏ

Notes

1. Do not confuse with similar part of the letter Ы, ы (romanized *Y, y*).

2. Letter is disregarded in romanization when found at the end of a word.

3. Letter is considered obsolete for the modern Russian Cyrillic alphabet; found primarily in prerevolutionary and emigré publications.

4. Church Slavic letter occasionally found in the modern Russian Cyrillic alphabet.

SPECIAL CHARACTERS AND CHARACTER MODIFIERS IN ROMANIZATION

Special Characters	*Name*	*USMARC hexadecimal code*
′	soft sign (prime)	A7
″	hard sign (double prime)	B7

Character Modifiers	*Name*	*USMARC hexadecimal code*
̄	macron	E5
̆	breve	E6
̇	dot above	E7
̈	umlaut (diearesis)	E8
͡	ligature, 1st half	EB
͡	ligature, 2nd half	EC
̦	right hook	F1

Sanskrit and Prakrit
(in Devanagari Script)

When Sanskrit is written in another script, the corresponding letters in that script are transliterated according to this table.

Vowels and Diphthongs (see Note 1)

अ	a		ॠ	r̥̄
आ	ā		ॡ	l̥
इ	i		ए	e
ई	ī		ऐ	ai
उ	u		ओ	o
ऊ	ū		औ	au
ऋ	r̥			

Consonants (see Note 2)

Gutturals		**Palatals**		**Cerebrals**		**Dentals**	
क	ka	च	ca	ट	ṭa	त	ta
ख	kha	छ	cha	ठ	ṭha	थ	tha
ग	ga	ज	ja	ड	ḍa	द	da
घ	gha	झ	jha	ढ	ḍha	ध	dha
ङ	ṅa	ञ	ña	ण	ṇa	न	na

Labials		**Semivowels**		**Sibilants**		**Aspirate**	
प	pa	य	ya	श	śa	ह	ha
फ	pha	र	ra	ष	ṣa		
ब	ba	ल	la	स	sa		
भ	bha	ळ	ḻa				
म	ma	व	va				

Anusvāra (see Note 3)		*Anunāsika*		*Visarga*		*Jihvāmūlīya*	
ं	ṃ	̐	m̐	:	ḥ	)(	ẖ

Upadhmānīya		*Avagraha* (see Note 4)	
̽	ḫ	ऽ	ʼ (apostrophe)

Notes

1. Only the vowel forms that appear at the beginning of a syllable are listed; the forms used for vowels following a consonant can be found in grammars; no distinction between the two is made in transliteration.
2. The vowel *a* is implicit after all consonants and consonant clusters and is supplied in transliteration, with the following exceptions:
    (a) when another vowel is indicated by its appropriate sign; and
    (b) when the absence of any vowel is indicated by the subscript sign ( ) called *halanta* or *virāma*.
3. Exception: *Anusvāra* is transliterated by:
    ṅ before gutturals,
    ñ before palatals,
    ṇ before cerebrals,
    n before dentals, and
    m before labials.
4. When doubled, *avagraha* is transliterated by two apostrophes (”).

SPECIAL CHARACTERS AND CHARACTER MODIFIERS IN ROMANIZATION

Special character	Name	USMARC hexadecimal code
’	apostrophe	27

Character modifiers	Name	USMARC hexadecimal code
Ć	acute	E2
C̃	tilde	E4
C̄	macron	E5
Ċ	dot above	E7
C̆	candrabindu	EF
C̣	dot below	F2
C̥	circle below	F4
C̠	underscore	F6
C̭	upadhmaniya	F9

Santali
(in Ol Script)

Vowels

꣕	a		꣖	u
꣕	ā		꣖	e
꣕.	ạ̄		꣖	o
꣕	i			

Consonants

꣕	k		꣕	p
꣕	g		꣕	b
꣕	ṅ		꣕	m
꣕	c		꣕	y
꣕	j		꣕	r
꣕	ñ		꣕	l
꣕	ṭ		꣕	w
꣕	ḍ		꣕	s
꣕	ṛ		꣕	h̲
꣕	ṇ		꣕	h
꣕	t		꣕	' (apostrophe)
꣕	d			(see Note 1)
꣕	n		꣕	ṃ
			꣕	m̐ (see Note 2)

Notes

1. The letter ꣕ is used with "checked" (voiceless) consonants and indicates a change in pronunciation. It is written following four consonants only, the letters ꣕, ꣕, ꣕, ꣕, which are romanized *g, j, d,* and *b* respectively.

2. The mark ꣕ (a dot written above the line after a vowel) is used to indicate nasalization and is romanized as *m̐* after the vowel it modifies. Another mark, ꣕ (written below the line after the vowel it modifies) is used to indicate low pitch and is omitted in romanization.

Other Marks Used in Ol Script

1.   The mark õ̃ , written over a letter, is used to indicate the prolongation of a vowel. It is omitted in romanization.

2.   The mark - (similar to a hyphen) is used to separate "checked" consonants from other consonants or vowels. It is omitted in romanization.

SPECIAL CHARACTERS AND CHARACTER MODIFIERS IN ROMANIZATION

Special character	Name	USMARC hexadecimal code
'	apostrophe	27

Character modifiers	Name	USMARC hexadecimal code
õ̃	tilde	E4
ō	macron	E5
ȯ	dot above	E7
ŏ̆	candrabindu	EF
ọ	dot below	F2
o̱	underscore	F6

Serbian and Macedonian

The romanization in the table below insures correspondence between the Serbian and present-day Croation alphabets.

Vernacular	Romanization	Vernacular	Romanization
Upper case letters		*Lower case letters*	
А	A	а	a
Б	B	б	b
В	V	в	v
Г	G	г	g
Ѓ	Ǵ	ѓ	ǵ
Д	D	д	d
Ђ	Đ	ђ	đ
Е	E	е	e
Ж	Ž	ж	ž
З	Z	з	z
Ѕ	Dz	ѕ	dz
И	I	и	i
Ј	J	ј	j
К	K	к	k
Ќ	Ḱ	ќ	ḱ
Л	L	л	l
Љ	Lj	љ	lj
М	M	м	m
Н	N	н	n
Њ	Nj	њ	nj
О	O	о	o
П	P	п	p
Р	R	р	r
С	S	с	s
Т	T	т	t
Ћ	Ć	ћ	ć
У	U	у	u
Ф	F	ф	f
Х	H	х	h
Ц	C	ц	c
Ч	Č	ч	č
Џ	Dž	џ	dž
Ш	Š	ш	š

SPECIAL CHARACTERS AND CHARACTER MODIFIERS IN ROMANIZATION

Special Characters	Name	USMARC hexadecimal code
Đ	D with crossbar (upper case)	A3
đ	d with crossbar (lower case)	B3

Character Modifiers	Name	USMARC hexadecimal code
́	acute	E2
̌	hachek	E9

Sindhi
(in Arabic Script)

Letters of the Alphabet (see Note 1)

Initial	Medial	Final	Alone	Romanization
ا	ـا	ـا	ا	omit
ب	ـب	ـب	ب	b
ٻ	ـٻ	ـٻ	ٻ	ḅ
ڀ	ـڀ	ـڀ	ڀ	bh
ت	ـت	ـت	ت	t
ث	ـث	ـث	ث	th
ٽ	ـٽ	ـٽ	ٽ	ṭ
ٿ	ـٿ	ـٿ	ٿ	ṭh
ث	ـث	ـث	ث	s̤
ڀ	ـڀ	ـڀ	ڀ	p
ج	ـج	ـج	ج	j
ڄ	ـڄ	ـڄ	ڄ	j̈
جھ	ـجھ	ـجھ	جھ	jh
-	ـڃ	ـڃ	ڃ	ñ
چ	ـچ	ـچ	چ	c
ڇ	ـڇ	ـڇ	ڇ	ch
ح	ـح	ـح	ح	ḥ
خ	ـخ	ـخ	خ	k͟h
د	ـد	ـد	د	d
ڌ	ـڌ	ـڌ	ڌ	dh
ڏ	ـڏ	ـڏ	ڏ	ḍ
ڊ	ـڊ	ـڊ	ڊ	ḍh
ذ	ـذ	ـذ	ذ	z
ر	ـر	ـر	ر	r
-	ـڙ	ـڙ	ڙ	ṛ
ز	ـز	ـز	ز	z
س	ـس	ـس	س	s
ش	ـش	ـش	ش	sh
ص	ـص	ـص	ص	ṣ
ض	ـض	ـض	ض	z̤
ط	ـط	ـط	ط	ṭ
ظ	ـظ	ـظ	ظ	z̤
ع	ـع	ـع	ع	ʻ (ayn)
غ	ـغ	ـغ	غ	gh
ف	ـف	ـف	ف	f
ڦ	ـڦ	ـڦ	ڦ	ph
ق	ـق	ـق	ق	q

ڪ	ڪ	ڪ	ڪ	k
ک	ک	ک	ک	kh
ڱ	ڱ	ڳ	ڳ	g
ڃ	ڃ	ڃ	ڃ	g̈
ڪه	ڪه	ڪه	ڪه	gh
	ڱ	ڱ	ڱ	ṅ
ل	ل	ل	ل	l
م	م	م	م	m
ن	ن	ن	ن	n
ٽ	ٽ	ٽ	ٽ	ṇ
و	و	و	و	v
ه	ه	ڇ ، ه ، ۔	ه ، ه	h
-	-	-	ء	omit
ي	ي	ي	ي	y

Vowels and Diphthongs (see Note 2)

◌َ	a	◌ِى	ī
◌ُ	u	◌ُو	o
◌ِ	i	◌ِي ، ◌ِ	e
◌ٰا ، ◌ٰى ، ◌َى	ā	◌ُو	au
◌ُو	ū	◌َى ، ◌ِ	ai

Notes

1. When Sindhi is written in the Devanagari script, it is romanized according to the Hindi table. The letters, ॼ , ॾ , ॾ , and ॻ are romanized ḇ, ǰ, ḍ, and g̈ respectively.
2. The rules of application of Urdu are to be used for Sindhi. Vocalization are those used for entry in Mewaram's *A Sindhi English Dictionary* (1st ed., Hyderabad, 1910), *Sindhī Ūrdū Lughāt* (Haidarābād, 1959), and *Jāmi'-i Sindhī Lughāt* (Karācī, 1931).

SPECIAL CHARACTERS AND CHARACTER MODIFIERS IN ROMANIZATION

Special Characters	*Name*	*USMARC hexadecimal code*
'	ayn	B0

Character Modifiers	*Name*	*USMARC hexadecimal code*
◌̃	tilde	E4
◌̄	macron	E5
◌̇	dot above	E7
◌̈	umlaut (dieresis)	E8
◌̣	dot below	F2
◌̤	double dot below	F3
◌̲	underscore	F6

Sinhalese

Vowels and Diphthongs (see Note 1)

අ	a	ඒ	ē
ආ	ā	ඔ	o
ඇ	ă	ඕ	ō
ඈ	â	ඍ	r̥
ඉ	i	ඎ	r̥̄
ඊ	ī	ඏ	l̥
උ	u	ඐ	l̥̄
ඌ	ū	ඓ	ai
එ	e	ඖ	au

Consonants (see Note 2)

Gutturals		**Palatals**		**Cerebrals**		**Dentals**	
ක	ka	ච	ca	ට	ṭa	ත	ta
ඛ	kha	ඡ	cha	ඨ	ṭha	ථ	tha
ග	ga	ජ	ja	ඩ	ḍa	ද	da
ඝ	gha	ඣ	jha	ඪ	ḍha	ධ	dha
ඞ	ṅa	ඤ	ña	ණ	ṇa	න	na

Labials		**Semivowels**		**Sibilants**		**Aspirate**	
ප	pa	ය	ya	ශ	śa	හ	ha
ඵ	pha	ර	ra	ෂ	ṣa		
බ	ba	ල	la	ස	sa		
භ	bha	ළ	ḷa				
ම	ma	ව	va				

Anusvāra (see Note 3)		*Visarga*		*Avagraha*		*Saññaka* (see Note 4)	
ං	ṃ	ඃ	ḥ	(	’ (apostrophe)	ʿ	

Notes

1. Only the vowel forms that appear at the beginning of a syllable are listed; the forms used for vowels following a consonant can be found in grammars; no distinction between the two is made in transliteration.
2. The vowel *a* is implicit after all consonants and consonant clusters and is supplied in romanization, with the following exceptions:
   (a) when another vowel is indicated by its appropriate sign; and
   (b) when the absence of any vowel is indicated by the sign ⊦ (or ⌐) called *virāma*.
3. Exception: *Anusvāra* is transliterated by:
   ṅ before gutturals,
   ñ before palatals,
   ṇ before cerebrals,
   n before dentals, and
   ṃ before labials.
4. Exceptions:
   (a) when *saññaka* represents a nasal. It is romanized according to the rule for *anusvāra*.
   (b) when *saññaka* is combined with an aspirated consonant, the combination is romanized as a non-aspirated, followed by an aspirated consonant.

SPECIAL CHARACTERS AND CHARACTER MODIFIERS IN ROMANIZATION

Special character	*Name*	*USMARC hexadecimal code*
ʼ	apostrophe	27

Character modifiers	*Name*	*USMARC hexadecimal code*
́◌	acute	E2
̂◌	circumflex	E3
̃◌	tilde	E4
̄◌	macron	E5
̆◌	breve	E6
̇◌	dot above	E7
◌̣	dot below	F2
◌̥	circle below	F4

Tamil

Vowels and Diphthongs (see Note 1)

அ	a	எ	e
ஆ	ā	ஏ	ē
இ	i	ஐ	ai
ஈ	ī	ஒ	o
உ	u	ஓ	ō
ஊ	ū	ஔ	au

Consonants (see Note 2)

ஃ	k̲a	ம	ma
க	ka	ய	ya
ங	ṅa	ர	ra (see Note 3)
ச	ca	ல	la
ஞ	ña	வ	va
ட	ṭa	ழ	l̲a
ண	ṇa	ள	ḷa
த	ta	ற	r̲a
ந	na	ன	n̲a
ப	pa		

Sanskrit Sounds

ஜ	ja	ஸ	sa
ஶ	śa	ஹ	ha
ஷ	ṣa		

Notes

1. Only the vowel forms that appear at the beginning of a syllable are listed; the forms used for vowels following a consonant can be found in grammars; no distinction between the two is made in transliteration.
2. The vowel *a* is implicit after all consonants and consonant clusters and is supplied in romanization, with the following exceptions:
   (a) when another vowel is indicated by its appropriate sign; and
   (b) when the absence of any vowel is indicated by the superscript dot (◌்) called *puḷḷi*.
3. This letter has the same form as the vowel sign for *ā* appearing after a consonant. Where ambiguity arises, it is written ர .

CHARACTER MODIFIERS IN ROMANIZATION

Character Modifiers	*Name*	*USMARC hexadecimal code*
Habout	acute	E2
Ĩ	tilde	E4
Ō	macron	E5
Ȧ	dot above	E7
Ọ	dot below	F2
Ụ	underscore	F6

Telugu

Vowels and Diphthongs (see Note 1)

అ	a		ఌ	ḷ̥
ఆ	ā		ఎ	e
ఇ	i		ఏ	ē
ఈ	ī		ఐ	ai
ఉ	u		ఒ	o
ఊ	ū		ఓ	ō
ఋ	r̥		ఔ	au
ౠ	r̥̄			

Consonants (see Note 2)

Gutturals		Palatals		Cerebrals		Dentals	
క	ka	చ	ca	ట	ṭa	త	ta
ఖ	kha	చ̄	ĉa	ఠ	ṭha	థ	tha
గ	ga	చ	cha	డ	ḍa	ద	da
ఘ	gha	జ	ja	ఢ	ḍha	ధ	dha
ఙ	ṅa	జ̂	ĵa	ణ	ṇa	న	na
		ఝ	jha				
		ఞ	ña				

Labials		Semivowels		Sibilants		Aspirate	
ప	pa	య	ya	శ	śa	హ	ha
ఫ	pha	ర	ra	ష	ṣa		
బ	ba	ఱ	r̲a	స	sa		
భ	bha	ల	la				
మ	ma	ళ	ḷa				
		వ	va				

Sunna (see Note 3)		*Visarga*		*Ardhasunna* (see Note 4)	
ం	ṃ	ః	ḥ	౸ , ౦̇	m̐

Notes

1. Only the vowel forms that appear at the beginning of a syllable are listed; the forms used for vowels following a consonant can be found in grammars; no distinction between the two is made in transliteration.

2. The vowel *a* is implicit after all consonants and consonant clusters and is supplied in transliteration, with the following exceptions:
   (a) when another vowel is indicated by its appropriate sign; and
   (b) when the absence of any vowel is indicated by the superscript sign (ᴇ) called *valapalagilaka*.

3. Exception: *Sunna* is transliterated by:
       ṅ before gutturals,
       ñ before palatals,
       ṇ before cerebrals,
       n before dentals, and
       m before labials.

4. *Ardhasunna* before gutturals, palatal, cerebral, and dental occlusives is transliterated *n̆*. Before labials, sibilants, semivowels, the aspirate, vowels, and in final position it is transliterated *m̐*.

CHARACTER MODIFIERS IN ROMANIZATION

Character Modifiers	Name	USMARC hexadecimal code
Ó	acute	E2
Ô	circumflex	E3
Õ	tilde	E4
Ō	macron	E5
Ȯ	dot above	E7
Ŏ	candrabindu	EF
Ç	cedilla	F0
Ọ	dot below	F2
Ọ̥	circle below	F4
O̲	underscore	F6

Thai

Vowels and Diphthongs

Vernacular	Romanization	Vernacular	Romanization
อะ, อ้	a	อ้วะ	ua
ยา	ā	อ้ว, ว	ūa
อำ	am	ไอ, ไอ, อัย, ไอย	ai
อิ	i	อาย	āi
อี	ĭ	เอา	ao
อึ	ʉ	อาว	āo
อื	ŭ	อุย	ui
อุ	u	โอย	ōi
อู	ū	ออย	ǫi
เอะ, เอ็	e	เอย	œi
เอ	ē	เอื้อย	ʉ̆ai
แอะ, แอ็	æ	อวย	ūai
แอ	ǣ	อิ้ว	iu
โอะ, อ	o	เอ็็ว	eo
โอ	ō	เอว	ēo
เอาะ	ǫ	แอว	ǣo
ออ	ǭ	เอี้ยว	ĭeo
เออะ	œ	ฤ	rʉ
เออ, เอ้	œ̄	ฤ	ri
เอี้ยะ	ia	ฤ	rœ̆
เอี้ย	ĭa	ฤๅ	rʉ̄
เอื้อะ	ʉa	ฦ	lʉ
เอื้อ	ʉ̄a	ฦๅ	lʉ̄

Consonants

Vernacular		Romanization when initial and medial	Romanization when final
ก		k	k
ข, ฃ, ค, ฅ, ฆ		kh	k
ง		ng	ng
จ		čh	t
ฉ, ช, ฌ, ฌ		ch	t
ญ		y	n
ด, ฎ, ฑ	(see Note 1)	d	t
ต, ฏ		t	t
ฐ, ฑ, ฒ, ท, ธ, ฒ	(see Note 1)	th	t
น, ณ		n	n
บ		b	p
ป		p	p
ผ, พ, ภ		ph	p
ฝ, ฟ		f	p
ม		m	m
ย		y	-
ร	(see Note 2)	r	n
ล, ฬ		l	n
ว		w	-
ซ, ทร, ศ, ษ, ส		s	t
อ	(see Note 3)	' (ayn)	-
ห, ฮ	(see Note 4)	h	-

Notes

1. ฑ is usually romanized *th*, occasionally *d*, depending on the pronunciation as determined from an authoritative dictionary.

2. When ร follows another consonant and ends a syllable, it is romanized *n*, and the inherent vowel of the preceding consonant is represented by ǭ (e.g., นคร *nakhǭn*).

   When รร follows another consonant and no other pronounced consonant follows in the same syllable, it is romanized *an* (e.g., สวรรค์ *sawan*), but if a pronounced consonant follows, it is represented by *a* (e.g., กรรม *kam*).

3.   In four common words อ occurs preceding another consonant to mark a certain tone and is then not romanized.

4.   When ห occurs preceding another consonant to mark a certain tone, it is not romanized.

RULES OF APPLICATION

Romanization

1.   Tonal marks are not romanized.

2.   The symbol ฯ indicates omission and is shown in romanization by " ... " the conventional sign for ellipsis.

3.   When the repeat symbol ๆ is used, the syllable is repeated in romanization.

4.   The symbol ฯลฯ is romanized *la*.

5.   Thai consonants are sometimes purely consonantal and sometimes followed by an inherent vowel romanized *o, a,* or *ǭ* depending on the pronunciation as determined from an authoritative dictionary, such as the Royal Institute's latest edition (1982).

6.   Silent consonants, with their accompanying vowels, if any, are not romanized.

7.   When the pronunciation requires one consonant to serve a double function--at the end of one syllable and the beginning of the next--it is romanized twice according to the respective values.

8.   The numerals are: ๐ (0), ๑ (1), ๒ (2), ๓ (3), ๔ (4), ๕ (5), ๖ (6), ๗ (7), ๘ (8), and ๙ (9).

9.   In Thai, words are not written separately. In romanization, however, text is divided into words according to the guidelines provided in *Word Division* below.

Word Division

1.   In general, Thai words formulated by romanization are made up of a single syllable (คำ *kham*; ไทย *Thai*), and thus each syllable is considered a separate word, with a space between each. (Exceptions are covered by rules 2 through 43.) This is in contrast to many multisyllabic words that are foreign to Thai but that are found written in the Thai script. These multisyllabic foreign words are written with the space closed up between the syllables as appropriate. Prominent examples are words of Pali and Sanskrit origin, as well as some words that are Thai in origin but have been formed according to the grammar of Pali or Sanskrit.

Examples of monosyllabic Thai words:

คำ	kham
ไทย	Thai
พูด	phūt

Examples of multisyllabic Thai words formed according to the rules of other languages:

กระทรวง	krasūang
ภาษา	phāsā
ปัญญา	panyā

Examples of multisyllabic words of Pali or Sanskrit origin:

วัฒนธรรม	watthanatham
มหาวิทยาลัย	mahāwitthayālai
กษัตริย์	kasat
พลเมือง	phonlamư̄ang
ภารโรง	phānrōng

2. In contrast to the preceding statement that Thai words are monosyllabic, note that there are multisyllabic Thai words in which the first syllable is used as a prefix; write the prefix and the succeeding element as a single word.

(a) Words with การ (*kān*) prefixed

การเดินทาง	kāndœ̄nthāng
การแปล	kānplǣ
การต่างประเทศ	kāntāngprathēt

(b) Words with ความ (*khwām*) prefixed

ความจริง	khwāmčhing
ความหมาย	khwāmmāi
ความเห็น	khwāmhen

(c) Miscellaneous cases with various words used as prefixes. The most common are:

พ่อ	phǭ	นาย	nāi
แม่	mǣ	นาง	nāng
ลูก	lūk	ข้อ	khǭ
พี่	phī	คำ	kham
น้อง	nǭng	บท	bot

ผู้	phū	เครื่อง	khrư̄ang
นัก	nak	แผน	phǣn
คน	khon	ท้อง	thǭng
ชาว	chāo	ขี้	khī
เด็ก	dek	ใจ	čai
ข้า	khā	ช่าง	chāng
ราย	rāi	วัย	wai
ต้น	ton	ดวง	dūang
ลาย	lāi	หมอ	mǭ

Note that the listing of miscellaneous cases covers only the most common ones. Other, less common cases may be handled in the same way.

บุญ	bun

Note also that some words, reflecting a transposition in normal Thai word order and consisting of a principal word and one or more words used with it as a prefix, may be considered as belonging to this category.

ราชบัณฑิตยสถาน	Rātchabandittayasathān
โบราณคดีวิทยา	bōrānnakhadīwitthayā
ไทยคดีศึกษา	Thaikhadīsưksā

3.   *Compounds.* Write compounds as a single word.

(a)   *General:* Identifying a compound is largely a matter of knowledge of the language together with the use of good judgment. Note that compounds generally result in concepts to one degree or another different from the meaning of either of the component words when used alone.

ใกล้ชิด	klaichit	ค้นหา	khonhā
เข้มงวด	khēmngūat	ทดลอง	thotlǭng
ภายนอก	phāinǭk	มองดู	mǭngdū
ชัดเจน	chatčēn	อดทน	ʻotthon
ชั่วคราว	chūakhrāo	กลางแจ้ง	klāngčhǣng
กล้าหาญ	klāhān	ครบถ้วน	khropthūan

เกี่ยวข้อง	kīeokhǭng	สุดท้าย	sutthāi
หมู่บ้าน	mūbān	ผลไม้	phonlamai
รถไฟ	rotfai	เสื้อผ้า	sūaphā
เงินเดือน	ngœndūan	ตนเอง	ton‘ēng
จัดทำ	čhattham	พูดคุย	phūtkhui
รับใช้	rapchai	ไปเยี่ยม	paiyīam
บอกรับ	bǭkrap	ตีพิมพ์	tīphim
ต่อสู้	tǭsū	จัดพิมพ์	čhatphim
รบกวน	ropkūan		

N.B.: Do not consider as compounds repeated words sometimes referred to as "reduplicated compounds."

ต่าง ๆ	tāng tāng
ช้า ๆ	chā chā
เร็ว ๆ	reo reo

(b) *Reduplicated Doublets:* When words are strung together for sound, write them as a single word.

เปลี่ยนแปลง	plīanplǣng
เรียบร้อย	rīaprǭi
อึกทึก	‘ukkathuk
รอบคอบ	rǭpkhǭp

4. *Geographical Names.* Divide geographical names into separate words according to the decisions of the U.S. Board on Geographic Names, as expressed in the *Gazetteer of Thailand.*

5. *Royal Language (rāchāsap).* Write as a separate word any word found as an entry in either of the following dictionaries unless otherwise directed by these rules.

Rāchāsap chabap sombūn / Rāchamānop. (Bangkok: Kāonā, 1965)

Rāchāsap chabap sombūn / Sangūan ‘Ānkhong. (Bangkok: Kāonā, 1964)

6. Generally separate all elements in terms of rank, privilege, address, etc., associated with names of persons unless another rule directs otherwise.

นายทหารตำรวจ	Nāithahān Tamrūat
ผู้ช่วยศาสตราจารย์	Phūchūai Sāttrāčhān
หม่อมราชวงศ์	Mǭm Rātchawong
รองอำมาตย์โท	Rǭng ʻAmāt Thō
พลตำรวจเอก	Phon Tamrūat ʻĒk
พระมหา	Phra Mahā
รองประธานาธิบดี	Rǭng Prathānāthibǭdi
พระปรมินทรมหา	Phraparaminthra Mahā
พระเทพรัตนราชสุดาฯ	Phrathēprattanarātchasudā
สยามบรมราชกุมารี	Sayāmbǭrommarātchakumārī
พระบาทสมเด็จพระเจ้าอยู่หัว	Phrabāt Somdet Phračhaoyūhūa
พระนางเจ้าพระบรมราชินีนาถ	Phranāng Čhao Phrabǭrommarāchinī Nāt

One arbiter of whether official pronunciations of royal ranks with กรม (*Krom*) require an extra syllable is *Photčhanānukrom nakrīan chalœ̄m phrakīat, Phǭ. Sǭ. 2530*, 2nd edition, 1988, p. 329. This officially approved work is based on proclamations of the Prime Minister's Office as well as on the Royal Institute's 1982 dictionary.

	กรมพระยา	Krom Phrayā
but	กรมหลวง	Krommalūang

7. Generally combine elements (covered by terms described in 6. above) which begin with เจ้า (*Čhao*) and combine elements in ท่านผู้หญิง (*Thānphūying*), เจ้าจอมมารดา (*Čhaočhǭmmāndā*), and พระเจ้าอยู่หัว (*Phračhaoyūhūa*)

	เจ้านาย	Čhaonāi
	เจ้าของ	Čhaokhǭng
	เจ้าฟ้า	Čhaofā
	เจ้าพระยา	Čhaophrayā
	ท่านผู้หญิง	Thānphūying
	เจ้าจอมมารดา	Čhaočhǭmmāndā
	พระเจ้าอยู่หัว	Phračhaoyūhūa
but	เจ้าฟ้าหญิง	Čhaofā Ying
	เจ้าฟ้าชาย	Čhaofā Chāi
	พระองก์เจ้าชาย	Phra ʻong Čhao Chai

หม่อมเจ้าหญิง	Mǭm Čhao Ying
เจ้าเมืองแปร	Čhao Mư̄ang Prǣ

8. Generally separate elements in personal royal titles and corporate names beginning with กรม (*Krom*) except as listed below. For these excepted cases only, although pronunciation with or without the extra syllable are correct in popular usage, proclamations of the Prime Minister's Office in recent years have approved pronunciations with the extra syllable (effectively combining the elements) as the only officially correct pronunciations.

	กรมพระ	Krommaphra
	กรมหลวง	Krommalūang
	กรมหมื่ม	Krommamư̄n
	กรมวัง	Krommawang
	กรมท่า	Krommathā
but	กรมพระยา	Krom Phrayā

9. Keep separate the Buddhist *samanasak* ranks พระมหา (*Phra Mahā*) and พระครู (*Phra Khrū*) as well as the conventional religious terms of address พระ (*Phra*) and พระอาจารย์ (*Phra ʻĀčhān*).

พระมหาประยุทย์	Phra Mahā Prayut
พระครูเลิศ	Phra Khrū Lœ̄t
พระสมหวัง	Phra Somwang
พระอาจารย์สมหวัง	Phra ʻĀčhān Somwang

10. พระ (*Phra*) should be separate as follows:

    (a) When connoting the Buddha, his image, a member of the Buddhist Order of the Sangha, etc.;

    (b) As the only element or one of the elements in a separately written conferred rank, or;

    (c) As an independent (complimentary, conventional, etc.) element immediately preceding a personal name (except the name of Buddha) but not an integral part of it. Otherwise, it should be written as a combined prefix to words (usually associated with royalty, gods, objects or worship, etc.).

พระแก้วมรกด	Phra Kǣo Mǭrakot
พระสยามเทวาธิราช	Phra Sayāmmathēwāthirāt
พระอาจารย์สมหวัง	Phra ʻĀčhān Somwang
พระอภัยมณี	Phra ʻAphaimanī
พระมหาประยุทย์	Phra Mahā Prayut
พระครูเลิศ	Phra Khrū Lœ̄t
กรมพระมหิดล	Krom Phra Mahidon

	พระพุทธยอดฟ้าจุฬาโลก	Phra Putthay\ōtfā Čhulālōk
	พระนั่งเกล้าเจ้าอยู่หัว	Phra Nangklao Čhaoyūhūa
	สมเด็จพระวรรณรัตน์	Somdet Phra Wannarat
but	พระพุทธเจ้า	Phraphutthačhao
	พระปรมินทรมหามงกุฎ	Phraparaminthra Mahā Mongkut
	กรมพระมหิดล	Krommaphra Mahidon
	กรมพระราชวังบวร	Krom Phrarātchawangbǭwǭn
	พระสังฆราช	Phrasangkharāt

11. มหา (*Mahā*) should be separate when as an independent (complimentary, conventional, etc.) element it immediately precedes and is not an integral part of a personal name. Otherwise, it should be treated as specified in paragraph 12. below.

พระปรมินทรมหามงกุฎ	Phraparaminthra Mahā Mongkut
พระปรมินทรมหาภูมิพลอดุลยเดช	Phraparaminthra Mahā Phūmiphon ʻAdunlayadēt
มหาธาตุ	mahāthāt

12. พระมหา (*Phra Mahā*) is a *samanasak* rank conferred on a lower-level Buddhist religious who has finished at least the third grade of parīan (Buddhist theology). It should not be confused with มหา- (*mahā-*) or พระมหา- (*phramahā-*), which are prefixes added to words associated with royalty, religious, gods, objects of worship, etc., such as titles of the supreme patriarch. The rank should be written separately; the prefix, combined.

พระมหาประยุทธ์	Phra Mahā Prayut
พระมหาสังฆราชเจ้า	Phramahāsangkharāt Čhao
พระมหาสมณเจ้า	Phramahāsamanačhao
มหาเถระ	Mahāthēra

13. Titles of honor with เจ้า (*čhao*) as the last element should be written separate or combined in accordance with whether the immediately preceding element is commonly used as a prefix.

พระองค์เจ้า	Phra ʻong Čhao
พระสังฆราชเจ้า	Phrasangkharāt Čhao
พระพุทธเจ้า	Phraphutthačhao
พระมหาสมณเจ้า	Phramahāsamanačhao
พระนางเจ้า	Phranāng Čhao
พระเจ้าวรวงศ์เธอพระองค์เจ้า	Phračhao Wǭrawongthœ Phra ʻong Čhao

14. Combine หลวง (*Lūang*) when used as a simple (non-conferred) title in combination preceding words for relatives supposed to be Buddhist priests.

หลวงพ่อ	Lūangphǭ
หลวงพี่	Lūangphī̌
หลวงพ่อปู่	Lūangphǭpū
หลวงลุง	Lūanglung

15. Generally separate คุณ (*Khun*) as first element, except in the courtesy titles คุณหญิง (*Khunying*) and คุณนาย (*Khunnāi*).

	คุณแม่	Khun Mǣ
	คุณพ่อ	Khun Phǭ
	คุณหนู	Khun Nū
but	คุณหญิง	Khunying
	คุณนาย	Khunnāi

16. Combine elements in personal pronouns or their equivalents.

ข้าพระพุทธเจ้า	khāphraphutthačhao
ข้าพเจ้า	khāphačhao
หม่อมฉัน	mǭmchan
กระผม	kraphom
ใต้ฝ่าละอองธุลีพระบาท	taifāla'ǭngtulīphrabāt

17. Elements in royal or noble titles and names are generally combined but should be separate when two distinct terms can be isolated in a noun/modifier or noun/noun-in-apposition configuration if the terms would not otherwise be combined, or if there is doubt about whether to combine them.

ดำรงราชานุภาพ	Damrongrāchānuphāp
ปราสาททอง	Prāsāt Thǭng
พุทธยอดฟ้าจุฬาโลก	Phutthayǭtfā Čhulālōk
พุทธเลิดหล้านภาลัย	Phutthalœtlā Naphālai
ตากสิน	Tāk Sin

18. Elements ordinarily combined should be separate when immediately followed by a proper name or its substitute.

แม่ทัพใหญ่	Mǣthap Yai
รองแม่กองงานพระธรรมทูต	Rǭng Mǣ Kǭng Ngān Phrathammathūt
เจ้าอาวาส	čhao'āwāt
เจ้าคณะภาค ๗	Čhao Khana Phāk 7

นายสุชาติ	Nāi Suchāt
เจ้าเมืองแปร	Čhao Mư̄ang Præ
เจ้าเมือง	čhao mư̄ang

19. นาย (*Nāi*) before a proper name as a *bandāsak* or roughly equivalent to *Mister* should be separate. Otherwise, it is combined as a prefix in accordance with paragraph 2.(c) above.

นายสุชาติ	Nāi Suchāt
นายร้อย	Nāirǭi
นายทหารตำรวจ	Nāithahān Tamrūat
นายแพทย์ปรัดเลย์	Nāiphæt Pratlē
นายพิทักษ์ราชา (โจ)	Nāi Phithakrāchā (Čhō)

20. In cases of doubt about whether miscellaneous words listed under 2.(c) above are functioning as prefixes, generally separate elements unless sufficient conventional usage has bestowed word status on the configuration. Always separate demonstrative adjectives, relative pronouns, and numerals from the first element.

คนพ้นคุก	khon phon khuk
ผู้ก่อการร้าย	phūkǭkānrāi
คนนั้น	khon nan
ผู้ลี้ภัย	phūlīphai
เครื่องนี้	khrư̄ang nī
ข้อหนึ่ง	khǭ nưng
but คนสี่เทา	khonsīthao

21. Combine elements in colors, days of the week, but not months of the year.

สีเหลือง	sīlư̄ang
วันจันทร์	Wančhan
เดือนพฤศจิกายน	Dư̄an Phrưtsačhikāyon

22. Combine numerals in the same way as in English; i.e., combine teens, combine first elements, and separate from the digital element if any in twenty through ninety-nine, etc. Separate ที่ (*thī*) in ordinals.

สิบสาม	sipsām
ยี่สิบสอง	yīsip sǭng
ร้อยเอ็ด	rǭi ʻet
วันที่สิบเจ็ด	wan thī sipčhet

23. Generally separate royal introductory verbs and verbs indicating royal courtesy, but combine elements in conventional phrases of courtesy.

ทรงประกอบพิธีเปิด	song prakọ̄p phithī pœ̄t
ทรงพระเจริญ	song phrač̌harœ̄n
ทรงพระกรุณาโปรดเกล้า	song phrakarunā prōt klao
ขอบใจ	khọ̄pč̌hai

24. In most cases separate หลาย (*lāi*), ชั่ว (*chūa*), ทั่ว (*thūa*), ทุก (*thuk*), ทั้ง (*thang*), บาง (*bāng*), ต่าง (*tāng*), etc., preceding words.

ทั้งประเทศ	thang prathēt
ทั่วราชอาณาจักร	thūa rātcha ʻānāč̌hak
ชั่วชีวิด	chūa chīwit
บางคราว	bāngkhrāo
ทุกสิ่ง	thuk sing
ต่างมารดา	tāng māndā
หลายคน	lāi khon
but ชั่วคราว	chūakhrāo
ทั่วไป	thūapai
ทั้งหมด	thangmot
ชั่วโมง	chūamōng
ต่างประเทศ	tāngprathēt

25. Generally separate งาน (*ngān*) preceding a word or phrase except in cases denoting literary or research activity when only two elements are present.

งานพระราชทานเพลิงศพ	ngān phrarātchathān plœ̄ng sop
งานธุรกิจ	ngān thurakit
งานเขียน	ngānkhīan
งานวิจัย	ngānwič̌hai

26. Combine or separate the following miscellaneous phrases as shown.

เนื้องใน	nūang nai	แค่ไหน	khǣ nai
ว่าด้วย	wādūai	ล่วงหน้า	lūangnā
ร่วมกับ	rūam kap	เบื้องต้น	būangton
ครบรอบ	khrop rọ̄p	ต่อไป	tọ̄pai
พร้อมด้วย	phrọ̄m dūai	ตั้งแต่	tangtǣ
ตนเอง	ton ʻēng	จนกระทั่ง	č̌honkrathang
เนื้องจาก	nūangč̌hāk	จนถึง	č̌hon thưng

27. Combine ตะวัน (*tawan*) not เฉียง (*chīang*) in compass points.

ตะวันออกเฉียงเหนือ	tawan'ǭk chīang nūa
ตะวันตกเฉียงใต้	tawantok chīang tai
ตะวันตกเฉียงเหนือ	tawantok chīang nūa
ตะวันออกเฉียงใต้	tawan'ǭk chīang tai

28. Generally separate geographical designations with เมือง (*mūang*).

	เมืองเหนือ	mūang nūa
	เมืองใต้	mūang tai
but	เมืองนอก	mūangnǭk

29. When ความ (*khwām*) is used in the legal context meaning "case" or "matter", it should be separate.

| ความแพ่ง | khwām phǣng |
| ความอาญา | khwām 'āyā |

30. Those elements equivalent to English hyphenated adjectival phrases (not clauses) should be combined although kept separate from any noun (not included under paragraph 2.(c)) that they might modify, the latter clause applying only to phrases that are clearly adjectival in nature and not including the phrase words whose role Thai syntax makes doubtful.

หนังสือปกสีขาว	nangsū poksīkhāo
เรือชายฝั่งทะเล	rūa chāifangthalē
ข้าวประดับดิน	khāopradapdin
สินค้าส่งออก	sinkhāsong'ǭk
พ่อค้าส่งออก	phǭkhāsong'ǭk
การเจรจาการค้าหลายฝ่าย	kānchērrachā kānkhā lāifāi

31. Many phrases consisting of predicate and object have attained single word status. But if there is doubt that the elements have attained single word status, do not combine them unless 30. above applies.

	ประเมินผล	pramœnphon
	ทำงาน	thamngān
	วางแผน	wāngphǣn
	อวยพร	'ūaiphǭn
but	การย้ายถิ่น	kānyāi thin
	การย้ายถิ่นฐาน	kānyāi thinthān
	ถิ่นใต้	thin tai

32. Generally separate phrases with ส่วน (*sūan*).

	ส่วนพระองด์	sūan phra ʻong
	ส่วนพลเมือง	sūan phonlamưang
but	ส่วนตัว	sūantūa
	ส่วนรวม	sūanrūam

33. Phrases with words indicating buildings as first element are generally combined.

หอศิลปะ	hǭsinlapa
ห้องประชุม	hǭngprachum
โรงพิมพ์	rōngphim
หอสมุด	hǭsamut
โรงเรียน	rōngrīan

34. For terms not of rank, privilege, address, etc., generally do not combine elements that might otherwise be candidates for combining when the second element is a proper name unless the first element appears in the list under 2.(c) above. Nevertheless, capitalize the first element in any case.

	หอภูมิพล	Hǭ Phūmiphon
	รถเบ็นซ์	Rot Ben
	คัมภีร์พระเวท	Khamphī Phrawēt
but	คนไทย	Khonthai

35. For phrases consisting of a verb and งาน (*ngān*), generally do not combine.

	ประสานงาน	prasān ngān
	รวมงาน	rūam ngān
	ปฏิบัติงาน	patibat ngān
but	ทำงาน	thamngān

36. รวม (*rūam*) as initial or final element should generally be separate.

	รวมเล่ม	rūam lēm
	รวมอยู่ด้วย	rūam yū dūai
but	ส่วนรวม	sūanrūam

37. Keep separate elements that purport to be translated phrases from other languages.

นครวัด	Nakhǭn Wat
สยามสแควร์	Sayām Sakhwæ

38. Generally, when applying word division rules, retain word division appearing in the Thai script only if there is doubt about the exact mean of the configuration. Otherwise, ignore the division in Thai script.

โครงการ พุทธ-ไทย ปริทรรศน์   Khrōngkān Phut-Thai Parithat

39. Phrases beginning with น่า (*nā*) should only be combined if convention has conferred word status on the configuration.

	น่าเสียดาย	nāsīadāi
	น่าสนใจ	nāsončhai
but	น่าจับตา	na čhap tā
	น่ารับรอง	nā raprǭng

40. Separate words beginning with ทหาร (*thahān*) for military, etc.

ทหารบก	thahān bok
ทหารเรือ	thahān rư̄a
ทหารอากาศ	thahān ʻākāt
ทหารตำรวจ	thahān tamrūat

41. Combine the generic element with all elements of a name for plants, animals, vegetables, etc.

นกขุนทอง	nokkhunthǭng
แตงกวา	tǣngkwā
สุนัขจิ้งจอก	sunakčhingčhhǭk
ผักกาดหัว	pakkāthūa
ต้นหมาก	tonmāk

42. For diseases, combine the generic term โรค (*rōk*) only if it appears as the final element of the configuration.

กาฬโรค	kānlarōk
กามโรค	kāmmarōk
โรคมะเร็ง	rōk marēng
โรคโลหิตน้อย	rōk lōhit nǭi
โรคทรพิษ	rōk thǭraphit
อหิวาตกโรค	ʻahiwātakarōk
โรคฝีดาษ	rōk fīdāt

43. Combine adjectival phrases with ใจ (*čhai*) as final element.

ร้อนใจ	rǭnčhai
เกรงใจ	krēngčhai
สุขภาพใจ	sukkhaphāpčhai
ดีใจ	dīčhai

SPECIAL CHARACTERS AND CHARACTER MODIFIERS IN ROMANIZATION

Special Characters	*Name*	*USMARC hexadecimal code*
Æ	digraph AE (upper case)	A5
Œ	digraph OE (upper case)	A6
Ư	U-hook (upper case)	AC
ʻ	ayn	B0
æ	digraph ae (lower case)	B5
œ	digraph oe (lower case)	B6
ư	u-hook (lower case)	BD

Character Modifiers	*Name*	*USMARC hexadecimal code*
◌̄	macron	E5
◌̌	hachek	E9
◌̧	right cedilla	F8

Tibetan

Internal capitalization of base consonants is not to be followed. When Tibetan is written in another script (e.g., 'Phags-pa) the corresponding letters in that script are romanized according to this table.

Vowels and Diphthongs (see Notes 1 and 2)

ཨ	a		[རྀ	r̥]
[ཀྵཱ	ā]		[རཱྀ	r̥̄]
ཀྀ	i		[ལྀ	l̥]
[ཀྀ	ī]		ཨེ	e
ཀུ	u		[ཨཻ	ai]
[ཀཱུ	ū]		ཨོ	o
			[ཨཽ	au]

Consonants (see Notes 2 and 3)

Gutturals		**Palatals**		**Cerebrals**		**Dentals**	
ཀ	ka	ཙ	ca	[ཊ	ṭa]	ཏ	ta
ཁ	kha	ཚ	cha	[ཋ	ṭha]	ཐ	tha
ག	ga	ཛ	ja	[ཌ	ḍa]	ད	da
[གྷ	gha]	[ཛྷ	jha]	[ཌྷ	ḍha]	[དྷ	dha]
ང	ṅa	ཉ	ña	[ཎ	ṇa]	ན	na

Labials		**Affricates**		**Semivowels**		**Sibilants**	
པ	pa	ཙ	tsa	ཝ	wa	ཞ	źa
ཕ	pha	ཚ	tsha	འ	'a (see Note 4)	ཟ	za
བ	ba	ཛ	dza	ཡ	ya (see Note 5)	ཤ	śa
[བྷ	bha]	[ཛྷ	dzha]	ར	ra	ས	sa
མ	ma			ལ	la	[ཥ	ṣa]

Aspirate

ཧ	ha

Anusvāra		*Anunāsika*		*Visarga*	
◦	ṃ	[◌	m̐]	◌	ḥ

Notes

1. Only the vowel forms that appear at the beginning of a syllable are listed. A syllable is defined as a graph or group of graphs followed by a *tsheg* (ⁱ). The forms used for vowels following a consonant can be found in grammars.

2. Letters enclosed within brackets in the table are used in Sanskrit words.

3. The vowel *a* is implicit after all consonants in independent form and is supplied in romanization, unless another vowel is indicated by its appropriate sign. *Tsheg* (ⁱ), the syllabic boundary marker, is represented by a hyphen in proper names and by a space in other words.

4. The *'a chuṅ* is represented by an apostrophe (') in *pre-initial* and *final* position unless marked with a vowel marker, in which case it is represented by the apostrophe plus the appropriate vowel. When *'a chuṅ* is written below any letter representing vocalic length, it is romanized according to the vowel table.

5. When ग॑ is preceded by ल॑, it is romanized *g'y* to distinguish it from झ॑ which is romanized *gya*.

SPECIAL CHARACTERS AND CHARACTER MODIFIERS IN ROMANIZATION

Special Characters	*Name*	*USMARC hexadecimal code*
’	apostrophe	27
′	soft sign (prime)	A7

Character Modifiers	*Name*	*USMARC hexadecimal code*
́	acute	E2
̃	tilde	E4
̄	macron	E5
̇	dot above	E7
̆	candrabindu	EF
̣	dot below	F2
̥	circle below	F4
̲	underscore	F6

Tigrinya

Syllables

1st Order	2nd Order	3rd Order	4th Order	5th Order	6th Order	7th Order
ha	hu	hi	hā	hé	he or h	ho
la	lu	li	lā	lé	le or l	lo
ḥa	ḥu	ḥi	ḥā	ḥé	ḥe or ḥ	ḥo
ma	mu	mi	mā	mé	me or m	mo
śa	śu	śi	śā	śé	śe or ś	śo
ra	ru	ri	rā	ré	re or r	ro
sa	su	si	sā	sé	se or s	so
ša	šu	ši	šā	šé	še or š	šo
qa	qu	qi	qā	qé	qe or q	qo
q̲a	q̲u	q̲i	q̲ā	q̲é	q̲e or q̲	q̲o
ba	bu	bi	bā	bé	be or b	bo
ta	tu	ti	tā	té	te or t	to
ča	ču	či	čā	čé	če or č	čo
ẖa	ẖu	ẖi	ẖā	ẖé	ẖe or ẖ	ẖo
na	nu	ni	nā	né	ne or n	no
ña	ñu	ñi	ñā	ñé	ñe or ñ	ño
'a	'u	'i	'ā	'é	'e	'o
ka	ku	ki	kā	ké	ke or k	ko
xa	xu	xi	xā	xé	xe or x	xo
wa	wu	wi	wā	wé	we or w	wo
‘a	‘u	‘i	‘ā	‘é	‘e	‘o
za	zu	zi	zā	zé	ze or z	zo
ža	žu	ži	žā	žé	že or ž	žo
ža	žu	ži	žā	žé	že or ž	žo
-	-	-	-	-	že or ž	-
ya	yu	yi	yā	yé	ye or y	yo
da	du	di	dā	dé	de or d	do
ǧa	ǧu	ǧi	ǧā	ǧé	ǧe or ǧ	ǧo
ga	gu	gi	gā	gé	ge or g	go
ṭa	ṭu	ṭi	ṭā	ṭé	ṭe or ṭ	ṭo
ċa	ċu	ċi	ċā	ċé	ċe or ċ	ċo
p̣a	p̣u	p̣i	p̣ā	p̣é	p̣e or p̣	p̣o
ṣa	ṣu	ṣi	ṣā	ṣé	ṣe or ṣ	ṣo
ṣ́a	ṣ́u	ṣ́i	ṣ́ā	ṣ́é	ṣ́e or ṣ́	ṣ́o
fa	fu	fi	fā	fé	fe or f	fo
pa	pu	pi	pā	pé	pe or p	po
va	vu	vi	vā	vé	ve or v	vo

Combinations with *w*:

1st Order		2nd Order	3rd Order		4th Order		5th Order		6th Order		7th Order
ቈ	qwa	-	ቊ	qwi	ቋ	qwā	ቌ	qwé	ቍ	qwe	-
ቈ	q̄wa	-	ቊ	q̄wi	ቋ	q̄wā	ቌ	q̄wé	ቍ	q̄we	-
ኈ	ḥwa	-	ኊ	ḥwi	ኋ	ḥwā	ኌ	ḥwé	ኍ	ḥwe	-
ኰ	kwa	-	ኲ	kwi	ኳ	kwā	ኴ	kwé	ኵ	kwe	-
ዀ	xwa	-	ዂ	xwi	ዃ	xwā	ዄ	xwé	ዅ	xwe	-
ጐ	gwa	-	ጒ	gwi	ጓ	gwā	ጔ	gwé	ጕ	gwe	-

SPECIAL CHARACTERS AND CHARACTER MODIFIERS IN ROMANIZATION

Special character	Name	USMARC hexadecimal code
ʾ	alif	AE
ʿ	ayn	B0

Character modifiers	Name	USMARC hexadecimal code
́	acute	E2
̃	tilde	E4
̄	macron	E5
̇	dot above	E7
̌	hachek	E9
̣	dot below	F2
̲	underscore	F6

Uighur

Letters of the Alphabet

Initial	Medial	Final	Alone	Romanization
غا	ل	ل	ا ، غا	a
ﺑ	ﺒ	ﺐ	ب	b
ﭙ	ﭙ	ﭗ	پ	p
ﺗ	ﺘ	ﺖ	ت	t
ﺟ	ﺠ	ﺞ	ج	j
ﭼ	ﭽ	ﭻ	چ	ch
ﺧ	ﺨ	ﺦ	خ	kh
ﺩ	ﺪ	ﺪ	د	d
ﺭ	ﺮ	ﺮ	ر	r
ﺯ	ﺰ	ﺰ	ز	z
ﮊ	ﮋ	ﮋ	ژ	zh
ﺳ	ﺴ	ﺲ	س	s
ﺷ	ﺸ	ﺶ	ش	sh
ﻏ	ﻐ	ﻎ	غ	gh
ﻓ	ﻔ	ﻒ	ف	f
ﻗ	ﻘ	ﻖ	ق	q
ﻛ	ﻜ	ﻚ	ك	k
ﮔ	ﮕ	ﮓ	گ	g
ﯕ	ﯖ	ﯔ	ڭ	ng
ﻟ	ﻠ	ﻞ	ل	l
ﻣ	ﻤ	ﻢ	م	m
ﻧ	ﻨ	ﻦ	ن	n
ﯟ	ﯞ	ﯞ	ۋ	v
ﻫ	ﻬ	ﺔ ، ﻪ	ە ، ة	h
ﻳ	ﻴ	ﻰ	ى	y

Vowels

Initial	Medial	Final	Alone	Romanization
ئا	ـا	ـا	ئا	a
ئه	ە ، ھ	ە ، ھ	ئه	ă
ئـ ، بـ	ـبـ	ى	ئى ، ى	i
ئـ ، بـ	ـىـ	ـى	ئـى ، ـى	e
ئو	ـو	ـو	ئو ، و	o
ئۆ	ـۆ	ـۆ	ئۆ ، ۆ	ö
ئوُ	ـوُ	ـوُ	ئوُ ، وُ	u
ئوْا	ـوْا	ـوا	ئوْا ، وا	ü

RULES OF APPLICATION

Letters Which May Be Romanized in Different Ways Depending on Their Context

1. Romanize initial ي followed by a vowel as *y*.

Yakhshi	ياخشى
yoldash	يولداش
yeqin	يبقن
yigană	يـگانه

2. Romanized medial ي followed by a vowel as *i*.

airoport	ئايروپوت
oiman	ئويمان

3. Romanize medial ي preceded and followed by a vowel as *y*.

ayăt	ئايـهت
ăyyam	ئەييام
oyush	ئويوُش

4. Romanized medial ي preceded and followed by ى as *y*.

qiyin	قيـين
jiyim	جيـيم
yiyim	يـيـيم

5.   Romanize medial ي preceded by a consonant and followed by a vowel as *y*.

        ăghyar   ئەغيار

        ăshya   ئەشيا

6.   Romanize final ى and ي as *i*.

        muqami   موقاى

        tili   تىلى

        ai   ئاي

        qarghai   قارغائى

        tarikhi   تاريخي

7.   Romanize ڭ when followed by گ as *n*.

        bilishing   بىلىشڭ

        bilishingă   بىلىشڭگە

        jăng   جەڭ

        jăngă   جەڭگە

        shojang   شوجاڭ

        shojangă   شوجاڭگە

8.   Do not romanize the *jazm* (ـ).

        turk   تۇرك

        qirq   قىرق

        ministr   مىنىستر

9a.   Romanize the diphthong ئاي as *ai*.

        airoport   ئايروپورت

        bailiq   بايلىق

9b.   Romanize the diphthong ئەي as *ăi*.

        băitulla   بەيتۇللا

        păishănbă   پەيشەنبە

        dăifu   دەيفو

10.   Use the single prime (′) to separate two letters representing two distinct consonantal sounds when the combination might be read as a digraph.

        uz′hal   ئۇزھال

11. Romanize foreign words that occur in an Uighur context and are written in uighur letters according to these rules for romanizing Uighur.

Vena (*not* Vienna)	ۋېنا
jughrapi (*not* geography)	جوُغراپى
sităin (*not* stein)	ستهٔين

12. Follow the rules for the capitalization of English.

SPECIAL CHARACTERS AND CHARACTER MODIFIERS IN ROMANIZATION

Special Characters	*Name*	*USMARC hexadecimal code*
ʹ	soft sign (prime)	A7

Character Modifiers	*Name*	*USMARC hexadecimal code*
̆	breve	E6
̈	umlaut (dieresis)	E8

Ukrainian

Vernacular	Romanization	Vernacular	Romanization
Upper case letters		*Lower case letters*	
А	A	а	a
Б	B	б	b
В	V	в	v
Г	H	г	h
Ґ	G	ґ	g
Д	D	д	d
Е	E	е	e
Є	I͡E	є	i͡e
Ж	Z͡H (see Note 1)	ж	z͡h (see Note 1)
З	Z	з	z
И	Y	и	y
І	I	і	i
Ї	Ï	ї	ï
Й	Ĭ	й	ĭ
К	K	к	k
Л	L	л	l
М	M	м	m
Н	N	н	n
О	O	о	o
П	P	п	p
Р	R	р	r
С	S	с	s
Т	T	т	t
У	U	у	u
Ф	F	ф	f
Х	Kh	х	kh
Ц	T͡S (see Note 2)	ц	t͡s (see Note 2)
Ч	Ch	ч	ch
Ш	Sh	ш	sh
Щ	Shch	щ	shch
Ь	′ (soft sign)	ь	′ (soft sign)
Ю	I͡U	ю	i͡u
Я	I͡A	я	i͡a

Notes

1. The ligature is necessary to distinguish ж from the combination зг.

2. The ligature is necessary to distinguish ц from the combination тс.

SPECIAL CHARACTERS AND CHARACTER MODIFIERS IN ROMANIZATION

Special Characters	*Name*	*USMARC hexadecimal code*
′	soft sign (prime)	A7

Character Modifiers	*Name*	*USMARC hexadecimal code*
̆	breve	E6
̈	umlaut (dieresis)	E8
͡	ligature, 1st half	EB
͜	ligature, 2nd half	EC

Urdu
(in Arabic Script)

Letters of the Alphabet

Initial	Medial	Final	Alone	Romanization
ا	ﻟ	ﻟ	ا	omit (see Note 1)
ﺑ	ﺒ	ﺐ	ب	b
ﭘ	ﭙ	ﭗ	پ	p
ﺗ	ﺘ	ﺖ	ت	t
ﭨ	ﭩ	ﭧ	ٹ	ṭ
ﺛ	ﺜ	ﺚ	ث	t̤
ﺛ	ﺜ	ﺚ	ث	s̲
ﺟ	ﺠ	ﺞ	ج	j
ﭼ	ﭽ	ﭻ	چ	c
ﺣ	ﺤ	ﺢ	ح	ḥ
ﺧ	ﺨ	ﺦ	خ	kh
ﺩ	ﺪ	ﺪ	د	d
ﮈ	ﮉ	ﮉ	ڈ	ḍ
ﺩ	ﺪ	ﺪ	ذ	ḍ
ﺫ	ﺬ	ﺬ	ذ	z̲
ﺭ	ﺮ	ﺮ	ر	r
ﮌ	ﮍ	ﮍ	ڑ	ṛ
ﺯ	ﺰ	ﺰ	ز	ṛ
ﺯ	ﺰ	ﺰ	ز	ṛ
ﺯ	ﺰ	ﺰ	ز	z
ﮊ	ﮋ	ﮋ	ژ	zh
ﺳ	ﺴ	ﺲ	س	s
ﺷ	ﺸ	ﺶ	ش	sh
ﺻ	ﺼ	ﺺ	ص	ṣ
ﺿ	ﻀ	ﺾ	ض	ż
ﻃ	ﻄ	ﻂ	ط	t̤
ﻇ	ﻈ	ﻆ	ظ	z̤
ﻋ	ﻌ	ﻊ	ع	' (ayn)
ﻏ	ﻐ	ﻎ	غ	gh
ﻓ	ﻔ	ﻒ	ف	f
ﻗ	ﻘ	ﻖ	ق	q
ﻛ	ﻜ	ﻚ	ك	k
ﮔ	ﮕ	ﮓ	گ	g
ﻟ	ﻠ	ﻞ	ل	l
ﻣ	ﻤ	ﻢ	م	m

نـ	ـنـ	ـن	ن	n
بـ	ـبـ	ـب	ب	ṉ (see Note 2)
و	ـو	ـو	و	v
ھ	ـھ	ـھ	ہ	h
-	-	ـة	ة	t (see Rule 10)
یـ	ـیـ (ـے ، ـی)	ـی (ے ، ی)	ی (ے ، ی)	y (see Note 3)

Digraphs Representing Urdu Aspirates (see Note 4)   **Value**

bh	بھ
ph	پھ
th	تھ
ṭh	ٹھ
jh	جھ
ch	چھ
dh	دھ
ḍh	ڈھ
ṛh	ڑھ
kh	کھ
gh	گھ

Urdu Vowels and Diphthongs (see Note 5)   **Value**

a	◌َ
u	◌ُ
i	◌ِ
ā	آ ، ◌َا
á	◌َی ، ◌َیٰ
ū	◌ُو
ī	◌ِی
o	◌و
e	◌ے ، ◌ی
au	◌َوْ
ai	◌ے ، ◌َیْ

Notes to the Tables

1. For the use of ا (*alif*) to support ء (*hamzah*) and آ (*maddah*) see rules 1 and 2, respectively. For the romanization of ء by ʼ (*alif*) see rule 12. For other orthographic uses of ا see rules 3-4.
2. For the distinction between ن and ں see rule 6.
3. For the distinction between ی and ے see rule 11(c) and (e).
4. For the form of the letter ہ in these digraphs, see rule 9.
5. Vowel points are used sparingly, and for romanization must be supplied from a dictionary.

RULES OF APPLICATION

Letters Which May Be Romanized in Different Ways Depending on Their Context

1. ا (*alif*), و and ی are used to support ء (*hamzah*); see rule 12. When so used, these letters are not represented in romanization.

2. ا (*alif*) is used to support ٓ (*maddah*); see rule 13. When so used, it is not represented in romanization.

3. ا (*alif*) is used after a consonant to indicate the long vowel romanized *ā*.

    | rāj | راج |
    | karnā | کرنا |

    In some words of Arabic origin this *alif* appears as a superscript letter over ی representing the *alif maqṣūrah*.

    | da'vá | دعویٰ |

    The *alif* is sometimes omitted in writing. It is always represented in romanization.

    'Abdurraḥmān   عبد الرحمن ، عبد الرحمان

    When the long vowel *ā* is initial, it is written آ. See rule 13(a).

4. ا (*alif*) may be used as an orthographic sign without phonetic significance. In these cases it is not represented in romanization. See rule 16.

    | 'ilman | علما |

5. ط appears as a superscript letter over ت, د, and ر when the latter represent the cerebral sounds romanized *ṭ*, *ḍ*, and *ṛ*, respectively.

6. Regardless of pronunciation, undotted forms of the letter ن are romanized *n̲* and dotted forms are romanized *n*.

    | jahān̲ | جہاں |

7. و is used:

    (a) To represent the consonant sound romanized *v*.

    | dev | دیو |
    | vujūd | وجود |

    In some words of Persian origin this consonant, though written, has ceased to be pronounced. It is retained in romanization.

    | k̲h̲vīsh | خویش |

(b) To represent the long vowel romanized *ū*.

ūkh	اوخ
Urdū	اردو

(c) To represent the long vowel romanized *o*.

os	اوس
dost	دوست

For the romanization of the conjunction و as *o* see rule 19.

(d) To represent the diphthong romanized *au*.

aur	اور
qaumī	قومی

(e) To support ء (*hamzah*). See rule 12.
For the use of ﳲ (*shaddah*) with و see rule 14.

8.   ە is used to represent the consonantal sound romanized *h*.

ham	ھم
gāh	گاہ

Final ە , though often not pronounced, is normally retained in romanization.

kih	کہ
guldastah	گلدستہ

Exception is made in the case of words whose final syllable ends in an aspirated consonant. When final ە is added to the letter ھ in this position, it is not represented in romanization.

mukh	مکھہ

9.   ە (usually written in the form ھ) is used to represent the aspirated element of the sounds romanized *bh, ph, th, ṭh, jh, ch, dh, ḍh, ṛh, kh, gh*.

phūl	پھول
acchā	اچھا

For the writing and romanization of words ending in an aspirated consonant, see rule 8.

10.   ة and ت, which are sometimes used interchangeably, are both romanized *t*.

ḥikmat	حکمة ، حکمت

11.   ى (often written ي) is used:

(a) To represent the consonant romanized *y*.

siyāsat	سیاست
dayā	دیا

(b) To represent the long vowel romanized *ī*.

taṣvīr   تصویر

īshvār   ایشوار

(c) To represent the long vowel romanized *e*.

sher   شیر

nevā   نیوا

When ى with this value is final, the form ے generally replaces ى.

se   سے

laṛke   لڑکے

(d) To represent the long vowel romanized *á*. See rule 3.

da'vá   دعوی

'uqbá   عقبی

(e) To represent the diphthong romanized *ai*.

maidān   میدان

bail   بیل

When ى with this value is final, it is sometimes written ے .

hai   ہے

(f) To support ء (*hamzah*). In this position ى is usually undotted. See rule 12.

For the use of ّ (*shaddah*) with ى see rule 14.

For the use of ى in a *muẓāf* see rule 17.

Romanization of Orthographic Symbols Other Than Letters and Vowel Signs

Although vowel signs are frequently omitted in printed texts, they are always taken into consideration in romanization. The rules for other symbols vary.

12. ء (*hamzah*)

(a) In initial position ء is not represented in romanization.

(b) In medial and final position, when ء represents a consonant, it is romanized ʼ (*alif*).

mu'min   مؤمن

li'e   لئے

bhā'ī   بھائی

(c) When ء represents the connective syllable joining a *muẓāf* to what follows, it is romanized *-yi*. See rule 17.

malikah-yi Inglistān   ملکۂ انگلستان

13. ⎺◌ (*maddah*)

    (a) At the beginning of a word, or following the Arabic article ال, آ is romanized *ā*.

        āb   آب

    (b) At the beginning of a syllable within a word, آ is romanized *'ā*.

        mir'āt   مرآت
        Qur'ān   قرآن

    (c) ⎺◌ is otherwise omitted in romanization.

14. ◌ّ (*shaddah* or *tashdīd*) indicates the doubling in pronunciation of the letter over which it is written. It is represented in romanization by doubling the letter or digraph concerned.

        caccā   چچّا
        khaṭṭā   کھتّا
        makkhī   مکّھی

When ◌ّ occurs over و and ی, these letters are regarded as representing consonants. They are romanized *vv* and *yy*, respectively.

        quvvat   قوّت
        sayyid   سیّد
        Zakariyyā   زکریّا

15. ◌ْ (*sukūn* or *jazm*) indicates the absence of a vowel following the letter over which it is written. It is not represented in romanization.

16. *Tanvīn* (written ◌ً, ◌ٍ, ◌ٌ (اً)) is romanized *un, in, an*, respectively, when it occurs in a word or expression borrowed from Arabic. Otherwise it is not represented in romanization.

        fauran   فوراً

Romanization as Affected by Grammatical Structure

17. *Iẓāfat.*

    (a) When the *muẓāf*, the first of two words in the grammatical relationship known as *iẓāfah*, ends in a consonant, *-i* is added to it in the romanization.

        tārīkh-i Hindūstān   تاریخ ہندوستان

(b) When the *muẓāf* ends in a vowel or in silent ہ, -yi is added.

daryā-yi shor	دریای شور
zabān-i Urdū-yi muʻallá	زبان اردو معلی
malikah-yi Inglistān	ملکۀ انگلستان

For the use of ء (*hamzah*) to indicate the *muẓāf*, see rule 12(c).

18. The Arabic article ال is romanized differently depending on the letters and context with which it is associated.

(a) When it is prefixed to a word beginning with a "moon letter" (ح ، ج ، ب ، ا ، ی ، ہ ، و ، م ، ك ، ق ، ف ، غ ، ع ، خ) it is romanized *al*.

al-Qurʼān	القران

(b) When it is prefixed to a word beginning with a "sun letter" (ر ، ذ ، د ، ث ، ت ، ن ، ل ، ظ ، ط ، ض ، ص، ش ، س ، ز) the *l* of the article is replaced in romanization by the same letter, or digraph, as that which begins the following word.

as-sijill	السجل

(c) When it occurs before the second element in a name, the vowel of the article is replaced by the final vowel of the preceding word.

ʻAbdulʻazīz	عبد العزیز
ʻAbdurrashīd	عبد الرشید
Abūlfaẓl	ابو الفضل
Ẕūlqarnain	ذو القرنین
Faẓlullāh	فضل الله

19. The conjunction و, when used to join two closely associated members of a phrase, is romanized *o*.

māl o asbāb	مال و اسباب

Otherwise و is romanized *va*.

20. Rules for the capitalization of English are followed, except that the Arabic article *al* is lowercased in all positions.

21. The macron is used with both capital and lowercase letters.

22. The hyphen is used:

(a) To connect a *muẓāf* with the following vowel or syllable. See rule 17.

(b) To connect the Arabic article *al* with the following word. See rule 18.

23.   Foreign words in an Urdu context, including Arabic and Persian words, are romanized according to the rules for Urdu.

جناب ہیڈ ماسٹر صاحب گورنمنٹ ہائی اسکول

Janāb-i Heḍ Māsṭar ṣāḥib-i Gavarnmanṭ Hā’ī Iskūl

For short vowels not indicated in the script, the Urdu vowels nearest the original pronunciation of the word concerned are supplied in romanization.

24.   A quotation in another language using the Arabic script is romanized according to the rules for the language concerned.

SPECIAL CHARACTERS AND CHARACTER MODIFIERS IN ROMANIZATION

Special Characters	Name	USMARC hexadecimal code
’	alif	AE
‘	ayn	B0

Character Modifiers	Name	USMARC hexadecimal code
Ó	acute	E2
Ō	macron	E5
Ọ	dot below	F2
Ọ̤	double dot below	F3
O̲	underscore	F6

Character Sets Used in Romanization

The transliterations produced by applying *ALA-LC Romanization Tables* are encoded in machine-readable form into USMARC records. Encoding of the basic Latin alphabet, special characters, and character modifiers listed in this publication is done in USMARC records following two American National Standards; the *Code for Information Interchange (ASCII)* (ANSI X3.4), and the *Extended Latin Alphabet Coded Character Set for Bibliographic Use (ANSEL)* (ANSI Z39.47). Each character is assigned a unique hexadecimal (base-16) code which identifies it unambiguously for computer processing.

The graphics for certain characters used in romanization are so similar that they are often confused. The apostrophe ('), soft sign (prime) ('), acute accent (´), alif ('), and ayn (') are typical of characters that are difficult to differentiate. A listing has been provided at the end of each romanization table that shows special characters and character modifiers that are used with it. The following list shows the entire basic Latin alphabet, and all special characters and character modifiers that are used in these romanization tables. Each unique character is presented with its graphic, hexadecimal code, and name. More information on the character sets used in USMARC records can be found in *USMARC Speci-fications for Record Structure, Character Sets, and Exchange Media* (Washington: Library of Congress, CDS, 1994).

Graphic	Hex Code	Name	Graphic	Hex Code	Name
	20	SPACE (BLANK)	?	3F	QUESTION MARK
!	21	EXCLAMATION MARK	@	40	COMMERCIAL AT
"	22	QUOTATION MARK	A	41	A
#	23	NUMBER SIGN	B	42	B
$	24	DOLLAR SIGN	C	43	C
%	25	PERCENT SIGN	D	44	D
&	26	AMPERSAND	E	45	E
'	27	APOSTROPHE	F	46	F
(	28	OPENING PARENTHESIS	G	47	G
)	29	CLOSING PARENTHESIS	H	48	H
*	2A	ASTERISK	I	49	I
+	2B	PLUS SIGN	J	4A	J
,	2C	COMMA	K	4B	K
-	2D	HYPHEN-MINUS	L	4C	L
.	2E	PERIOD (DECIMAL POINT)	M	4D	M
/	2F	SLASH	N	4E	N
0	30	0	O	4F	O
1	31	1	P	50	P
2	32	2	Q	51	Q
3	33	3	R	52	R
4	34	4	S	53	S
5	35	5	T	54	T
6	36	6	U	55	U
7	37	7	V	56	V
8	38	8	W	57	W
9	39	9	X	58	X
:	3A	COLON	Y	59	Y
;	3B	SEMICOLON	Z	5A	Z
<	3C	LESS THAN SIGN	[	5B	OPENING SQUARE BRACKET
=	3D	EQUAL SIGN	\	5C	REVERSE SLASH
>	3E	GREATER THAN SIGN	]	5D	CLOSING SQUARE BRACKET

Graphic	Hex Code	Name
\	5C	REVERSE SLASH
[	5D	OPENING SQUARE BRACKET
^	5E	SPACING CIRCUMFLEX
‾	5F	SPACING UNDERSCORE
‵	60	SPACING GRAVE
a	61	a
b	62	b
c	63	c
d	64	d
e	65	e
f	66	f
g	67	g
h	68	h
i	69	i
j	6A	j
k	6B	k
l	6C	l
m	6D	m
n	6E	n
o	6F	o
p	70	p
q	71	q
r	72	r
s	73	s
t	74	t
u	75	u
v	76	v
w	77	w
x	78	x
y	79	y
z	7A	z
{	7B	OPENING CURLY BRACE
|	7C	VERTICAL BAR (FILL)
}	7D	CLOSING CURLY BRACE
~	7E	SPACING TILDE
Ł	A1	UPPERCASE POLISH L
Ø	A2	UPPERCASE SCANDINAVIAN O
Đ	A3	UPPSERCASE D WITH CROSSBAR
Þ	A4	UPPERCASE ICELANDIC THORN
Æ	A5	UPPERCASE DIGRAPH AE
Œ	A6	UPPERCASE DIGRAPH OE
′	A7	SOFT SIGN (PRIME)
·	A8	DOT IN MIDDLE OF LINE
♭	A9	MUSICAL FLAT
®	AA	SUBSCRIPT PATENT MARK
±	AB	PLUS OR MINUS
Ơ	AC	UPPERCASE O-HOOK
Ư	AD	UPPERCASE U-HOOK
'	AE	ALIF

Graphic	Hex Code	Name
'	B0	AYN
ł	B1	LOWERCASE POLISH L
ø	B2	LOWERCASE SCANDINAVIAN O
đ	B3	LOWERCASE D WITH CROSSBAR
þ	B4	LOWERCASE ICELANDIC THORN
æ	B5	LOWERCASE DIGRAPH AE
œ	B6	LOWERCASE DIGRAPH OE
″	B7	HARD SIGN (DOUBLE PRIME)
ı	B8	LOWERCASE TURKISH I
£	B9	BRITISH POUND SIGN
ð	BA	ETH
ơ	BC	LOWERCASE O-HOOK
ư	BD	LOWERCASE U-HOOK
°	C0	DEGREE SIGN
ℓ	C1	LOWERCASE SCRIPT L
℗	C2	PHONO COPYRIGHT MARK
©	C3	COPYRIGHT MARK
♯	C4	SHARP
¿	C5	INVERTED QUESTION MARK
¡	C6	INVERTED EXCLAMATION MARK
	E0	PSEUDO QUESTION MARC
◌̀	E1	GRAVE
◌́	E2	ACUTE
◌̂	E3	CIRCUMFLEX
◌̃	E4	TILDE
◌̄	E5	MACRON
◌̆	E6	BREVE
◌̇	E7	SUPERIOD DOT
◌̈	E8	UMLAUT (DIERESIS)
◌̌	E9	HACEK (CARON)
◌̊	EA	CIRCLE ABOVE (ANGSTROM)
◌͡	EB	LIGATURE, FIRST HALF
◌͡	EC	LIGATURE, SECOND HALF
◌̓	ED	HIGH COMMA, OFF CENTER
◌̋	EE	DOUBLE ACUTE
◌̆	EF	CANDRABINDU
◌̧	F0	CEDILLA
◌̨	F1	RIGHT HOOK (OGONEK)
◌̣	F2	DOT BELOW
◌̤	F3	DOUBLE DOT BELOW
◌̥	F4	CIRCLE BELOW
◌̳	F5	DOUBLE UNDERSCORE
◌̲	F6	UNDERSCORE
◌̦	F7	LEFT HOOK (COMMA BELOW)
◌̧	F8	RIGHT CEDILLA
◌	F9	UPADHMANIYA
◌͠	FA	DOUBLE TILDE, FIRST HALF
◌͠	FB	DOUBLE TILDE, SECOND HALF
◌̓	FE	HIGH COMMA, CENTERED

Index to Languages

This index lists the names of languages covered by romanization schemes in this publication. After each name is an indication of where the table for that language can be found. Some tables are applied to more than one language (e.g., the table for Hindi is used also for Awadhi, Bihari, Braj, Kashmiri in Devanagari script, Maithili, Pahari, and Rajasthani). In these cases, an instruction to use a specific romanization table is given. A table is generally named for the language for which it was first developed. *See* references from alternate names and spellings of languages have been included in the index when they differ significantly from the preferred form.

Language		*page*
Romany	see **Non-Slavic Languages**	152
Russian		184
Sanskrit		186
Santali		188
Selkup	see **Non-Slavic Languages**	152
Serbian		190
Shor	see **Non-Slavic Languages**	152
Sindhi		192
Sinhalese		194
Sonthal	see **Santali**	188
Sundanese	see **Javanese**	86
Syriac (in Cyrillic script)	see **Non-Slavic Languages--Aisor**	139
Syriac (in Hebrew script)	see **Hebrew and Yiddish**	68
Tabasaran	see **Non-Slavic Languages**	153
Tajik	see **Non-Slavic Languages**	153
Tamil		196
Tat	see **Non-Slavic Languages**	153
Tatar	see **Non-Slavic Languages**	153
Tegulu		198
Thai		200
Tibetan		216
Tigre	see **Amharic**	8
Tigrinya		218
Tua Tham	see **Pali**	164
Turkish	see **Ottoman Turkish**	158
Turkmen	see **Non-Slavic Languages**	153
Tuva	see **Non-Slavic Languages**	154
Udekhe	see **Non-Slavic Languages**	154
Udmurt	see **Non-Slavic Languages**	154
Uighur (in Arabic script)		220
Uighur (in Cyrillic script)	see **Non-Slavic Languages**	154
Ukrainian		224
Urdu		226
Uzbek	see **Non-Slavic Languages**	154
White Russian	see **Belorussian**	34
Xanty	see **Non-Slavic Languages--Khanty**	146-147
Yakut	see **Non-Slavic Languages**	154
Yiddish	see **Hebrew and Yiddish**	68
Yuit	see **Non-Slavic Languages--Eskimo**	143

☆ U. S. GOVERNMENT PRINTING OFFICE: 1997-424-978/70198